# ✝ Courageous Faith

# Courageous Faith

## Trusting God When Times Are Tough

Keith Bower, Ph.D.

HENSLEY
PUBLISHING

Tulsa, OK

HENSLEY
PUBLISHING

ISBN 1-56322-085-7

Courageous Faith: Trusting God When Times Are Tough

✠

# About Photocopying

First Timothy 5:17-18 instructs us to give the laborer his wages, specifically those who labor in the Word and doctrine. Hensley Publishing has a moral, as well as legal, responsibility to see that our authors receive fair compensation for their efforts. Many of them depend upon the income from the sale of their books as their sole livelihood. So, for that matter, do the artists, printers, and numerous other people who work to make these books available to you. Please help us by discouraging those who would copy this material in lieu of purchase.

To my wife, Julie,
and my children,
Emily and Stephen

Your lives and love
have blessed me
beyond words.

# Contents

# Introduction

"Julie's on line one."

Phone calls from my wife are never interruptions. Usually they're vacations. But this call was different, as every call would be until we got the results of her biopsy.

"M. D. Anderson called," she told me. The results were in, four days early. The test was positive.

Julie had breast cancer.

In many ways we were prepared for the news. Julie's family history had more than alerted us to the possibility. The onset of pain, the process of setting up the appointment, the mammogram, the initial report, the biopsy, the trips to M. D. Anderson Cancer Center — these things had long since shaken us free from our routines. In the meantime, countless hours of reading had informed our thinking and prepared us for the days and months ahead. In many ways we were well prepared for the news.

The most important preparation, though, had taken place several years earlier when God taught us a simple but profound lesson. Long before the diagnosis, God had taught us how to trust Him.

Don't get me wrong — trusting God was not even a remotely new concept for either of us. I had been taught from childhood that God loved me, that He cared about the big things and the little things in my life, and that whenever a crisis came, I could trust Him. Understanding that I should trust God was old news. What was new for both of us was what trusting Him actually meant in practice — in real life.

Like so many people, and without even realizing it, Julie and I had previously gotten hung up on the knotty question: What does "trusting God" actually mean? To begin with, what were we trusting Him to do? In this instance, would "trusting God" mean that we should trust Him to heal Julie? We had known cancer victims who had endured difficult struggles and died (my brother, Kevan), and we had known cancer victims who had endured equally difficult struggles and lived (Julie's sister Sherry). On what basis, then, should we trust God to heal Julie?

As if grappling with that question weren't difficult enough, we also wondered what we should actually do. What would trusting God look like when we put it into action? Suppose we should decide to trust Him to heal Julie; how would we act on that? Would we continue to pursue the best medical treatment available, trusting God to heal her through the doctors? Would we pursue some alternative therapies, trusting that God had brought us into contact with just the right people who knew of just the right treatment? Or would trusting God mean trusting Him to heal Julie's cancer directly through a miraculous intervention? Dear friends were recommending each of these approaches. To whom should we listen? What should we do? Which course of action should we follow?

The phrase *trusting God* sounds great. But what does it mean?

The good news, and really the wonder of our entire experience with cancer, is that Julie and I didn't struggle with any of these questions, not for a moment. From the day Julie was diagnosed to the day she was declared cancer free, we were able to trust God boldly, some would even say courageously, for one simple reason: God had already taught us how to trust Him.

It was a lesson He brought into focus for us through the Old Testament story of Esther. And it's a lesson I am excited to share with you.

Over the next nine weeks we will learn how to trust God boldly. We will learn to trust a God we cannot see, to "lean on the everlasting arms," as the old hymn puts it, even when those arms are invisible. The story of Esther will show us how because, through her example, you and I will learn how to live with courageous faith.

# Why the Story of Esther Is So Special

The reason the story of Esther is so wonderfully helpful is that the ways of God in her times are so much like the ways of God today. As you read the story of Esther, you will notice something remarkable: The name of God is never mentioned, not even once. There are no overt miracles — no divine appearances or manifestations. If God is acting, and it is unmistakable that He is, He is acting very much behind the scenes. He plays a major role, to be sure, but He remains "off stage."

This is exactly how God acts in our time and in our lives. We see few if any overt miracles — I've never seen one. God doesn't appear to us in person, in pillars of fire, or even, I think most of us would say, in our dreams. Yet as we look back on our lives, we see that God has been hard at work all along, guiding us and going ahead of us at every turn.

But in that very fact lies the problem: We see God's work in our lives, but too often only in retrospect, only after the fact. God acts in our lives, but He stays behind the scenes, working in ways that are often frustratingly difficult to detect at the time. We see His provision for us and His coming through for us as only He can, but we usually recognize this only after the crisis and the opportunity to trust Him actively have passed.

To put the matter simply, how do we trust — how do we place courageous faith — in a God we cannot see?

A young woman named Esther will show us how to do just that. The beauty of the book of Esther is that it teaches us how to see God at work and trust Him not only in retrospect, but at the time, in the midst of the crisis, at the crucial moment when courageous faith can make such a difference.

# Welcome to Courageous Faith

We will be spending nine exciting weeks together. Each week includes five daily studies for you to complete on your own, and a weekly small group discussion guide that will give you the chance to share your insights and make personal applications. Let me encourage you to be faithful and consistent both with your daily studies and your weekly small group meetings. You will learn and grow so much more if you do!

Before we begin our study, let me make one final and very odd request, maybe the first such request in the history of Bible study: Do not read ahead. The story of Esther has more amazing twists, turns, and dramatic reversals than even Alfred Hitchcock could have imagined, and I would hate for you to spoil it by getting ahead of the rest of us. Stay with us and resist the temptation to rush ahead.

Welcome to *Courageous Faith: Trusting God When Times Are Tough!* Let's get started.

# Real Life, Real Problems

You might expect that a book entitled *Esther* would begin with someone named Esther: "Once upon a time, there was a girl named Esther." Well, perhaps it wouldn't be that obvious, but something like that. Yet that is not at all what we find. Although the book of Esther in the Bible bears her name, Esther does not even make an appearance until chapter two. (If that strikes you as strange, remember that God is never mentioned, not even once, in the entire book!) Instead, chapter one of the book of Esther focuses on two people — two very unusual people: Xerxes, king of the Persian Empire, and Vashti, his queen.

But weren't these people, well, a little too unusual? What could people like us — average people living average lives — possibly have in common with an ancient Near Eastern despot and his queen? These were some of the most powerful people who have ever lived, people of unimaginable wealth and influence. What could their lives possibly teach us?

First of all, as powerful as these people were, they were still just human beings who, like the rest of us, had real problems. Second, as we will see, these powerful people tried to handle their problems pretty much the way we try to handle ours — without God.

Chapter one, then, is a kind of mirror. Although what we will see in that mirror isn't very flattering, it will show us what we often do during times of crisis, even though we know better.

# Ordinary People

**PASSAGE: Esther 1:1-4**

We will learn a number of important life lessons in Esther 1 — lessons about tough times and how *not* to handle them! As we begin, let's introduce ourselves to one of the key players and to his world.

If you love history as much as I do, you will enjoy placing the story of Esther in its historical and cultural context. If you do not happen to be a history buff, let me encourage you to stay with me anyway. Although this lesson will involve a lot of history, it is impossible to fully benefit from the book of Esther without some familiarity with the people and places involved.

**READING ASSIGNMENT: Esther 1:1-4**

**FOCUS FOR TODAY: Esther 1:1-4**

> *This is what happened during the time of Xerxes, the Xerxes who ruled over 127 provinces stretching from India to Cush.* (1:1)

*Xerxes* was the Greek name for the Persian king *Khshayarsh* (I can't pronounce it either) who ruled the Persian Empire almost 2,500 years ago, from 485 to 465 B.C. The Hebrews called him *Ahasuerus,* which is how he is identified in a number of English translations. Xerxes controlled an immense empire extending from the borders of India in the east to ancient Cush, or modern Ethiopia, in the southwest. To the northwest, the empire extended to the borders of modern Greece. If you have a globe or a world map, locate the western border of India, and the eastern borders of Greece and Ethiopia.

**Based on what you see on the map, the Persian Empire embraced the territory of what modern countries?**

_____

_____

_____

As you can see, the Persian Empire was vast, embracing what is today Pakistan, Afghanistan, Iran, Iraq, Jordan, Syria, Israel, Turkey, parts of the Balkan Peninsula, and Egypt to the borders of Sudan and Ethiopia. The Persian Empire was enormous even by modern standards. It was by far the largest and most powerful empire the world had ever seen at that time. And Xerxes was its absolute ruler.

How did this enormous empire come into being and how did Xerxes become its ruler? Prior to Xerxes' time, that part of the world was ruled by a succession of empires, each one larger than its predecessor. The first was the Assyrian Empire, which God used to punish the northern kingdom of Israel. The Assyrian Empire was replaced by the larger and more powerful Babylonian Empire. God used Babylon to punish the southern tribes of Judah and Benjamin. It was during the Babylonian period that many Jews were removed from Israel and taken into exile. These Jews, both those who remained in exile and those who would later return home, were central to the story of Esther.

Isn't this all a bit pedantic? How really important were all these empires to God's work among His people anyway?

**Using a complete concordance or an online tool such as www.biblegateway.com, look up the words *Assyria/Assyrian*, *Babylon/Babylonian*, and *Persia/Persian*.**

**How many books of the Bible include references to these empires and people? _____**

**What does this suggest to you about the importance of these empires to the unfolding story of God's work among His people?**

_____

_____

As you discovered, a great deal of the Old Testament is devoted to telling the story of the ancient empires, including most of 1 Kings, all of 2 Kings, most of 2 Chronicles, all of Ezra, Nehemiah, and Esther, and virtually every book of the prophets. Add it up and you will see that these empires and events were crucial to over half of the Old Testament books! The story of these empires is vitally important.

During the reign of the Babylonian king Nabonidus, a Persian named Cyrus began the step-by-step conquest of the Babylonian Empire. The final overthrow of Babylon is an amazing story, one that is recorded in Daniel 5. If you have not read the story lately, you might want to do so in preparation for our further study of Esther. For now, let me give you the highlights.

Belshazzar was ruling the city on behalf of his father, Nabonidus, who seemed to have been away at the time. Belshazzar took the opportunity of his father's absence to throw a wild party — the same type of party that we will be reading about in tomorrow's lesson. It was during Belshazzar's party that God did something genuinely frightening. At the height of the party, a hand appeared in the banquet room — not an entire body, just a hand — and wrote a message on the wall.

The prophet Daniel, aging and all but forgotten, was summoned to explain the meaning of the message. Daniel explained that God had measured Belshazzar's character and he had come up short; therefore his kingdom was being taken away from him and handed over to the Persians. At that very moment the forces of Persia were crawling under a wall — an opening they had created by diverting a river — and shortly thereafter they conquered the city. With the fall of Babylon, the Babylonian Empire became the Persian Empire, eventually to be ruled by King Xerxes.

What about Xerxes? Who was he and how did he come to power? Briefly, the Persian Empire, though not ethnically Persian, was ruled by seven Persian families who intermarried extensively and who ruled over 127 ethnically diverse provinces. The leader of this group of ruling families was Xerxes. He had inherited the throne from his father, Darius I (not the Darius of Daniel 5). As the curtain opens on chapter one of Esther, Xerxes was ruling over the vast and powerful Persian Empire.

*At that time King Xerxes reigned from his royal throne in the citadel of Susa.* (1:2)

Xerxes had five palaces, including a summer palace in the mountains near the Caspian Sea and a winter palace in Susa. The city of Susa was located in modern Iran, about 150 miles north of the Persian Gulf, near the border with Iraq. (It is amazing how that small and desolate part of the world continues to be important.) In the center of Susa was a walled citadel, or fortress, that served as Xerxes' winter home, and it is here in this palace that the story of Esther began to unfold.

> *In the third year of his reign he gave a banquet for all his nobles and officials. The military leaders of Persia and Media, the princes, and the nobles of the provinces were present.* (1:3)

The third year of Xerxes' reign would have been 483 B.C. It is important to note these dates because they show us that God doesn't always do things on man's timetable. We tend to focus on the problems and struggles of the moment, while God always looks and plans far ahead. To understand how God works, then, we should keep a close eye on the passage of time throughout the story of Esther. Quite a few years will elapse between chapters one and two, and many more between these and later chapters. So let's start keeping track of time right now.

Verse three mentions a banquet. We will discuss the banquet in greater detail in our next lesson, but for now it is important that we understand the reason for this enormous gathering. The Greek historian Herodotus recorded these events about thirty years after they took place, and he tells us that Xerxes called this meeting to plan an invasion of Greece.[1] Why would Xerxes invade Greece? In a word, pride. Years before, Xerxes' father, Darius I, had just conquered the regions north of the Greek Peninsula, when he encountered the Athenians. This first encounter went against the Persians when a storm sent the Persian navy to the bottom of the Aegean Sea. A second invasion went against the Persians when the Athenians defeated them at the battle of Marathon. This defeat embarrassed and enraged Darius, since Athens was nothing more than a tiny city-state. But Darius died before he could mount another campaign. The task of avenging Persian pride would fall to his son, Xerxes.

Upon taking the throne, Xerxes' first order of business was the brutal suppression of a rebellion in Egypt. But once the Egyptians had been crushed, he turned his attention elsewhere. Determined to uphold both Persian and family pride, Xerxes called a meeting of leaders from throughout his empire to plan another campaign — a decisive campaign, he was confident — against the Greeks. It is this meeting that is recorded in Esther 1.

> *For a full 180 days he displayed the vast wealth of his kingdom and the splendor and glory of his majesty.* (1:4)

That's six months!

**Why might Xerxes have been so eager to display his power and wealth to the rulers from throughout his empire? What purpose might this display have served?**

_____

_____

I suspect that, as a relatively new king, Xerxes needed to convince the outlying rulers, many of whom were fellow members of the seven ruling Persian families, that he had the resources necessary to mount yet another campaign against the Greeks. If he were calling on them to contribute men and material to the campaign, they needed to know that he was in a position to make substantial contributions himself.

In *Book Seven* of his *History*, Herodotus summarized the key speeches delivered at the meeting, beginning with a rousing and enthusiastic speech from Xerxes. The mood darkened when an uncle who had been with Xerxes' father at Marathon warned the assembly of the superior capabilities of the Greeks both on land and sea. According to Herodotus, however, Xerxes regained his confidence when, in a dream, a heavenly personage not only assured him of victory over the Greeks, but of worldwide dominion as well. The campaign against the Greeks was to go forward.[2] But as in the previous campaigns, the Persians would ultimately suffer defeat.[3]

Few people in history have lived the life of a Xerxes. We don't usually rule empires or conquer nations. People like us live our lives at a far less pretentious level. Yet, however modest our position in life, we all face challenges — challenges to our position, our power, our prestige, our personhood, and our sense of significance or well being. And when we face these challenges, we all, like Xerxes, tend to fall back on our perceived strengths. We try to impress ourselves and, we hope, the people around us with our talents, our accomplishments, our possessions — with whatever it is about us that we feel will enable us to meet the challenge.

When faced with challenges, we don't all face those challenges in precisely the same way. Each of us tends to depend on our own unique mix of personal strengths and resources to pull us through. When you face a challenge, what do you depend on apart from God?

**What challenges or difficulties are you facing right now?**

_____

_____

_____

_____

**How is your sense of significance, security, or self-worth being threatened? Be as specific as possible.**

_____

_____

_____

_____

**As you face these challenges, upon what personal strengths and resources do you find yourself drawing? Apart from God, on what achievements, capabilities, or qualities do you tend to depend to pull you through?**

_____

_____

_____

## PRAYER SUGGESTION

Tell God about the challenges you are facing today. Tell Him how they are affecting you and what you are doing to overcome them. If you don't know the right words to pray, go back and read your answers to the previous questions. Just say, *God, today I'm struggling with...*, and read what you wrote under the first question. Then say, *God, I don't know if this is the right way to respond to these challenges, but here's what I'm doing about them*, and read what you wrote under the second question.

You may wish to conclude your study time with the following prayer:

> *God, You know that I like to look strong and confident, when often I am overwhelmed and even scared. I try to impress people, when often I don't know what to do or how things will turn out. I want You to be involved in my life. I want to trust You more, but I'm not sure how. God, please use this Bible study to teach me how to depend on You more, how to trust You more courageously. Thank You for hearing and answering this prayer. Amen.*

# Why Are These People Celebrating?

**PASSAGE: Esther 1:5-9**

We love celebrations. And it doesn't really matter whether there is anything in particular to celebrate. Just the chance to set aside the routine of the day and be with friends and family is reason enough. But sometimes "parties" are not so much celebrations as they are painkillers. We aren't celebrating our blessings; we're numbing ourselves to our problems. And it is especially tragic when we can no longer tell the difference.

In today's passage we will witness a "party" like nothing we have ever seen before. In fact, it is not even so much a party as it is a seven-day drinking bout. The spectacle will give us a clearer picture of who the Persians were and how they approached life — and we will learn something about ourselves along the way.

**READING ASSIGNMENT: Esther 1:1-9**

Notice that I have asked you to begin your reading today with verse one. There is a good reason for this. Each day I will ask you to begin your reading at the beginning of the chapter because it will help you keep the story in mind and the day's passage in context.

**FOCUS FOR TODAY: Esther 1:5-9**

> *When these days were over, the king gave a banquet, lasting seven days, in the enclosed garden of the king's palace, for all the people from the least to the greatest, who were in the citadel of Susa.* (1:5)

King Xerxes, his fellow nobles, and the military leaders of the Persian Empire spent 180 days, or six months, planning the military campaign against the Greeks. But when the planning was over, it was time for a party! In this immediate context, the word translated *banquet* refers to a drinking bout.[4] It was, essentially, a seven-day frat party in which the only question at issue was who could drink the most.

The party was held in the enclosed garden of the palace. Such gardens were called *paradises*,[5] and they were some of the great wonders of the ancient world. Although most of the surrounding countryside was austere and barren, these enormous enclosed parks were lush and spectacular. Some even included wild animals for hunting.

Who was invited to Xerxes' party? The guest list included every male — the word *people* here refers only to men — who lived in the palace, including, of course, all of Xerxes' guests. The word *least* here would not include commoners since they did not live in the palace.

> *The garden had hangings of white and blue linen, fastened with cords of white linen and purple material to silver rings on marble pillars. There were couches of gold and silver on a mosaic pavement of porphyry, marble, mother-of-pearl and other costly stones. (1:6)*

The description now turns to the pavilions where the party was being held. The *hangings* were large canopies suspended between marble pillars and attached with silver rings. Under these pavilions, the guests reclined on couches made of silver and gold. (Presumably they had cushions.) The floor of the pavilion was a mosaic of costly stones. Now picture these pavilions in an equally extravagant private park, and you begin to appreciate the breathtaking setting for Xerxes' banquet.

> *Wine was served in goblets of gold, each one different from the other, and the royal wine was abundant, in keeping with the king's liberality. By the king's command each guest was allowed to drink in his own way, for the king instructed all the wine stewards to serve each man what he wished. (1:7-8)*

Now we come to the true guest of honor: the wine. The wine was served in goblets, or flagons, of gold, each one large, shaped like a drinking horn, and unique in design. The wine was also served in abundance — yet another demonstration of the king's wealth and generosity. To say that *each guest was allowed to drink in his own way* was to say that there were no rules, no limits. No one was there to say, "I think you've had enough."

And so after six months of languishing in their wealth and power and reveling in the prospect of crushing the Greeks, Xerxes and his male guests drank continuously for seven days. We can only imagine the atmosphere.

But where were the ladies?

*Queen Vashti also gave a banquet for the women in the royal palace of King Xerxes.* (1:9)

Meanwhile, Xerxes' queen was acting as hostess to the ladies. It is highly unlikely that the women were holding a drinking bout of their own. In fact, it was doubtless due to the inappropriateness of the behavior of the men that the women were separated in the first place.

A word about Queen Vashti: This particular name does not appear outside of Scripture. According to Herodotus, Xerxes' queen at this time was named *Amestris*.[6] Is this a contradiction? Not necessarily. As we previously saw with Xerxes, ancient Near Eastern leaders were often referred to by a variety of names. It is also possible that the name *Vashti* was a term of endearment since it does seem to be associated with the Persian words for *beloved* or *desired one*.[7] This would make sense, because, as we will learn in Esther 2, Xerxes was in the habit of elevating his favorite concubine to the status of queen. It would not be at all surprising, then, if Xerxes were to refer to Amestris, his favorite concubine, as *Vashti*, or *desired one*.

If this is Amestris, as we will assume, Queen Vashti is well known to history.[8] Not only would she become the mother of King Artaxerxes I, the son and successor of King Xerxes, she may even have been pregnant at the time of these events. By all accounts, Amestris, or Vashti, was brilliant, cunning, and cruel. But above all, she was beautiful. And it is her beauty that will lead to the crisis that we will study in tomorrow's lesson.

What were Xerxes and his guests celebrating? They were celebrating themselves. Or to put it more precisely, they were celebrating in order to prop up their self-perception, to convince themselves that power and wealth such as theirs was worth celebrating.

People today do the same types of things — measure themselves against others in order to make them feel better about themselves. But God doesn't make such comparisons. He loves us despite all of our sins, flaws, and insecurities.

**Take a moment right now to read Ephesians 2:1-10.**

Did you read it? Great! As you saw in that passage, God loves us even though we are not all that lovable. And because He loves us, He sent His Son to deal with the sin that would separate us from Him. Those who, through faith, accept the free gift of Christ's death in our place have a new standing before God. We are no longer the objects of God's wrath; we are instead the objects of His love. Our standing before Him is no longer that of a sinner, but that of the saved — of people raised up with Christ and seated with Him in heaven.

Even so, despite this incredible truth of our position in Christ, we still choose to measure ourselves against other people. Why? In order to feel good about ourselves. And since our human standards are always flawed, they need propping up from time to time. We might even feel a need to do something tangible to "celebrate" our supposed superiority. Xerxes propped up his way of feeling superior by throwing a fantastically expensive, week-long frat party.

Let's ask ourselves a nasty question.

**On a nonspiritual level, apart from Christ, how do you tend to prop up, or reinforce, your own self-esteem? What do you do to display, or "celebrate," your area of supposed superiority over others?**

_____

_____

_____

_____

**How do these demonstrations impact the people around you, both positively and negatively?**

_____

_____

_____

_____

**How does God look at us? Before you answer, reread Ephesians 2:1-10. If you have put your faith in Christ, what is your position, or your standing, before God?**

_____

_____

_____

_____

**PRAYER SUGGESTION**

Ask God to give you His perspective on the ways that you tend to reinforce your self-esteem, especially the negative ways. Pray something like this: *God, I know You love me, even when I don't feel particularly impressive or important. But when I'm having trouble loving myself, or when I think other people aren't loving me, I sometimes do things to make myself feel better.* In your prayer, list the ways you seek to improve your self-esteem. *God, I want You to help me to see these actions as You see them. Are they legitimate or are they harmful? Please let me know.*

Also, ask God to help you understand the impact these actions might be having on the people around you. Here is a suggestion: *God, I know that my actions and attitudes have an impact on the people around me, and that that impact isn't always good. Sometimes my attempts to build myself up can actually tear someone else down. Please show me how I might be hurting the people in my life.*

**Take a moment to allow Him to bring something to mind, and when He does, write it down.**

_____

_____

_____

Finally, ask God to help you understand what it means to be "in Christ" and to help you see yourself that way more consistently. You might pray like this: *God, I understand that in and of myself I am a sinner. But I am learning that through faith in Christ I have a new standing before You — that I am no longer Your enemy, but Your beloved child, seated with You in heaven with Christ. Help me understand more and more each day what that means. Show me how I try to feel good about myself by comparing myself with others, and when I do, remind me how wrong that can be. Amen.*

# ☩
# Nowhere to Hide

**PASSAGE: Esther 1:10-15**

"There is no unfallen turf." A seminary professor told me that years ago, and I have never forgotten it. No matter how hard we try to insulate and isolate ourselves from this sinful and fallen world, no matter how high we build the walls or how much we try to control what gets through the gates, we will still face problems. And even if we could guard the gates and control the people around us, we could never succeed in controlling ourselves.

**In what ways may you have built a "fortress" in your life? What do you keep inside that fortress? Who or what are you trying to keep out?**

_____

_____

_____

Today's passage gives us two examples of this principle in action. Vashti, the queen of Persia, was about to face an unsought but unavoidable moment of truth. Entirely apart from any actions on her part — and despite her intelligence and high position — Vashti was about to be drawn into a crisis that could, quite literally, lead to her death. Likewise, Xerxes, the most powerful man the world had ever seen at that time, was about to learn "up close and personal" that despite his dreams of conquering the Greeks, he could not even control his own wife. He could crush his enemies with his military might, but he could not bend the will of his queen. Xerxes would be forced to choose between his reputation and his wife.

It seems that, despite their power and position, the king and queen of the Persian Empire were real people who faced real problems. Just like the rest of us.

Today's passage should convince us that, despite enormous resources and resourcefulness, everyone is still vulnerable to the real problems of real life. Some of those problems are self-imposed, and some are imposed upon us. But whether they come from within or without, we can't always depend on ourselves to solve them. We will eventually have to look elsewhere.

**READING ASSIGNMENT: Esther 1:1-15**

Again, I would like to ask you to read from the beginning of Esther 1. This will help you keep the story clearly in mind and the passage firmly in context.

**FOCUS FOR TODAY: Esther 1:10-15**

> *On the seventh day, when King Xerxes was in high spirits from wine, he commanded the seven eunuchs who served him — Mehuman, Biztha, Harbona, Bigtha, Abagtha, Zethar and Carcas... (1:10)*

Xerxes was on his seventh day of heavy drinking, and he was in *high spirits*. The Hebrew word translated as *high spirits* (literally, *a good heart*) is a lot like its English translation in the sense that it can mean either *in a merry mood* or, as in Ecclesiastes 9:7, *drunk*.[9] In this context, it probably means both.

In his drunken state, Xerxes summoned the seven eunuchs who served him. The word translated as *eunuch* could simply refer to an official — as in the reference to Potiphar, a married man, in Genesis 37:36 — or it can refer to a literal eunuch. The latter is probably the case in this context since these men were granted access to the king's harem. Why had Xerxes summoned them?

> *...to bring before him Queen Vashti, wearing her royal crown, in order to display her beauty to the people and nobles, for she was lovely to look at. (1:11)*

King Xerxes wanted to show his guests that the queen was as beautiful as they had heard, so she was summoned to appear. The queen faced a crisis.

**Try to sympathize with Queen Vashti's position. How might she respond to this request and why?**

_____

_____

_____

Let's see what she does.

> *When the attendants delivered the king's command, Queen Vashti refused to come. Then the king became furious and burned with anger. (1:12)*

Now Xerxes' crisis hit: Queen Vashti declined to appear. Why? We are not told, though many have speculated. Some have suggested that Vashti was being asked to appear wearing *only* her crown. We should remind ourselves that Queen Vashti was a proud and intelligent woman who may well have been quite visibly pregnant. But from a literary standpoint it is significant that no reason for her refusal is provided in the text, so that the focus remains on her defiance rather than on her reasons. It is, of course, her defiance that confronted the king.

What was the king's reaction? Rage. After all, how often had King Xerxes heard the word, *No*? The merry drunk is merry no more. What would he do?

> *Since it was customary for the king to consult experts in matters of law and justice, he spoke with the wise men who understood the times and were closest to the king — Carshena, Shethar, Admatha, Tarshish, Meres, Marsena and Memucan, the seven nobles of Persia and Media who had special access to the king and were highest in the kingdom.* (1:13-14)

These seven nobles were Xerxes' closest and most valued advisors. In fact they continued to advise Xerxes' successor, his son Artaxerxes, even twenty-three years later. (See Ezra 7:14.) The king consulted these "wise men" not so much as lawyers, but as men who knew the right thing to do, perhaps based on the position of the stars.[10] That's what it means to say that they *understood the times*.

What legal action did these wise and trusted astrologers believe that Xerxes should take in this no doubt unprecedented situation?

> *"According to [the] law, what must be done to Queen Vashti?" he asked. "She has not obeyed the command of King Xerxes that the eunuchs have taken to her."* (1:15)

Persian law may not have addressed this situation since it is doubtful that anyone would have ever anticipated it. So Xerxes asked the wise men what legal action he should take. Notice how he referred to himself in the third person. Vashti had not merely defied her husband. She had defied the throne.

We all work hard to insulate ourselves from problems and crises. We use our ingenuity, our education, our resources, our influence — any and every resource at our disposal — to build a fortress around ourselves and our families. But despite our best efforts, problems still find us.

Or we still find them. Whatever the case, problems, crises, and struggles of all kinds are inevitable. They are part of the fabric of life.

**What recent problems or struggles have you brought upon yourself and why?**

_____

_____

_____

**What recent problems or struggles have been imposed on you by others? What, if anything, did you do to contribute to the situation?**

_____

_____

_____

**What problems or struggles in your life just seem to have come out of nowhere, with no one to blame?**

_____

_____

_____

## PRAYER SUGGESTION

Ask God to show you the extent to which your current crises are self-imposed: _God, sometimes I bring problems on myself, I know that. Please show me where I'm tripping up. Help me recognize the self-destructive patterns that I keep repeating so easily._

Of course, not every problem you face is the result of your own actions. Sometimes they are the result of the actions of others. Ask God to give you an honest and accurate view of the problems caused by other people in your life: _God, I know that it's easy to blame others, to act like a victim, but sometimes I blame myself for things that really were not my fault. Please give me the ability to tell the difference, to know when I am at fault and when I am just paying the price for someone else's mistakes. Teach me to be forgiving and to trust You for help and hope._

Finally, ask God to give you the ability to accept problems that just seem to come out of the blue: _God, that problem may have seemed to have come from nowhere, but I know that You saw it coming. When unexpected problems come into my life, help me learn to trust in You. Remind me that You haven't stopped loving me, and that You are still bigger than any problem that comes my way. Amen._

# Imperfect Strength

**PASSAGE: Esther 1:16-20**

Both Vashti and Xerxes were facing problems, and particularly humiliating ones at that. The most influential woman in the world — a woman of great intelligence and legendary beauty — was being threatened with either abject humiliation or certain punishment. What would she do? At the same time, the most powerful man in the world — a man who for six months had been meeting with his generals and noblemen planning the conquest of the Greeks and then for seven days had been drinking in celebration of his prowess — this man had been told *no*. And this by none other than his wife, right in front of his drinking buddies. What would he do?

As it turns out, both Vashti and Xerxes did essentially the same thing: They confronted their crisis by falling back on their perceived strengths. Vashti confronted her crisis by relying on her strength of will, while Xerxes confronted his by drawing on his authority as king. What both Vashti and Xerxes failed to recognize was that the reason they were facing these crises was because their respective strengths had already failed them. And as a solution to those crises, their strengths would once again prove inadequate.

We are a lot like Vashti and Xerxes. We tend to confront every problem as though the correct solution were the one provided by what we regard as our greatest strength. Why can't we recognize that our greatest strength failed to prevent the problem in the first place?

Let's take a closer look at Vashti and Xerxes, then a closer look at ourselves.

**READING ASSIGNMENT: Esther 1:1-20**

As always, remember to begin your reading at the beginning of the chapter.

**FOCUS FOR TODAY: Esther 1:16-20**

> *Memucan replied in the presence of the king and the nobles, "Queen Vashti has done wrong, not only against the king but also against all the nobles and the peoples of all the provinces of King Xerxes. (1:16)*

Xerxes had asked what he should do in light of Vashti's defiance of the king's command. One advisor, Memucan, responded that the king wasn't seeing the full picture. Vashti's offense, he argued, was not only against the throne, but *"also against all the nobles and the peoples of all the provinces."* How could that be? What was he thinking?

**As ridiculous as it might seem, can you think of any way that Vashti's offense might be considered *"against all peoples of all the provinces?"***

_____

_____

_____

> *"For the queen's conduct will become known to all the women, and so they will despise*
> *their husbands and say, 'King Xerxes commanded Queen Vashti to be brought before*
> *him, but she would not come.'* (1:17)

Here we find the real explanation. Memucan was worried about how Vashti's actions would influence wives throughout the Persian Empire. In that culture, women were considered little more than possessions, but Memucan was concerned that every wife would be able to say to her husband, "If Vashti doesn't have to obey the king, why should I obey you?" If the most powerful man in the world didn't act quickly, wives all over the Persian Empire would begin to defy their husbands. Forget about the Greeks! Xerxes had real problems a lot closer to home.

> *"This very day the Persian and Median women of the nobility who have heard about*
> *the queen's conduct will respond to all the king's nobles in the same way. There will be*
> *no end of disrespect and discord.* (1:18)

Memucan was concerned that Vashti's defiance might already have become known to the wives of the nobles. But how could this have been? The incident had just taken place.

**How could the other women possibly have known about it so quickly? What do you think?**

_____

_____

_____

Recall that the wives of the nobles, who were attending Vashti's banquet at that very moment, may have been eyewitnesses to her defiance. You can almost hear the panic in Memucan's voice: "Do you realize what this means? Our own wives won't obey us!" (And these guys had thought they were going to defeat the Greeks!)

*"Therefore, if it pleases the king, let him issue a royal decree and let it be written in the laws of Persia and Media, which cannot be repealed, that Vashti is never again to enter the presence of King Xerxes. Also let the king give her royal position to someone else who is better than she. (1:19)*

Look again at the middle of verse nineteen. Note how Vashti's title has been dropped. The question is not whether Vashti should be dethroned — that much seems certain — but what additional punishment she should suffer.

Memucan had a suggestion: Let Vashti's decision become her punishment. She didn't want to appear before the king? So be it. She would never again appear before the king for as long as she lived. Of course that would require that her position be taken from her and given to someone else, which opened the way for Esther. But that comes later.

What did this mean for Vashti? As one who was possibly pregnant with the king's heir, Vashti would be permitted to remain in the palace. But she would forfeit her title and never again be in the presence of the king. If Vashti was indeed Amestris, she disappeared from the pages of history until Xerxes was dead and Artaxerxes, her son, took the throne. At that time Amestris reappeared as a powerful and influential "queen mother" figure.[11]

It is important to note here that Vashti's courage could not save her. But why not? Isn't this study all about courage? Well, yes, it's about courage; but more precisely, it's about *courageous faith*.

**What's the difference between "courage" and "courageous faith?"**

_____

_____

Often courage alone can't save us. You see, the power of "courageous faith" lies not in our courage or even in our faith, but in the One in whom we put that faith: God. Esther's courage was no greater than Vashti's — it might even have been less. The difference, as we will see, is that Esther's courage was based on her faith in God.

Finally, keep in mind that this decree also had consequences for Xerxes.

**Put yourself in the king's position. What consequences did he have to face?**

_____

_____

If Vashti were indeed Xerxes' *desired one,* as she clearly was, his decree deprived him of the companionship of the woman he desired above all others. Although Xerxes was anything but a family man,[12] Vashti was likely pregnant with his son and heir. But even if this worked no hardship on Xerxes, the fact remained that this woman, his own queen, had defied his will and had done so publicly. No decree of banishment would ever change that. So while the consequences in Xerxes' life were far less severe than for Vashti, there were consequences for him nonetheless.

> *"Then when the king's edict is proclaimed throughout all his vast realm, all the women will respect their husbands, from the least to the greatest."* (1:20)

What effect did this have on the women of the empire? It was hoped that the divorce and banishment of the former queen would dissuade them from treating their husbands with the same disregard with which Vashti had treated hers.

When Vashti faced a crisis, she did the only thing she knew to do: She drew on her inner strength and refused to yield — and for this she was banished and replaced as queen. When Xerxes faced a crisis, he did the only thing he knew to do: He wielded raw power — and for this he lost the companionship of his *desired one.* When things went wrong, each of these people used what they regarded as their greatest strength to carry them through. And in a very real sense, both of them paid a price.

Most of us do that. When we face a crisis, we depend on our areas of strength to pull us through. Look back at your study guide for Day One of this week. Remind yourself of what you listed there as your greatest areas of strength. Then ask yourself these questions.

**How do you use your areas of greatest strength to confront the problems and crises of your life? Try to provide a specific example.**

_____

_____

_____

_____

_____

_____

_____

Has that dependence on your own strength and abilities ever disappointed you or resulted in any unwanted consequences? Explain.

_____

_____

_____

_____

In 2 Corinthians 12:9, the apostle Paul wrote that God's strength is made perfect in our weakness. Look that verse up and read it in context. What does this verse mean? Has your weakness ever given God a chance to show His strength? Give an example.

_____

_____

_____

_____

_____

## PRAYER SUGGESTION

Ask God to show you all the ways that you depend on your own strength, instead of His, to confront the problems and crises in your life. Then ask Him to show you where your strength has failed you, or where it has brought about unfortunate and unintended consequences: *God, I know that when a crisis comes, my first instinct is not to turn to You, but to depend on my own strength and resourcefulness. When I do that, point it out to me, prick my conscience. And please use the times when dependence on myself has failed to teach me to turn to You sooner, to ask for Your involvement from the beginning. Amen.*

# Who Is in Control?

**PASSAGE: Esther 1:21-22**

Vashti made her decision, and it cost her the crown. The crisis came upon her suddenly and without warning, but she stood strong, demonstrating the courage of her convictions. Yet courage alone could not deliver Vashti from the crisis, and at that point she disappeared from the pages of Scripture.

Xerxes, too, had made his decision, and now that decision was promulgated throughout the vast Persian Empire. True, by dealing with the problem of Vashti's defiance from his area of greatest strength, Xerxes preserved the social hierarchy in Persian households; yet he also lost the companionship of his *desired one.*

But, quite apart from his intention, Xerxes did more than that — a great deal more. Xerxes could never have realized that he was acting not merely in the interests of the Persian social order, but in the interests of the God of Abraham, Isaac, and Jacob — a God whose purpose was not to place wives in bondage to their husbands, but to save His people. What is even more fascinating is that this God was saving His people from a threat that wouldn't even materialize for many years.

**READING ASSIGNMENT: Esther 1:1-22**

**FOCUS FOR TODAY: Esther 1:21-22**

> *The king and his nobles were pleased with this advice, so the king did as Memucan proposed.* (1:21)

Memucan had advised not only that Xerxes issue an edict deposing Vashti and banishing her from his presence, but also that the edict be announced throughout the kingdom. The suggestion seemed good to Xerxes and his nobles, so the edict was issued.

Before we move on, let's pause for a moment to assess the moral character of Xerxes' decree.

**Would you say that the decree, particularly as a response to Vashti's actions, was just and well-founded, or unjust and arbitrary?**

_____

**Would you, then, characterize the decree as good and moral, or as evil and immoral?**

_____

We are about to argue that God used Xerxes' decree to open the way for Esther to become queen — a move that would, some years later, prove vitally important to the continued existence of the Jewish people.

**If, in your judgment, Xerxes' decree was immoral and arbitrary, was God wrong to use that decree in the interests of His people? Why or why not?**

_____

_____

**Does the fact that God used Xerxes' decree for good mean that the decree itself was good? To help you think this through, I suggest that you look at Joseph's words to his brothers in Genesis 50:19-20.**

_____

_____

Regardless of the immorality of Xerxes' decree or its eventual impact on God's people, the decree had become law. It remained only for the news of it to spread throughout Xerxes' empire.

> _He sent dispatches to all parts of the kingdom, to each province in its own script and to each people in its own language, proclaiming in each people's tongue that every man should be ruler over his own household._ (1:22)

How was this edict promulgated throughout the empire? With amazing efficiency! Persia had a system of couriers as well as a network of signal towers that could spread a message throughout the empire with astonishing speed.[13] It is certain, then, that word of the king's edict arrived throughout the empire far in advance of any rumors of Vashti's defiance.

**What was the content of this decree?**

_____

_____

Note that Xerxes' edict made explicit the authority of each man over his wife. He was not going to risk his decision about Vashti's punishment being misunderstood. The significance of Vashti's banishment was made abundantly clear to wives throughout the empire. Xerxes had acted swiftly and powerfully to keep the wives of Persia in subjection to their husbands. Now for the Greeks!

Finally, notice the multicultural nature of the Persian Empire. There were actually relatively few true Persians in the Persian Empire. Most of Xerxes' subjects were conquered peoples: men, women, and children of other nations and languages. This was equally true of his soldiers — an important reason that the Persian army failed to defeat the Greeks, as we will see in a future lesson.

Xerxes' crisis seems to have been resolved. He may have lost the companionship of his *desired one,* but he preserved his authority as well as the authority of husbands throughout the empire. Yet Xerxes could not have realized how significant that decision would be for reasons having nothing to do with the defiance of Vashti. Xerxes was hard at work on the surface of events, trying to control people and outcomes in a way that would please his own purposes. But the God of Israel was also at work, although behind the scenes and years in advance, in a way that is impossible to see no matter how closely we look at chapter one.

There are two major lessons to be learned from this chapter. First, real people have real problems. It is a part of life. No matter how powerful or successful we are, regardless of our resources or resourcefulness, no matter how high or how strong we build the walls of our fortresses, our lives will be marked by crises of all kinds. Some of them we bring on ourselves. Some come as the result of the actions of others. And some seem to come from nowhere. But come they will. There is no avoiding them.

Second, most of us confront these crises depending almost entirely on our own resources, our own talents, and our own strengths. God is available to help us, but we don't turn to Him, at least not fully and seldom right away. Instead, we depend on ourselves — and that is never enough. No matter how hard we try, we cannot control people, events, or outcomes.

**What are some of the ways, good and maybe not so good, that you have tried to control the people, events, and outcomes in your life?**

_____

_____

_____

**How does God get your attention? What does He do to bring you back around to trusting Him?**

_____

_____

One final question, and for this, I want us to get ahead of ourselves just a bit. Most of us would agree that Xerxes' actions against Vashti were unjust. Yet we will argue that God will use those evil actions for good. Has that ever happened to you? Has God ever used an evil action on someone else's part to bring good things into your life? I'm confident that He has, so I will ask you to describe the situation.

**Describe a time when the evil actions of someone else actually ended up bringing you something good.**

_____

_____

_____

## PRAYER SUGGESTION

It's natural and often wise to try to prevent problems by taking control. But sometimes we go too far or depend on that too exclusively. Ask God to show you the extent to which you try to live as the king of your world, as the master of your universe, instead of trusting Him as the one true King: _God, I am grateful that You have given me the sense and ability to avoid even more crises than I already face in life. But I admit to You today that sometimes I take the business of control a little too far and depend on it a little too much. Sometimes it hurts the people around me. And often it keeps me from trusting You as I should. Help me to see when and where I cross that line. Amen._

Now pause for a moment. Did He remind you of something that you might need to add to your answer to the first of today's questions? If He did, go back and include that in your answer right now.

# Preparing for Your Small Group Discussion

Assuming that you are doing this study with others, this is the final lesson before you meet with your class or small group. Before you meet with the others, take a moment to preview the questions included in the Small Group Discussion Guide included on the following pages. If you notice that some of the questions look familiar, that's deliberate. These "repeat questions" will draw on some of the answers you have already given in your daily study, but this will give you the opportunity to share some of the insights you've gained this week with the rest of your group.

If you are going through this Bible study as an individual, don't assume that the Small Group Discussion Guide has no benefit for you. Use it instead to review the things you have learned and solidify the truths God may be imparting to your heart.

✟

# Small Group Discussion Guide

In real life, real people have real problems. And while it's comforting to know that we have a God who cares, at one time or another most of us will wonder where He is when we need Him. The truth is that often God's help isn't nearly as visible as we would like it to be. If God does care, if He is involved, is there a way that we can learn to see Him at work in our lives? Yes, there is! That's what the book of Esther is all about — learning to see God at work so that we can trust Him more courageously.

Today we take a look at two people who faced real problems and who made the same mistakes we make. The only difference between them and us is that they made their mistakes on a larger scale. We may not learn very much from them about what we should be doing, but we can learn from them what we should *not* be doing!

**TODAY: Esther 1:1-22**

**I. Be realistic about your ABILITIES and ACCOMPLISHMENTS.**
**KEY PASSAGE:** Esther 1:1-5a (read it aloud)

**DISCUSSION QUESTION:** What abilities or accomplishments did Xerxes like to emphasize?

_____

_____

_____

**SUPPORT PASSAGE:** Romans 12:3 (read it aloud)

**PRINCIPLE:** It's great to recognize and exercise our God-given strengths, but we need to work a lot harder at guarding against arrogance and overconfidence.

**APPLICATION:** Which of your abilities or accomplishments do you like to emphasize?

_____

_____

_____

_____

## II. Don't expect your ABILITIES to PREVENT problems.

**KEY PASSAGE:** Esther 1:10a, 11-12 (read it aloud)

**DISCUSSION QUESTION:** In what ways did Xerxes' and Vashti's abilities fail to prevent problems?

_____

_____

_____

**SUPPORT PASSAGE:** Job 5:7 (read it aloud)

**PRINCIPLE:** No amount of talent, education, experience, resources, or diligence will prevent us from running into real problems.

**APPLICATION:** Personalize this point by writing in the blank one of your specific abilities or accomplishments: "I shouldn't expect my _____ to prevent problems." Look at what you wrote in that blank. How have you tried to use that specific ability or accomplishment to prevent problems? Share an example with the group.

_____

_____

_____

## III. Above all, don't depend on your ABILITIES to SOLVE your problems.

**KEY PASSAGE:** Esther 1:16-20 (read it aloud)

**DISCUSSION QUESTION:** In what ways did Xerxes and Vashti depend on their abilities to solve their problems?

_____

_____

_____

**PRINCIPLE:** It may be natural for us to tackle our problems from the area of our greatest strength, but it seldom does much good. In fact it often makes things worse. Learn that lesson!

**APPLICATION:** Again, personalize point three by writing a specific ability or accomplishment in the blank: "I shouldn't expect my _____ to solve my problems." Specifically, how have you depended on that ability to solve your problems? Again, share an example.

_____

_____

_____

Let's end on a positive note. Here are some verses that remind us of what we should be depending on. Read these verses aloud and discuss how you can apply them in your day-to-day life.

> Trust in the LORD with all your heart and lean not on your own understanding; in all your ways acknowledge him, and he will make your paths straight.
>
> —Proverbs 3:5-6


> "I have told you these things, so that in me you may have peace. In this world you will have trouble. But take heart! I have overcome the world."
>
> —John 16:33

✦

# Unplanned, But Never Unexpected

**Day 1** — Riding Out Life's Ripple Events

**Day 2** — Surviving Life's Ambush Events

**Day 3** — Wrestling Life's Gorilla Events

**Day 4** — Pondering Life's Polaroid Events

**Day 5** — Noticing Life's Non-Events

The first chapter of Esther taught us two things. First, real people have real problems and there is nothing we can do to change that. No amount of money, education, hard work, or resourcefulness can prevent or even solve most of the bigger personal challenges we face in life. Second, when real people face real problems, they tend to depend on their areas of strength — their own abilities and resources — instead of on God. Even those of us who have a relationship with God through Christ too often respond to the challenges of life by trusting ourselves first and Him only later.

In chapter two we are going to discover how to trust God at the onset of and during a crisis, not just after it is resolved. We will see how God allows the unexpected and sometimes painful events in our lives as part of His plan. But more than that, we will learn to recognize this process while it is underway, allowing us to trust God much sooner.

In this week's study, we will see God at work through five different kinds of crises or events that take place in Esther 2. We will call them "Ripple Events," "Ambush Events," "Gorilla Events," "Polaroid Events," and "Non-Events." In each of these, God works in distinct and recognizable ways. Although we don't typically plan our crises, God knows they are coming. He expects them, and He is always ready. In a real sense, then, our crises may be unplanned, but they are never unexpected. We can begin to trust God more readily by learning to recognize the kinds of crises He allows to come our way.

# Riding Out Life's Ripple Events

**PASSAGE: Esther 2:1-4**

Some events don't seem to involve us at all, at least not at first. They're just too far away. Even if we do hear about something that happened to someone else somewhere, we are usually unconcerned because the impact could not possibly reach us. Or so we tell ourselves. But then our own boat begins to rock. And when the rocking finally gets our attention, we look up to discover that we're riding the ripples.

The event may have been far away at first, but somehow the ripples have reached your life. A corporate scandal in another state becomes a very personal financial loss that could delay your retirement. A political crisis a world away becomes a very personal parting as a beloved soldier is deployed overseas. An act of terrorism thousands of miles away becomes a sleepless night for a frightened child. Someone else's crisis has become your own.

This is precisely what we see as we open Esther 2. Vashti and Xerxes had faced and resolved their crisis in chapter one. Yet as the ripples of that crisis spread, the effects reached into villages and homes and rocked innocent lives throughout the empire. How can we learn to recognize and survive such "ripple events"?

**READING ASSIGNMENT: Esther 2:1-4**

Since we begin a new chapter today, you can begin your reading with chapter two, verse one.

**FOCUS FOR TODAY: Esther 2:1-4**

> *Later when the anger of King Xerxes had subsided, he remembered Vashti and what she had done and what he had decreed about her.* (2:1)

How much later does chapter two begin? We can't be sure. It could be as short a time as it took for Xerxes to sober up or as long as a year or so. The text doesn't say. But when the king's anger and the alcohol wore off, he remembered Vashti. In this context, the word translated *remembered* has the nuance of remembering with obligation or regret.[1] Xerxes remembered Vashti, what she had done, and what he had decreed in response, and he regretted it.

**Why might Xerxes have regretted his actions?**

_____

_____

It could be that Xerxes felt that he had overreacted and that the punishment didn't fit the crime, but that seems unlikely given that he could quite easily have had Vashti executed for her defiance. It seems more likely that Xerxes regretted the impact that his decree was having on him personally. After all, in his moment of rage he had permanently deprived himself of the company of an incredibly beautiful woman.

Why couldn't the king just reverse his ruling? It might not have been possible for him to do so. Although there is no record of this principle outside of the Bible, Esther 1:19 tells us that *the laws of Persia and Media…cannot be repealed.*[2] If our understanding of this is correct, then Xerxes' decision regarding Vashti was final.

> The king's personal attendants proposed, "Let a search be made for beautiful young virgins for the king. (2:2)

The response of the king's attendants supports our understanding of verse one. Seeing the king's regrets, his personal attendants knew just what was needed to lift the king's spirits: some fresh female companionship. Although the Hebrew word translated *virgin* refers to a young woman of marriageable age, in this context actual virginity is certainly implied.[3] And since the king was, after all, the king, not just any young woman — or even any beautiful young woman — would do. No, indeed! A search must be conducted.

> "Let the king appoint commissioners in every province of his realm to bring all these beautiful girls into the harem at the citadel of Susa. Let them be placed under the care of Hegai, the king's eunuch, who is in charge of the women; and let beauty treatments be given to them. (2:3)

How would this search be conducted? First, the search would span the entire empire. Every one of the 127 provinces must be forced to yield its most beautiful young women. Second, the search would be conducted by specially appointed royal commissioners.

**Why might this have been necessary? Why do you suppose they didn't just ask for volunteers?**

_____

_____

Being appropriated for use in the harem was not exactly considered an honor. Most of the subjects of the Persian Empire were conquered peoples — people of different races, different cultures, different customs, and different religions. Also keep in mind that these girls, most of whom were almost certainly engaged, were giving up all hope of marriage, a family, and a home, for a life of isolation, loneliness, and occasional "one night stands." Although the hopes and dreams of a young woman in that day and age were far different from the goals that modern young women aspire to, they most certainly did not include the isolation of life in a harem. These girls, their fiancés, and their families would not yield willingly.[4] Families typically hid their daughters.[5] A royal official would have to be present to enforce the royal will.

According to the plan, the girls would be transported to the palace in Susa where they would be placed under the care of Hegai, a eunuch, who would prepare each one for her visit with the king.

> *"Then let the girl who pleases the king be queen instead of Vashti." This advice appealed to the king, and he followed it.* (2:4)

One girl, the king's favorite, would be crowned queen — just one girl. What would become of the others? A few lucky ones might be judged unsuitable and sent home immediately. The others would have their year of preparation, their one night "date" with the king, then spend the rest of their lives in the harem, never again to see their families and never to enjoy the love of a family of their own. The "winner" would spend her life as the king's favorite, but not as the king's one and only.

*This advice appealed to the king.* No kidding.

One man's self-indulgence was about to radically and permanently alter the lives of countless young women and their families. Their hopes, their plans, their dreams — these things would no longer matter. All that would count was what one man did, what one man wanted. His life was about to become an irresistible force in shaping theirs. One of these young women was named Esther. We will meet her in our next lesson.

This happens in our world each and every day: Events far removed from us send their ripples and rock our lives. We think we are in control, that we have set our own course, when our lives are suddenly, radically, and permanently changed by the actions, often the sinful actions, of others. It may be as innocent as a corporate restructuring or as culpable as international terrorism. Whatever form it takes, our lives are unavoidably and profoundly shaped by the decisions and actions of others. Let's identify some of the "ripple events" that take place in our lives.

**What "ripple events" — crises that seemed far away at first, but that somehow reached you — have rocked your life? How has your life changed as a result?**

_____

_____

_____

_____

_____

**How has this "boat-rocking" experience made you feel? Do you feel like an innocent victim? How about resentment? What emotions are you struggling with as you suffer through a crisis of someone else's making?**

_____

_____

_____

_____

_____

Finally, remember that we have a tremendous advantage over Esther and the other young women whose lives would be forever changed. As we read the story, we already know that God is up to something, even if we may not know what that something is. We suspect that these events are headed somewhere, even though we may not be sure where. We understand that these events are not mere ripples that have reached out indiscriminately, but rather, they are events permitted by a loving God who has not forgotten to care for His children. If only these young women could have seen it that way as the ripple — or tidal wave — of Xerxes' decree began to rock their world.

What if we were to adopt that same perspective as we face the ripple events in our lives? What difference would that make? That is our final question for today.

How would your feelings change if you knew — absolutely knew — that God had allowed that "ripple event" into your life for a reason? Even if you weren't sure what that reason was, how would it make a difference knowing that the ripples were not an accident, but were instead part of God's specific plan for your life?

_____

_____

_____

_____


**PRAYER SUGGESTION**

As you encounter a "ripple event," tell God about it, then ask Him to help you see that He is the One who is in ultimate control of your life. Begin by telling God about any recent "ripple events" in your life and about how you feel as you "ride the waves." You may wish to pray something like this: *God, right now I'm riding the waves of someone else's crisis.* Then read the specific recent events you listed in the first question. *To be honest, I'm struggling,* then tell Him how.

Next, acknowledge to Him that He has *ordained your days,* and that you will trust Him. One way to do this is by "praying Scripture." You can simply read a passage of reassurance back to God as your prayer. For example: *God, all the days ordained for me were written in Your book before one of them came to be* (Psalm 139:16). *So I am going to be strong and courageous. I will not be afraid or terrified because of them, for You, my Lord and my God, go with me; You will never leave me nor forsake me* (Deuteronomy 31:6). *Amen.*

# Surviving Life's Ambush Events

**PASSAGE: Esther 2:5-9**

Have you ever noticed how some of the biggest events in our lives just seem to come out of the blue? We plan, prepare, and work for years to create for ourselves the lives we are hoping to enjoy. Then, without warning, something happens, something completely unexpected, that changes everything — and our lives are never the same again. These are life's "ambush events." If "ripple events" come from a distance, "ambush events" come out of nowhere. They strike like a bolt of lightening on a clear day.

This is exactly what happened to Esther, the heroine of our story, whom we finally meet in today's passage. We know little of her early life. Nothing, in fact, beyond what we read in these few verses. Yet it is clear that the crisis that is about to overtake her is completely unexpected. Whatever her plans might have been, they surely did not include the bizarre and doubtless unwelcome series of events that would utterly reshape her life and set her on a new course of eternal significance in the plan and purpose of God.

Let's take a look at this "ambush event" in Esther's life. We just might learn something about dealing with the "ambush events" in our own.

**READING ASSIGNMENT: Esther 2:1-9**

**FOCUS FOR TODAY: Esther 2:5-9**

> *There was in the citadel of Susa a Jew of the tribe of Benjamin, named Mordecai son of Jair, the son of Shimei, the son of Kish.* (2:5)

Right there in the citadel of the king was a Jew named Mordecai, of the tribe of Benjamin. The name *Mordecai* is not of Hebrew origin. It is almost certainly a Babylonian name based on the name of the god *Marduk*.[6] Does this pagan name suggest anything about Mordecai's spirituality?

Not necessarily. It wasn't unusual for Jews to bear pagan names during the period of the exile, even names based on the names of pagan gods. One example of this can be found in Daniel 1:6-7.

**What pagan names are given to Daniel and his friends and what is the meaning of each name? (The meanings might be listed in your Bible's margin.)**

**Daniel's name is changed to** _____**, meaning** _____.

**Hananiah's name is changed to** _____**, meaning** _____.

**Mishael's name is changed to** _____**, meaning** _____.

**Azariah's name is changed to** _____**, meaning** _____.

Daniel's Babylonian name, as well as the names of his friends, all had pagan religious significance. So it would be unwarranted to draw inferences about Mordecai's religious devotion solely from his name.

Although Mordecai is identified as a Jew of the tribe of Benjamin, he chose to keep his ethnic origin a secret, as we shall soon see.

> *Who had been carried into exile from Jerusalem by Nebuchadnezzar king of Babylon,*
> *among those taken captive with Jehoiachin king of Judah. (2:6)*

Verse five traces Mordecai's ancestry back to the Babylonian exile. Prior to the rise of the Persian Empire, God had used the Babylonian Empire to bring judgment on the southern kingdom of Judah and Benjamin, much as He had used the Assyrians to judge the northern kingdom of Israel. Among the Jewish kings taken prisoner by King Nebuchadnezzar was Jehoiachin (also known as Jeconiah and Coniah) who reigned for three months during the winter of 598/597 B.C.

Take a moment to read 2 Kings 24:8-17 and Jeremiah 22:24-30; 24:1.

**What do these events tell you about the spiritual state of the leaders of God's people at the time of the exile to Babylon?**

_____

_____

Apparently Mordecai's great-grandfather, Kish, was taken into captivity along with Jehoiachin. Now, almost 120 years and three generations later, Mordecai was working in the palace of the king whose empire had overthrown the Babylonians.

One of the truly marvelous facts about the Jews is their distinct and enduring presence as a people throughout history. Join me in a little experiment.

**How many Assyrians do you know?** _____

**How many Babylonians?**_____

**Any Hittites or Canaanites?** _____

Now try this one:

**How many Jews do you know?** _____

Do you ever find yourself wondering whether the Jews really are a uniquely chosen people, a treasured possession of God? If you do, just ask yourself this question: How many people do you know who have survived such unimaginable persecution and suffering to celebrate a heritage that goes back literally thousands of years?

Of course God's preservation of the Jewish people is the great miracle of the book of Esther. But that part of the story comes later.

> *Mordecai had a cousin named Hadassah, whom he had brought up because she had neither father nor mother. This girl, who was also known as Esther, was lovely in form and features, and Mordecai had taken her as his own daughter when her father and mother died. (2:7)*

Now we meet our heroine, Esther. Her Hebrew name is *Hadassah*, which means *myrtle*, a beautiful shrub with fragrant white flowers.[7] The name *Esther* is probably based on a Persian word meaning *star*.[8] It is, of course, by her Persian name that she is known throughout the book.

Although Mordecai was older, he and Esther were cousins. Esther's father, Abihail, was Mordecai's uncle. (See Esther 2:15.) Although no details of the tragedy are given, Esther's parents had died, and Mordecai had taken her in and raised her as his own daughter. The text tells us that Esther was a beautiful young woman.

> *When the king's order and edict had been proclaimed, many girls were brought to the citadel of Susa and put under the care of Hegai. Esther also was taken to the king's palace and entrusted to Hegai, who had charge of the harem. (2:8)*

There is no indication how long the empirewide search for beautiful young women lasted, but it doubtless took some time, possibly many months. Apparently the search included the capital city of Susa because the official appointed to search Susa discovered Esther. Since Mordecai worked in the citadel itself, he and his young cousin Esther likely lived within walking distance of the palace. Even so, Esther was not permitted to remain at home. Along with the other young women, Esther was taken from her home and placed in the palace.

The man in charge of the harem was Hegai, a eunuch. It was his responsibility to prepare the young women for their appointment with the king. How many girls were in this group? The text doesn't say, but estimates range from a few hundred to over a thousand.[9]

> *The girl [Esther] pleased him [Hegai] and won his favor. Immediately he provided her with her beauty treatments and special food. He assigned to her seven maids selected from the king's palace and moved her and her maids into the best place in the harem. (2:9)*

Hegai took an immediate liking to Esther. Although all of the girls would undergo the twelve months of preparation, Esther's preparation began immediately. She not only received the best treatment and special foods, she was also assigned seven handmaidens from the palace as well as special living quarters.

**How did Esther win Hegai's favor? This man worked with beautiful women all the time. What do you think might have made Esther so special?**

_____

_____

From the overall tone of the book, as well as a few hints that will come later, it seems clear that it is more than just Esther's physical beauty that sets her apart. Perhaps it was her demure and solicitous attitude toward those in authority that was so endearing. Whatever it was, it won her the favor of Hegai, a man who knew quite well how to prepare a young woman to be the next queen.

Let's remind ourselves not to get too romantic here. Despite the favor and special privileges, Esther's situation was far from ideal. She was separated from Mordecai, the only family she knew, and she was being prepared for a life far different from the one she and Mordecai had no doubt planned. It was anything but clear how the purpose and plan of God was involved, if at all. The direction of Esther's life had changed dramatically and unexpectedly. And there wasn't a thing she or Mordecai could do about it.

Some of the most significant events in our lives are completely unexpected and completely outside of our control. One minute our plans are made and our future seems secure, and the next minute everything is up in the air. It may be a job change, a diagnosis, the death of a loved one, or even a single phone call that causes the turmoil. But whatever form they may take, "ambush events" can change our lives in a moment. Let's take a look back at some of the more important "ambush events" in our lives.

**What have been some of the major "ambush events" that have shaped your life?**

_____

_____

_____

**Select one of these events and describe how your life might have been different had this event never taken place.**

_____

_____

_____

_____

As we will see in weeks to come, God may not warn us of life's ambush events, but He always prepares us. Wouldn't it be incredible if we could grasp that truth and cling to it right now? Let's ask ourselves a final question today:

**How might your reaction to life's "ambush events" be different if you were absolutely confident that God had seen the ambush coming and had prepared you for it in advance?**

_____

_____

_____

_____

_____

**PRAYER SUGGESTION**

Ask God to remind you that nothing that has happened in your life has ever taken Him by surprise. You might pray something like this: *God, I know that, from Your point of view, there is no such thing as an ambush. Nothing could ever surprise You or sneak up on You. But I admit that sometimes I forget that. I'm caught off guard, so I feel like You must have been caught off guard, too. I know that could never happen, so please help me remember that. Remind me each and every time I get ambushed that You knew what was coming and that You chose to let it come.*

Which brings us to the second point: Thank Him for His providence — for His sovereignty over the events of your life. Then ask Him to help you trust Him during the times that His plans differ from yours. Pray a prayer such as this: *God, I want to thank You for being in charge of my life and for the way ambush events remind me of that. When those reminders come, though, I need You to help me trust in You. I know that my plans are often very different from Your plans. Help me to recognize that ambush events are simply times when Your plans win out, and help me trust You during those times. Amen.*

✟

# Wrestling Life's Gorilla Events

**PASSAGE: Esther 2:10-14**

We like to think that we are in control of our lives, that we're in charge, the masters of our personal universe. But then something happens that shatters that illusion. A major event takes place in our lives that has overwhelming power, and we are left feeling utterly helpless. Suddenly our lives are turned upside down by someone or something far bigger and far stronger than we are. And there isn't a thing we can do to resist.

You've heard the joke: Where does an 800-pound gorilla sit? Answer: Wherever it wants! Some events are like that. They are 800-pound gorillas, and they sit wherever they want.

Esther and Mordecai must have had that feeling. Whatever their plans, hopes, and dreams might have been, control of their lives had been wrested from them and handed over to King Xerxes. What can we do at times like that to keep helplessness from turning into hopelessness? We will gain some insights into wrestling with life's "gorilla events" in today's study.

**READING ASSIGNMENT: Esther 2:1-14**

**FOCUS FOR TODAY: Esther 2:10-14**

> *Esther had not revealed her nationality and family background, because Mordecai had forbidden her to do so.* (2:10)

**Why was Mordecai concerned that Esther's *nationality and family background* not become known? How might her ethnic background have placed her at risk? What do you think?**

_____

_____

Most commentators believe that Mordecai was concerned about antisemitism. A major event later in the book suggests that a virulent antisemitism was resting just beneath the surface in

Susa, if not empirewide. Why Mordecai might have suspected this is not explained. But he was concerned enough to warn Esther to keep her Jewish identity to herself. This decision would prove to be enormously significant later on.

> *Every day he walked back and forth near the courtyard of the harem to find out how*
> *Esther was and what was happening to her. (2:11)*

**What does this tell us about Mordecai's attitude toward Esther? _____**
**What does it tell us about his access to Esther? _____**

As Esther's cousin, guardian, and adoptive father, Mordecai was deeply concerned about Esther, and he took advantage of his employment in the citadel to loiter near the harem courtyard in the hope of hearing news of her fate. Notice, though, that even an employee who worked within the citadel itself couldn't get near the harem. This demonstrates how completely isolated these girls were, not only from their families, but from anyone in the outside world.

> *Before a girl's turn came to go in to King Xerxes, she had to complete twelve months*
> *of beauty treatments prescribed for the women, six months with oil of myrrh and six*
> *with perfumes and cosmetics. (2:12)*

Apparently being one of the most beautiful young women in the empire wasn't quite enough. But did we read that right? Six months of skin conditioning, followed by six months of treatment with perfumes and cosmetics — that's what it says. We know that the Persian aristocracy, including the men, made heavy use of cosmetics,[10] but this seems bizarre even by Persian standards.

**How can we explain this? We might imagine how skin could be softened or perhaps lightened over a period of time, but what is gained by six months of application of perfumes and cosmetics? Any guesses?**

_____

_____

The answer would seem to be permanence. The objective was to virtually tattoo both the cosmetics and the fragrances into the girl's skin. Burners, much like incense burners, were used to fill the air and permeate the skin with the aroma of spices.[11] So for six months a girl would be rubbed with oils and then for six months she would be fumigated with fragrances — all for one night with the king.

*And this is how she would go to the king: Anything she wanted was given her to take with her from the harem to the king's palace. (2:13)*

After a year of this kind of preparation, a girl would be taken to the king. But before she went, she was allowed to select *anything she wanted...from the harem* to bring with her. We don't know what might be in view here, but it almost certainly included a choice of attire and jewelry. The young women were evaluated for their aesthetic sense as well as for their beauty.

*In the evening she would go there and in the morning return to another part of the harem to the care of Shaashgaz, the king's eunuch who was in charge of the concubines. She would not return to the king unless he was pleased with her and summoned her by name. (2:14)*

This verse makes the nature of these meetings all too clear. The young woman would go to the king in the evening and return the next morning. When she returned, she would report to another part of the harem, one occupied by the concubines under the oversight of a man named Shaashgaz. Because these concubines had had similar encounters with the king, they were in what we might describe as a semimarried state: no longer a virgin, yet certainly not available to marry anyone else.

**Put yourself in their place, if you can. What would your state of mind be?**

_____

_____

_____

_____

These young women would remain in lonely isolation with nothing to break the monotony but an occasional and doubtless unwelcome summons from the king.

Esther was helpless. If her Jewish background became known, she might be in danger. Even if she did manage to keep her ethnic identity a secret, she could hope for nothing more than a life of lonely, impersonal, emotionless luxury. And nothing she could do could change that. It wasn't just a crisis; it was an 800-pound gorilla!

God often chooses to allow "gorilla events" into our lives: situations that leave us feeling completely overmatched, even helpless. But helpless doesn't have to mean hopeless. It's true that we cannot control events, but God can and does. And that should give us hope.

**What "gorilla events" in your past left you feeling helpless?**

_____

_____

_____

**How did God wrestle that gorilla? (Translation: How did He give you victory?)**

_____

_____

_____

**What "gorilla events" have you feeling helpless right now?**

_____

_____

_____

**How might God's victory over your previous "gorilla event" give you hope today?**

_____

_____

_____

_____

**PRAYER SUGGESTION**

Thank God for the helpless times in your past when He came through for you. And don't use generalities; be specific. Look again at your answers to the first two questions above and tell God the story. Pray something like this: *God, I remember the time that…*, then relive it with Him, remembering to tell all about how He came through for you. Now tell God all about your current "gorilla event," about how you're feeling helpless, then ask God to give you hope through trust in Him.

# Pondering Life's Polaroid Events

**PASSAGE: Esther 2:15-18**

Has a crisis ever arisen in your life that seemed to have no spiritual significance at all? Maybe it was job related or had something to do with the kids' schoolwork. Maybe it was a sudden change in vacation plans or a costly home or car repair. Whatever it was, it just didn't seem to be the kind of thing that would warrant God's attention. Life is filled with day-to-day crises that don't seem the least bit spiritual — or at least not at first.

But then something happens. Events continue to unfold. Things develop, and before long the situation that you didn't consider "spiritual" is presenting you with some significant spiritual challenges.

Let's call these "Polaroid events." Even in a digital world, most of us are familiar with Polaroid cameras: You just point, shoot, and watch as the picture slowly develops and becomes clear. You don't even need to download it to a computer for printing! A lot of crises are like that — they develop slowly and become clear only later. Like a Polaroid photograph, you don't see the picture right at first. But after the situation has had some time to develop, its spiritual significance becomes perfectly clear.

Esther was facing just such a "Polaroid event" in her life. While it was clear that her crisis was truly and permanently life-changing, there was no way she could have discerned its greater spiritual importance. How can we learn to trust God for the true, though hidden, spiritual significance of the "Polaroid events" in our lives? We will find out in today's study.

**READING ASSIGNMENT: Esther 2:1-18**

**FOCUS FOR TODAY: Esther 2:15-18**

*When the turn came for Esther (the girl Mordecai had adopted, the daughter of his uncle Abihail) to go to the king, she asked for nothing other than what Hegai, the king's eunuch who was in charge of the harem, suggested. And Esther won the favor of everyone who saw her. (2:15)*

Here we learn the name of Esther's father and the precise nature of her relationship with Mordecai — Esther's father was Mordecai's uncle, so Esther and Mordecai were cousins.

The time had now come for Esther's visit with the king. How many of the girls had preceded Esther? We don't know. But when her turn came, Esther asked Hegai what she should take, what clothing and jewelry she should wear. We are also learning a bit more about Esther's character and attitude.

**What does this passage reveal about Esther?**

_____

_____

This passage provides a glimpse of Esther's solicitous attitude toward those in authority over her. Of course, it might also suggest a shrewd mind, given that no one would be in a better position to know the preferences of the king than Hegai. In any event, the results were stunning. Esther's appearance was so striking that she *won the favor of everyone who saw her.*

*She was taken to King Xerxes in the royal residence in the tenth month, the month of Tebeth, in the seventh year of his reign. (2:16)*

Remember to pay attention to dates because very soon the story of Esther is going to teach us an important lesson about God's timing. Four years had passed since the king had deposed Vashti. According to the Greek historian Herodotus, Xerxes devoted two years of this time to his campaign against the Greeks. It was presumably during those years that the search for and preparation of the beautiful young women was conducted. Keep in mind that Xerxes' army was made up of young men from throughout the empire, conquered peoples, pressed into military service for the king. Yet at the very time that these soldiers were in the field of battle fighting for King Xerxes, representatives of the king were back in their villages conscripting their fiancées into a different kind of service. It is really no surprise that the Greeks, free men fighting to defend their homes and families, were able to defeat the Persian army.

Following the decisive defeat of his navy at the Battle of Salamis, Xerxes abandoned the bulk of his army in Greece and fled for home,[12] where the process of selecting his new queen was underway. It was during the winter of 479 B.C. that Esther was taken to the king.

This raises a question in the minds of many readers: Should we be disturbed that Esther is yielding to a process that we would regard as immoral? Should she, rather, have refused the king, much as Vashti had done, and trusted God with the consequences?[13]

**That is a tough question. How would you respond?**

_____

_____

_____

I would respond to this concern in two ways. First, our culture tends to sensitize us to some moral issues while desensitizing us to others. For example, racism was widely accepted in the early 1960s, while sexual exhibitionism was not. Today racism is taboo and sexual exhibitionism is rampant. Whether we approve or not, concubinage was widely practiced and socially accepted in ancient Near Eastern culture, including among the patriarchs of Israel and in the courts of Saul, David, Solomon, and others.[14] While Jewish families typically hid their daughters from foreign kings, they willingly yielded them to the kings of Israel.[15] It might be a mistake, then, to impose the "moral values" of one culture on the "moral failings" of another.

Second, we should keep in mind that Esther was a real person — one who was going to grow enormously through these events. She was a hero, but not a superhero, and like virtually every other hero of the faith, she was a work-in-process. True, Esther would one day become the great model of courageous faith, but that wouldn't happen for some time yet. When the time did come, we will see her struggle and waver, then finally step forward — in other words, we will see her growing just like the rest of us. This is enormously encouraging for us since we, too, are very much works-in-process. We may not always do the right thing the first time, but it is encouraging to know that we can grow in our faith — that we have the opportunity to improve — to do better the next time.

> _The king was attracted to Esther more than to any of the other women, and she won_
> _his favor and approval more than any of the other virgins. So he set a royal crown on_
> _her head and made her queen instead of Vashti. (2:17)_

When the king's time with Esther ended, so did his search for a queen. Or at least that is how most interpreters understand this verse. It is possible that the search continued and that the king made the choice later on, but the tone of the passage makes it more likely that the king made his decision right away. So Esther, a young Jewish girl who had lost her parents and been raised by her cousin, was crowned queen of the Persian Empire.

It is clear that something pretty amazing is happening here, but what? Remember, today's study is about "Polaroid events" — events whose ultimate significance is not yet clear. Let's look at this event in Esther's life: She has been appointed queen.

**If you had no clue where this story was headed, what would you make of that? How might you speculate as to its significance? What might you suggest that God is up to?**

_____

_____


Does it feel like guesswork? Sure it does! You probably know that feeling all too well from trying to figure out what God is up to in the "Polaroid events" in your own life.

Esther was now the queen of the Persian Empire, yet she wasn't a queen in the usual sense.

**Based on what you're learning about Persian culture, how might her life and role differ from that of a more modern queen?**

_____

_____


We should recall that the position of "queen" meant that of all the king's wives, concubines, and harem girls, and there may have been thousands, Esther was the king's favorite. As we learned in verse fourteen, the king was entirely free to summon any of these other women at his whim. In fact Esther was even deprived of the privilege of bearing the royal heir, since Vashti's son, Artaxerxes, was by this time three years old. Yet her title did allow her some access to the king, something that would prove very important very soon.

> *And the king gave a great banquet, Esther's banquet, for all his nobles and officials. He proclaimed a holiday throughout the provinces and distributed gifts with royal liberality. (2:18)*

To celebrate the appointment of his new queen, Xerxes hosted a great banquet. The guest list no doubt included most of the same people we met in chapter one. In addition to the banquet, the king proclaimed a holiday throughout the empire. It is hard not to see in this banquet a foreshadowing of the Jewish "Feast of Purim" which was instituted later as a celebration and remembrance of the events recounted in the book of Esther. Whether that is what the writer intended is impossible to say.

Some amazing things have happened to Esther. It's not every day that a girl is crowned queen! Yet we still do not know what God might be up to. If there is a divine purpose in all this, we can't see it. Pieces of the puzzle are coming together, but we have no idea what the completed picture will look like.

Sound familiar? These are life's "Polaroid events." Things happen, sometimes dramatic things, yet we don't have the slightest idea of what God is up to or if He is even involved. No matter how hard we think about it, the spiritual significance, if there is any, remains completely obscure — at least at first. But over time the picture begins to develop. New events, new experiences, new perspectives, new insights — the pieces gradually come together so that what had been obscure has become clear. Now you can see it. God was at work all along!

The spiritual significance of the events in Esther's life won't become clear for some time yet. But what about you? Are there some "Polaroid events" in your life that have now fully developed? Let's consider how God can use the clarity of those events to help us trust Him with the "Polaroid events" we're facing today.

**What "Polaroid events" has God used in your life — events that at first seemed to have little or no spiritual significance, but later turned out to have great importance in your spiritual life?**

_____

_____

_____

_____

**What significant events has God allowed into your life more recently that, so far at least, seem to have no real spiritual purpose?**

_____

_____

_____

_____

_____

**How can the "Polaroid events" of your past encourage you to trust God with the "Polaroid events" of today?**

_____

_____

_____

_____

_____

## PRAYER SUGGESTION

Ask God to remind you of some of the major "Polaroid events" of your past so that you can more easily trust Him through the events of today. Then thank Him for how He brought clarity to those events in His time.

Next, thank God that *He has made everything beautiful in its time* (Ecclesiastes 3:11), including the "Polaroid events" you are facing right now. Be sure to mention them by name. Finally, ask Him to use the events of your past to help you trust Him with the specific events of today.

# Noticing Life's Non-Events

**PASSAGE: Esther 2:19-23**

Esther had experienced some amazing things. She had been snatched from her home, isolated in the king's harem, given numerous beauty treatments, taken to the king, and finally crowned queen. In just over a year she had gone from happy obscurity to a position of immense and, in all likelihood, unwelcome prominence and privilege. Using our terminology, she rode out the ripple, survived the ambush, wrestled the gorilla, and pondered the obscure. How do you follow that?

The answer, as it turns out, was with an equally important yet in some ways thoroughly unremarkable event. We might even call it a non-event. Esther heard some important news and passed it along to the king. That's it. The incident came and just as quickly it went. It never occurred to Esther that there would be any consequences, good or bad, for her or for her people, nor did there appear to be any right away. Yet, amazingly, that single act was as significant as anything else that had taken place in God's unfolding plan for her life and for the survival of her people.

We've all experienced these "non-events." At first they seem to be of little or no importance. We hardly give them a thought. Yet remarkably these non-events prove to be turning points in our lives. How do we trust God with non-events given that they seem at first to call for no response at all?

**READING ASSIGNMENT: Esther 2:1-23**

**FOCUS FOR TODAY: Esther 2:19-23**

> *When the virgins were assembled a second time, Mordecai was sitting at the king's gate.* (2:19)

Were more virgins being assembled? That's one way to read this. But why? Hadn't the king selected Esther as his queen? Yes, he had. So, why was he gathering still more virgins? We could speculate, but the fact is that there may not have been another gathering in view here at all. The

Hebrew is notoriously awkward — so awkward in fact that the phrase was omitted from the Septuagint, the Greek translation of the Old Testament in use in Jesus' day. It is probably best, then, not to try to make too much of this phrase.

The emphasis of this verse is Mordecai's service. From the time of the gathering of the virgins, Mordecai had been *sitting at the king's gate*, meaning that he was a minor official working in the palace. One ancient Persian inscription actually mentions a Mordecai who served in the palace at Susa in a low-level role similar perhaps to that of an accountant.[16] It's fascinating to think that this inscription just might refer to the Mordecai of our story.

> *Esther had kept secret her family background and nationality just as Mordecai had told her to do, for she continued to follow Mordecai's instructions as she had done when he was bringing her up.* (2:20)

Esther kept her background a secret during her time of preparation and continued to keep it a secret after she became the queen.

**Speculate for a moment. If you could ask Esther at this point in her life just why she felt it was so important to keep her ethnicity a secret, what do you think she might have said?**

_____

_____

_____

_____

Just why it was so important that she keep this secret will become clear when the major crisis of the book unfolds. It was significant that, although she was now queen of the Persian Empire, Esther continued to follow Mordecai's instructions just as she had done when she was growing up. This is another hint of the character that, in addition to her physical beauty, made Esther so attractive.

> *During the time Mordecai was sitting at the king's gate, Bigthana and Teresh, two of the king's officers who guarded the doorway, became angry and conspired to assassinate King Xerxes.* (2:21)

A crisis erupted, but not for Esther. This crisis was for Mordecai. Two officers of the palace guard were conspiring to assassinate the king. Why? We don't know. The text simply reports that they had become angry. No details are provided. We might be tempted to recall the ruthlessness of

Vashti and wonder whether she might have had a hand in the plot, though no hint of this is given. Their anger suggests that their reason might be more personal.

In any event, these particular officers guarded the doorway to the king's private apartments.

**Why would a plot by these two men be especially dangerous to the king?**

_____

_____

As the king's personal security detail, these men were the last line of defense. No one stood between them and the king. Their access was unimpeded. Xerxes was in real danger.

> _Mordecai found out about the plot and told Queen Esther, who in turn reported it to the king, giving credit to Mordecai._ (2:22)

Somehow Mordecai learned of the plot and notified Queen Esther. Apparently Esther was more accessible to Mordecai now that she was queen than she had been when she was in the harem. This accessibility worked out well for Xerxes because Mordecai was able to report the plot directly to the queen. We will learn later on in the book that Esther's access to the king was not unrestricted. Nevertheless she managed to get this important information to Xerxes.

Significantly, she gave the credit for discovering and exposing the plot to Mordecai. Why was this significant? It seems like such a small detail.

**Suppose that you do not know how the story will unfold. Why might the mention of Mordecai be so significant? What do you think?**

_____

_____

It is impossible to tell at this point. In time we will see the significance very clearly, but now it is completely obscure. The mention of Mordecai seems like an unimportant and thoroughly unremarkable detail, when in fact it is an indispensable piece of the puzzle that is gradually coming together. Although we still cannot see the big picture, the pieces are falling into place.

> _When the report was investigated and found to be true, the two officials were hanged on a gallows. All this was recorded in the book of the annals in the presence of the king._ (2:23)

The report was investigated, it was found to be true, and the officers were executed. The phrase *hanged on a gallows* could also be translated *impaled on a spike*. The Persians did both.

One more seemingly insignificant detail is added: *All this was recorded in the book of the annals in the presence of the king.* The fact that Mordecai saved the life of the king was recorded in the official historical record of the king's court. Nothing was done to thank Mordecai; his actions were simply recorded. Why was this important? We are not told. It is another non-event. Yet another vital piece of the puzzle has fallen into place.

It is wonderful how effortlessly God was moving through these seemingly random and unrelated events to rescue His people from a crisis that had not yet even occurred. God was using non-events to set the stage for something amazing, yet Mordecai and Esther could not possibly see it. They didn't even know that a crisis was coming, let alone how the non-events they were experiencing might be involved. But God did, and at that point that was all that mattered.

God does the same thing in our lives. He uses seemingly insignificant events and experiences in our lives to do incredible things, often years later. At the time we may have no hint that anything of real significance has happened. But when the real crisis begins to unfold, we look back and realize that God was hard at work all along, often months or even years in advance.

Let me share a personal example. Months before my wife, Julie, was diagnosed with breast cancer, we decided to exercise more consistently. Some time later Julie began to experience sharp, nonmuscular pain in the breast tissues. It was that pain that caused her to go in for a mammogram, and the doctors discovered cancer. As it turns out, the pain had nothing whatever to do with the cancer; it was caused entirely by the workouts. Without that pain, however, the cancer might not have been discovered until much later. But instead, God used a non-event — our decision to exercise more consistently — to reveal the cancer at a very early and very treatable stage. At the time we could not possibly have imagined the significance of our decision, but in retrospect it is perfectly clear. God was working through a non-event to address a crisis in our lives that hadn't even appeared yet.

I am absolutely confident that God has done that in your life, too. You have a story to tell of a seeming non-event that God used in an incredibly significant way.

Think back on a crisis in your life; it can even be one you mentioned earlier. Now, try to identify something that happened prior to that crisis — something that seemed insignificant at the time, a non-event — that God used in a strategic way to resolve your crisis.

_____

_____

_____

_____

By definition, it is impossible to recognize the significance of seeming non-events in advance. In retrospect, though, it is easy. How can God's faithfulness through the non-events of your past encourage you to trust God in the crises of today?

_____

_____

_____

_____

_____

## PRAYER SUGGESTION

Ask God to remind you of the non-events that He used in significant ways in your life. You could pray something like this: _God, You've cared for me in so many ways through the years, often in ways I've hardly even noticed. When You do that, I don't want to miss it. I want to see Your hand at work in my life, even in the smallest details, so that I can thank You for it and tell others. Please remind me today of some of the ways You've worked in my past._ When He does, write them down. Otherwise you'll just forget them again!

Next thank God for how He has worked through these seemingly irrelevant events to care for you today: _God, I know that just as You have used the smallest events to care for me in the past, You are using equally small events to bless me today. Even though I cannot yet see the full significance of those events, I know that You are working through them for my good. So I want to thank You for all the little things You are doing in my life right now. Even though I can't see their significance, I know that I will someday, so I want to thank You today._

Finally, ask Him to help you trust Him for what is yet ahead: _Father, as You show me the small but significant things You have done in my past, please help me trust You with the small things of today and tomorrow. Remind me that You see the full significance of the smallest event, even when I don't. Convince me that it is really OK that I don't understand what You're up to sometimes, because You always know exactly what You're doing. Amen._

# Preparing for Your Small Group Discussion

You have now completed week two of *Courageous Faith*. Next week things begin to get exciting! But first comes one of the most important aspects of this study: your Bible study class or small group.

If you are completing this study with a group, I encourage you to be an active participant. Share your insights. Tell your stories. Encourage others, and let them encourage you. Remember, *As iron sharpens iron, so one man sharpens another* (Proverbs 27:17).

But again, if you have committed to this Bible study as an individual, please do not skip over these discussion questions. Use them as a guide for personal reflection on the things God is teaching you about your own *Courageous Faith*.

✝

## WEEK TWO
### UNPLANNED, BUT NEVER UNEXPECTED
# Small Group Discussion Guide

Some of the biggest, most significant events in our lives are ones we never planned. You know how it goes. You had it all figured out. Your life was on track. You were thinking and working in a very definite direction. Then suddenly it happened. It might have been a single, overwhelming event or a series of small, scarcely noticeable ones. Either way, the result was the same: Your life had been changed.

Esther surely knew that feeling — the feeling of being overtaken by the unplanned and the unexpected. What could Esther do in the face of such overwhelming events? What can we do when our lives take sudden, dramatic, and entirely unexpected turns? The answer lies in a simple realization: Although the crisis might have come as a surprise to us, it came as no surprise to God. We may not have expected this turn of events, but God did. And we can find strength and hope in that.

In today's study, we are going to look at five distinctive ways that crisis events can invade our lives. You might even have noticed in your personal study this week that Esther's crisis was actually a combination of several of these types of events. That shouldn't surprise us, because the worst crises usually are. Today we will learn how to recognize each type of event and see how God works through it for our good. By understanding these distinctions, we will be better able to trust God when a crisis comes.

**TODAY: Esther 2:1-23**

**I. RIPPLE EVENTS: Expect to be ROCKED, but refuse to be CAPSIZED.**
**KEY PASSAGE:** Esther 2:1-4 (read it aloud)

**What do we mean by a "Ripple Event"?**

_____

_____

**DISCUSSION QUESTION:** How was Esther's world rocked by the actions of a faraway king?

_____

_____

**SUPPORT PASSAGE:** Deuteronomy 31:6 (read it aloud)

**PRINCIPLE:** Like ripples in a pond, sometimes the actions of others can reach out and rock our world. When they do, look to God for stability.

**APPLICATION:** How is your world being rocked by people or events far away? How is God keeping your boat from capsizing?

_____

_____

## II. AMBUSH EVENTS: Expect the UNEXPECTED, but never be FEARFUL.
**KEY PASSAGE:** Esther 2:5-9 (read it aloud)

**What do we mean by an "Ambush Event"?**

_____

_____

**DISCUSSION QUESTIONS:** How was Esther ambushed? What unexpected event radically and permanently altered the course of her life?

_____

_____

**SUPPORT PASSAGE**: Psalm 139:16 (read it aloud)

**PRINCIPLE:** Some of the biggest events in your life may have been complete surprises to you, but not to God. Look to Him for courage.

**APPLICATION:** What unexpected event has altered the course of your life? How has God given you courage through that crisis?

_____

_____

**III. GORILLA EVENTS: Expect to feel HELPLESS, but refuse to feel HOPELESS.**
**KEY PASSAGE:** Esther 2:10-14 (read it aloud)

**What do we mean by a "Gorilla Event"?**

_____

_____

**DISCUSSION QUESTIONS:** As Esther was overpowered by her crisis, what were her options? In what ways was she empowered? What could she do for hope?

_____

_____

**SUPPORT PASSAGE:** Isaiah 46:9-10  (read it aloud)

**PRINCIPLE:** Some crises are bigger than we are, but they are not bigger than God. Look to Him for hope.

**APPLICATION:** What crisis left you feeling completely overpowered, yet still enjoying the peace of God?

_____

_____

**IV. POLAROID EVENTS: Expect God to DO SOMETHING, but don't expect to UNDERSTAND IT.**
**KEY PASSAGE:** Esther 2:15-18 (read it aloud)

**What do we mean by a "Polaroid Event"?**

_____

_____

**DISCUSSION QUESTION:** What events in Esther's life were obviously significant and life changing, yet obscure in their true significance?

_____

_____

**SUPPORT PASSAGE:** Romans 11:33-36 (read it aloud)

**PRINCIPLE:** God will allow significant events into your life without bothering to explain them to you. Look to Him for wisdom.

**APPLICATION:** What dramatic event or crisis grabbed your attention without giving you any sense of its true spiritual significance? How did God finally reveal to you the true significance of that event?

_____

_____


## V. NON-EVENTS: Expect God to ACT, but don't expect to always SEE IT right away.

**KEY PASSAGE:** Esther 2:19-23 (read it aloud)

**What do we mean by a "Non-event"?**

_____

_____


**DISCUSSION QUESTION:** Without reading ahead, what seemingly insignificant "non-event" in this passage might prove to be of immense spiritual significance as God's plan unfolded?

_____

_____


**SUPPORT PASSAGE:** Isaiah 55:8-9 (read it aloud)

**PRINCIPLE:** Although we don't always detect how God chooses to help us, we can depend on Him to act on our behalf. Look to Him for deliverance.

**APPLICATION:** What seemingly irrelevant event has God used to bring you through a crisis?

_____

_____

✝

# When the Crisis Hits

Day 1 — When the Right Thing Goes Wrong

Day 2 — Out of the Frying Pan

Day 3 — Into the Fire

Day 4 — Hitting Bottom

Day 5 — The Christian and Civil Disobedience

God might have seen it coming, but you didn't. And for whatever reason, He allowed it to come. It's a crisis. It's here. And there is nothing you can do to stop it. We can't prevent or control the crises that come our way, but we can control how we respond to them. In this week's passage we will learn how to respond when the crisis hits.

In the first two chapters of Esther, we saw God preparing the solution to a problem that hadn't even happened yet. These preparations have put us on the alert. But as you study the passage this week, try to put that out of your mind. Let yourself be surprised, even shocked. This crisis needs to hit us the same way it hit Esther and Mordecai, and the same way our crises hit us in our lives.

# When the Right Thing Goes Wrong

**PASSAGE: Esther 3:1-4**

Sometimes, in the midst of the storm, it can be difficult to discern God's will. At other times, when His will is clear, it can be difficult to obey. But toughest of all are those times when obedience only seems to make matters worse. Following God always pays off; but it doesn't always pay off right away. What can we do — how can we continue to follow God — when the right thing seems to go the wrong way?

Mordecai was about to face that challenge. His godly response to a personal crisis did not resolve that crisis. Indeed it triggered a far greater crisis, one that threatened the very survival of his people. How could Mordecai continue to do the right thing when the right thing went wrong?

**READING ASSIGNMENT: Esther 3:1-4**

**FOCUS FOR TODAY: Esther 3:1-4**

> *After these events, King Xerxes honored Haman son of Hammedatha, the Agagite,*
> *elevating him and giving him a seat of honor higher than that of all the other nobles.* (3:1)

As we learned in the previous chapter, Mordecai exposed a plot to assassinate Xerxes, and for this service to the king, his name was recorded in the court records. *After these events....* Exactly how long after isn't important. What is important is that God had been preparing for the upcoming crisis for nine years, ever since Vashti had been removed from the throne.[1] Yet, remarkably, the crisis itself still hadn't hit. God works in advance — well in advance!

Now we meet the other major character in our story: Haman. We don't know Haman's background, but it is surprising in light of his promotion that we don't see his name listed among the nobles and chief advisors in chapter one. He is identified here as the *son of Hammedatha,* but that tells us nothing. He is also identified as *the Agagite,* so Haman was probably from Agag, a province in the Persian Empire.[2] Identifying Haman as an Agagite may suggest more about his character than his identity. The Hebrew Old Testament is highly nuanced in its allusions and word plays. Calling Haman an *Agagite* would almost certainly remind the ancient Jewish reader of King Agag, king of the Amalekites.[3]

**Read 1 Samuel 15, especially verses 9, 20, and 32-33. What was King Agag's relationship to Israel?**

_____

_____

**For the Jewish reader, what would an allusion to Agag suggest about Haman?**

_____

_____

The allusion to Agag is apropos. Haman, *the Agagite,* would quickly prove to be no friend of the Jews.[4] Whatever his background, Haman is promoted to a position similar to that of prime minister or even "chief executive officer" of the Persian Empire.

> *All the royal officials at the king's gate knelt down and paid honor to Haman, for the king had commanded this concerning him. But Mordecai would not kneel down or pay him honor.* (3:2)

The *officials at the king's gate* were simply the government officials working in the palace who were below Haman on the organizational chart. As part of Haman's promotion, the king issued a decree that officials below Haman must *kneel down and pay him honor.*

What precisely did that mean? We're not sure, in part because no such decree would seem to be necessary. Persians greeted one another in three ways. When greeting a social equal, Persians kissed one another on the lips. When greeting someone of a somewhat higher social position, the person of lower standing would kiss the person of higher standing on the cheek. When one person was of significantly higher standing, the person of lower standing wouldn't be standing at all; he would be prostrate on the ground. So any low-level official *at the king's gate* would have already prostrated himself before Haman simply as a matter of Persian custom. There was, by the way, no element of worship in these customs. They were simple social conventions.[5] Why, then, were these special instructions regarding Haman even given?

**We might find a clue in Mordecai's reaction. Look again at the last sentence of verse two. What does it say?**

_____

_____

If nothing more than the ordinary Persian social custom was occurring, why did Mordecai refuse to participate? One might speculate that the Jews would consider bowing before someone a violation of the first and second commandments. But did they?

**Look at 1 Samuel 24:8. What does this verse tell you?**

_____

The fact is that the Jews had no objection to bowing before people as a social matter.[6] What exactly, then, had the king commanded concerning Haman? Mordecai's reluctance alerts us that something more, possibly something bordering on religious worship, must have been taking place.

> *The royal officials at the king's gate asked Mordecai, "Why do you disobey the king's command?" (3:3)*

**Why would Mordecai's fellow officials have been concerned? What hint has the story given us that the consequences of defiance might be severe?**

_____

_____

Recall the consequences of Vashti's disobedience in chapter one. She was the queen of the Persian Empire, the king's *desired one,* the mother of the royal heir. Yet for a single act of defiance she was dethroned and banished from the presence of the king. Imagine what the consequences would have been for Mordecai! Willful disobedience to the king's command was no small thing, especially when the act of defiance was committed repeatedly, publicly, and by a low-level bureaucrat.

It is not surprising, then, that Mordecai's fellow officials were concerned and asked him the reason for his disobedience. How did Mordecai answer? We are not told. But the next verse provides some fascinating insights.

> *Day after day they spoke to him but he refused to comply. Therefore they told Haman about it to see whether Mordecai's behavior would be tolerated, for he had told them he was a Jew. (3:4)*

Apparently this business of bowing in honor of Haman took place with enough frequency that Mordecai's refusal to comply became an issue. *Day after day* Mordecai's fellow officials urged him to participate, but he would not yield.

**What did these officials do in response?**

_____

In one sense these officials had no choice. They could not afford to risk complicity in rank disobedience against the king. Yet the passage also notes that they were particularly interested in whether Mordecai's behavior would be tolerated given that he was a Jew. That's interesting.

**What does this suggest?**

_____

Why would Mordecai's fellow officials wonder whether the disobedience of a Jew in particular would be tolerated? Perhaps they had detected the same incipient antisemitism that had alarmed Mordecai.

A more important question is this: How did they find out that Mordecai was a Jew? According to verse four, he told them.

**What had Mordecai told Esther in Esther 2:10?**

_____

**Why, under these circumstances, would Mordecai have shared the secret of his ancestry with his fellow officials? What do you think?**

_____

_____

It seems likely that Mordecai disclosed his Jewish heritage to explain why he refused to bow down in honor of Haman. If so, it would lend support to the notion that Mordecai's objections were religious.

One final question: Why was it even necessary to tell Haman that Mordecai was refusing to bow in his honor? Didn't he notice? The need to inform Haman of Mordecai's disobedience would have been difficult to explain if the issue were merely one of ordinary social greetings. After all, how could Haman miss the fact that, of all the people in the room, only Mordecai was standing? It is possible that Mordecai was being asked to bow in honor of Haman even when Haman was not present, and for a Jew that might seem perilously close to worship. This verse, then, provides helpful clues as to the nature of the "bowing" and Mordecai's subsequent objection.

A storm was brewing, and Mordecai was about to get caught in the middle of it. But what could he do? Violating his religious principles didn't seem like a very good solution. But holding to those principles was the very thing that was getting him into trouble. Sometimes we can do the right thing, even the godly thing, but the storm just keeps on building. When that happens, what can we do?

**Are there any storms building in your life? What right and godly things have you done that, so far, have failed to head off this crisis?**

_____

_____

**What right and godly things have you done that actually seem to be making the situation worse?**

_____

_____

_____

**How do you react when doing the right thing seems to backfire?**

_____

_____

_____

**There are times when the right thing seems to go wrong at first, but then things turn around and God gives us a victory. Has that ever happened to you? Explain.**

_____

_____

_____

## PRAYER SUGGESTION

As the crisis approaches, start asking God to give you the courage to do the right thing, even if, at first, the right thing seems to go wrong. Pray something like this: _Father, I understand that there is a right way and a wrong way to handle the crisis that has come into my life. And I admit that sometimes the wrong way seems to offer the easy way out. Please help me not only to know Your will, but to do Your will, even when the payoff isn't obvious. If the situation doesn't improve right away, or if it gets worse, keep my confidence in You strong. Use the victories of my past to remind me that You know what You're doing and that I can trust You. Amen._

# ✛Out of the ✛Frying Pan

**PASSAGE: Esther 3:5-7**

He was an official in the palace of the king and his own adopted daughter was the queen. But that wasn't enough. Mordecai had powerful enemies, and he was vulnerable. We would like to think that we can insulate and isolate ourselves from the ill will or influence of others, but the truth is we can't. No matter who we are, our life is inextricably intertwined with the lives of the people around us. Their thoughts, their actions, their opinions, their prejudices — all of these things have a huge impact on our sense of security and well-being.

In today's passage, we will see how Mordecai's response to the emerging crisis only took that crisis to a new and more threatening level. We will see how easily Haman was able to undermine Mordecai's security, if only at a human level. And we will be warned against thinking that our security and well-being can be guaranteed by anyone or anything but God.

**READING ASSIGNMENT: Esther 3:1-7**

**FOCUS FOR TODAY: Esther 3:5-7**

> *When Haman saw that Mordecai would not kneel down or pay him honor, he was enraged. (3:5)*

Having been alerted to Mordecai's defiance, Haman investigated the matter and discovered that the report was true. Haman was enraged. In a nice example of Hebrew word play, the name *Haman* is followed immediately by the word translated *enraged*, and they sound very much alike — *Haman hĕma* — hinting that rage was part of Haman's character.

> *Yet having learned who Mordecai's people were, he scorned the idea of killing only Mordecai. Instead Haman looked for a way to destroy all Mordecai's people, the Jews, throughout the whole kingdom of Xerxes. (3:6)*

**Look again at this verse. For one man's refusal to bow down in his honor, what punishment has Haman decreed?**

_____

This should stagger us. It should send us reeling. Such hatred! The incipient antisemitism was fully exposed. For Mordecai the man, the punishment would be death. For Mordecai the Jew, the punishment would be genocide.

Keep in mind that _all the Jews throughout the whole kingdom of Xerxes_ would include whom? Recall our discussion in week one.

**What was the extent of the Persian Empire? What were its borders?**

_____

**At that time, how many Jews do you suppose might have been living outside of those borders, say in central or southern Africa, in western Europe, or in the Far East?**

_____

The fact is that few, if any, Jews would have been living outside of the boundaries of the Persian Empire, which even included Israel itself. Suddenly virtually the entire Jewish race was marked for murder. In his rage, Haman was proposing nothing short of the extermination of the Jewish people. After all, Haman likely reasoned, if being Jewish were the cause of the problem, then all Jews were potential traitors.[7]

**To some, such an outrageous idea might have seemed like little more than racist bluster. But why was this a serious threat coming from Haman?**

_____

Remember that Haman was the prime minister — the chief executive officer, if you will — of the world's only superpower. He had available to him the authority, the personnel, and the resources to make the threat a reality. And if the twentieth century taught us anything, it taught us that threats of genocide must be taken seriously.

What provoked this ancient Near-Eastern Hitler to plan his personal holocaust? The determination of one man — one Jew — to stay true to his principles. Mordecai did not know it yet, but his refusal to obey the king was about to threaten the very existence of his race.

This is the great crisis of the story of Esther: the threat to the continued existence of the Jewish race. Why, then, didn't the story begin in chapter three?

**Why do you suppose the book of Esther contains the seemingly irrelevant and far less exciting events that we have studied for the past two weeks?**

---

*In the twelfth year of King Xerxes, in the first month, the month of Nisan, they cast the pur (that is, the lot) in the presence of Haman to select a day and month. And the lot fell on the twelfth month, the month of Adar. (3:7)*

The twelfth year of King Xerxes was 474 B.C., nine years after the incidents of chapter one and four years after Esther became queen.

**The crisis had just hit, but how long had God been working behind the scenes preparing for this moment?**

---

Haman may have been planning genocide, but God was way ahead of him!

The text says that *they* cast lots in the presence of Haman. Who were *they*? We don't know. The nearest antecedent might be Mordecai's fellow officials, but that seems unlikely. More likely is that the lots were cast by Haman's advisors or perhaps some magi.[8] It is significant that Haman chose the Hebrew month of Nisan — our late March and early April — to select a date to carry out the genocide. It was customary at that time of year for practitioners of the Babylonian religion to cast lots. According to the Babylonian religion, the gods convened at that time each year to determine the fate of all men for the coming months.[9] Lots were then cast here on earth to discover what the gods had determined.

So, on which month did the gods of Babylon decree that the genocide of the Jews would take place? The lot fell to the Hebrew month of Adar — late February and early March on our calendar — the very last month of the year, eleven full months away. The God of Israel was meddling. As Proverbs 16:33 says, *The lot is cast into the lap, but its every decision is from the LORD.* Haman might have believed that the gods of Babylon had set the date, but the God of Abraham, Isaac, and Jacob — and Mordecai — was firmly in control.

We might ask a final question, one that brings out a bit of irony: Why would a high-level Persian official practice the Babylonian religion? Haman was a high official in the Persian Empire, but he was not himself a Persian. He was an Agagite and apparently a practitioner of the Babylonian religion. Although the Persians practiced the religion of Zoroastrianism, they never attempted to impose it on conquered peoples. Ironically, Haman was completely free to practice his own religion while planning the extermination of the Jews for practicing theirs.

Mordecai was helpless. Events were utterly out of his control, even though, at that point, he didn't realize it. The good news is that Mordecai was standing strong, maintaining his principles with great courage. The bad news, tragically, is that his courageous stance was causing his opponent to raise the crisis to a new and higher level.

It often happens that a crisis hits and then seems to escalate. Sometimes the things we do or say can actually contribute to the problem. What should we do when our response to a crisis only seems to be making the situation worse? Should we back down and rethink our approach, or should we go forward with confidence, accepting what comes? In the questions below, we are going to assume that an action should not be measured by its immediate consequences, but by whether it truly honors or dishonors God. After all, if an action on our part truly honors God, as Mordecai's actions so plainly do, then we can trust God with the consequences.

**Have you ever experienced a crisis that escalated, no matter what you did? In what way did the risk seem to increase?**

_____

_____

_____

**What actions on your part might have contributed to that escalating threat?**

_____

_____

**In what way were those actions honoring to God?**

_____

_____

_____

**How might those same actions have been dishonoring to God?**

_____

_____

_____

**As you look at the answers to the two previous questions, can you see any ways in which you should have responded differently?**

_____

_____

_____

### PRAYER SUGGESTION

Talk to God about your reactions to the crises of life. Ask Him to show you what He thinks of your response. Ask Him to give you the strength and confidence to do the right thing even when the right thing seems to be making matters worse. And finally, ask Him for the wisdom to know how and when you should weigh immediate consequences as you consider what to do next.

Here is a suggested prayer: _Father, I know that You allowed this crisis into my life for a reason. I may not know what that reason is, but I am confident that You do, and that's good enough for me. I know that what You want from me more than anything else is a response of faith, a response that shows You and the world that I believe in You. Yet I admit that too often I want to weigh the pros and cons, look at the consequences, and decide what to do based on how it is going to impact me and my life. Lord, get my eyes off the consequences and onto You. When I respond in ways that displease You, let me know about it. And when I respond in ways that please You, keep me on track, even if the consequences become intimidating. Thank You for loving me. I know that You are with me in this and that You won't let me down. Amen._

**PASSAGE: Esther 3:8-11**

Mordecai and his fellow Jews weren't just up against Haman. They were up against the immense, almost immeasurable, power and resources of the Persian Empire. Do you ever feel that the other side is holding all the cards? Do you ever look at the power and influence or sheer determination of the forces arrayed against you, and just lose hope? In today's passage we will begin to get a sense for just how hopeless a situation can be, at least from a human standpoint. But then we will examine what we can do when we face these seemingly hopeless situations to turn them around.

**READING ASSIGNMENT: Esther 3:1-11**

**FOCUS FOR TODAY: Esther 3:8-11**

> *Haman said to King Xerxes, "There is a certain people dispersed and scattered among the peoples in all the provinces of your kingdom whose customs are different from those of all other people and who do not obey the king's laws; it is not in the king's best interest to tolerate them. (3:8)*

Despite his enormous power as the prime minister, Haman could not order genocide on his own authority alone. He needed to take his plan to the king.

**Notice how Haman identified the Jews simply as "*a certain people.*" Why do you think he did this? Do you think it was deliberate or unintentional?**

_____

If he had believed that Xerxes was also an antisemite, Haman would have identified the Jews by name. The truth is, though, it probably didn't matter to Xerxes which conquered people Haman was talking about. Their identity was of no consequence. Whatever his reasons, Haman's failure to mention the Jews by name would prove to be important in God's ultimate deliverance of His people. Once again, God was way ahead of His enemies.

To better capture the nuance of the Hebrew, the phrase translated *dispersed and scattered* could be expressed, *among us, yet unassimilated.*[10] It was almost certainly intended as an accusation: These people — unnamed throughout the interview — live all over the empire, but they haven't blended in. They have kept to themselves. Worse, they have kept their own customs, literally, their own laws, and they *"do not obey the king's laws."* This, of course, was an outright fabrication.

**What evidence did Haman possess that showed the Jews to be a race of lawbreakers?**

_____

It was true that Mordecai obeyed his own religious laws and had disobeyed the king's command, but there was absolutely no evidence whatsoever to suggest that the Jews as a whole were anything but a law-abiding people. Why was Haman lying? Why was he portraying an entire race as rebels and insurrectionists?

**What do you think?**

_____

_____

Perhaps Haman knew that the king would not have ordered genocide as punishment for the crime of one man, no matter how personally offended Haman might have been. So Haman lied in order to depict the Jewish people as insurrectionists and thereby secure the authority to murder an entire race.

Haman concluded with the assertion that *"it is not in the king's best interest to tolerate them."* Notice how Haman acted as though he had only the king's interests at heart. Again, there wasn't even a remote possibility that Xerxes would authorize genocide simply because Haman felt insulted. Haman had to tie his proposal to the interests of the king. What would Haman suggest as an appropriate remedy? That an example be made of a few of them? That the disobedience of some be punished as a warning to the others?

> *"If it pleases the king, let a decree be issued to destroy them, and I will put ten thousand talents of silver into the royal treasury for the men who carry out this business."* (3:9)

Haman was proposing that they *all* be killed — every single one of them. He even offered to pay for it himself, offering a fantastic sum. The amount he mentioned was roughly 750,000 pounds of silver. If the figures provided by Herodotus are correct, Haman's offer was equal to two-thirds of the annual tribute paid to the imperial government by the provinces.[11]

What a good and loyal prime minister this Haman was! Not only was he concerned about the defiance of the king's authority, he was willing to put up his own money to right the wrong!

> *The king took his signet ring from his finger and gave it to Haman son of Hammedatha, the Agagite, the enemy of the Jews.* (3:10)

What did King Xerxes do? He gave Haman, his loyal prime minister, the use of his signet ring.

**What was the significance of this? (Hint: Look at Genesis 41:41-43.)** _____

The signet ring was a symbol of imperial authority recognized throughout the empire.[12] Haman was given complete freedom to implement his plan. Notice that Haman was called *the Agagite, the enemy of the Jews.* Once again the writer reminded the Jewish reader of the character of this man by linking him, if only coincidentally, with the ancient Amalekite king.

> *"Keep the money," the king said to Haman, "and do with the people as you please."* (3:11)

What became of Haman's offer to fund the massacre? Commentators differ on this point, because the phrase translated as *keep the money* can be understood in several ways. Literally, the verse reads, *And the king said to Haman, "The silver and the people are given to you to do with as is pleasing in your eyes."* Did this mean that Haman's offer to fund the slaughter was being declined, as some commentators believe? Possibly, but there is an indication in the next chapter that Haman's money was actually used. (See Esther 4:7.) Besides, the fact that Haman donated the money to the treasury would not give him the authority to use it as he pleased. Both the people and the money, once donated, were under the authority of the king. It seems more likely that Xerxes, having accepted the gift to the royal treasury, was granting Haman the full authority to do as he proposed both with the money and with the people.

But wait. Isn't something missing?

**When Xerxes heard about the assassination plot, what was the first thing he did? (See Esther 2:23.)**

_____

**When Haman heard that Mordecai was refusing to bow down, what did he do? (See Esther 3:4-5.)**

_____

_____

When Haman accused this unnamed people of treason and proposed genocide, no investigation was carried out. Why not?

For the simple reason that Haman was the prime minister and Xerxes believed him. According to the Greek historian Herodotus, there were three things that the Persians took great care to teach their sons: to ride a horse, to draw the bow, and to tell the truth.[13] One of the most disgraceful things a person could do in Persian culture was to tell a lie. Despite their murderous and depraved lifestyles, the Persians had no tolerance for liars. It probably never occurred to Xerxes that Haman, his trusted friend and prime minister, might not have been telling him the truth or that his motives might have been entirely personal.

Mordecai didn't realize it, but a bad situation had just become worse — far worse. His personal crisis of refusing to bow in honor of Haman had developed into a crisis beyond anything he could have imagined. Although Mordecai could control whether or not he would willingly bow the knee to Haman, he could not control Haman's response.

We hate to lose control, to have a situation deteriorate in a way that leaves us feeling helpless. Yet there is one good thing about losing control: It leaves us no choice but to open the door to God. Wouldn't it be great if we could be convinced of our helplessness a little earlier? We might actually turn our problems over to God without first having to collapse in despair! Let's get some ideas on how to do that — how to bypass the "hopeless despair" stage of dealing with our problems.

**Think back to the crisis you described last week. What aspects of that crisis were outside of your control?**

_____

_____

_____

**What do you ordinarily do to hold on to control as situations seem to deteriorate?**

_____

_____

_____

_____

**What could you do differently in the future that would invite God's involvement sooner in the process?**

_____

_____

_____

_____

## PRAYER SUGGESTION

Tell God about a recent crisis in your life and admit to Him that, despite your best efforts, you can already see that you need Him. Describe to Him the usual things you do to maintain control over situations and other people. Ask Him to remind you that you need Him despite such efforts, and that the sooner He becomes involved, the better. Ask Him to show you exactly how to let Him take control. Finally, thank Him for allowing the crises of life to get bad enough that you are finally convinced to turn to Him.

Here is a suggested prayer: _Father, as I look at what I'm facing right now, I can already see that it's going to be too big for me. Even before things reach the meltdown stage, it's obvious that I need You. Thank You for opening my eyes to that. Usually at this point in a crisis I'm still totally focused on what I can do and how I can keep things under control. But I need You right now, and I see that. Please show me how to involve You early in the process. Help me understand what to expect from You and how I should cooperate with Your plan. Finally, I want to thank You for letting things go so haywire sometimes that I finally turn to You. Whatever it takes for You to get my attention, I know it's worth it. So thanks. Amen._

# Hitting Bottom

**PASSAGE: Esther 3:12-4:1**

When the full weight and enormity of the crisis finally hit, Mordecai was desolate. What had he done? What had he brought upon his people? And what would he do since there apparently was nothing that he *could* do? Little did Mordecai realize that God had already been at work resolving the crisis even before it occurred. How would it change our responses to the crises in our lives if we believed — *really believed* — that God had been at work for years on the perfect solution?

**READING ASSIGNMENT: Esther 3:1-4:1**

**FOCUS FOR TODAY: Esther 3:12-4:1**

> *On the thirteenth day of the first month the royal secretaries were summoned. They wrote out in the script of each province and in the language of each people all Haman's orders to the king's satraps, the governors of the various provinces and the nobles of the various peoples. These were written in the name of King Xerxes himself and sealed with his own ring.* (3:12)

Haman's plan had become the king's decree. Along with the authority, Haman had the personnel to carry it out. So *on the thirteenth day of the first month* — ironically, the day before Passover — *the royal secretaries were summoned.* These secretaries translated the decree, just as Haman dictated it, into every language of the empire. Copies were made for every provincial governor and even the nobles of the various peoples. In other words, a copy of the decree would be translated and sent to every "official" in the empire, right down to the tribal leaders.

**What did it mean that the decree was written in the king's name and sealed with his signet ring? Why was this so significant?**

_____

_____

_____

_____

Sealed with the signet ring, the decree was, in effect, signed by the king. Legally, it was not Haman who was taking this action, but Xerxes himself. There was no indication in the text of the decree that the will of anyone but the king was being carried out. The order was coming, literally, from the top. There was no one — absolutely no one — to whom an appeal of this decree could be made.

We are not accustomed in our culture to having utterly no recourse, no avenue of appeal. Ours is a government of checks and balances where the actions of one branch can be challenged by another. Even if the branches of government were somehow to unite against us, the government itself is ultimately accountable to the people, so we can always appeal to the press or to popular opinion. But the Jews had no avenue of appeal because at that time, the authority of the king was absolute. It could not be challenged. They had, literally, no recourse.

> *Dispatches were sent by couriers to all the king's provinces with the order to destroy, kill and annihilate all the Jews — young and old, women and little children — on a single day, the thirteenth day of the twelfth month, the month of Adar, and to plunder their goods.* (3:13)

As I mentioned in week one, the Persians had a remarkable system of couriers similar to, but far more extensive than, the pony express. Copies of the decree were on their way to every corner of the empire.

**How does the wording of the decree strike you? What do you notice?**

_____

_____

_____

The order to *destroy, kill and annihilate* reflected the redundancy typical of legal language, but it also reflected the coldbloodedness of the decree. Note that the order specified all Jews, young and old, including women and children. Make no mistake: This was not just mass murder. This was genocide.

The decree further specified that this genocide was to be carried out on a single day. Even Hitler wasn't that ambitious, but Hitler was trying to do the job with a relatively small network of death camps, whereas Haman was mobilizing the resources of the entire Persian Empire. The day specified was the thirteenth day of the twelfth month, or on our calendar, the end of February of the following year. As we learned in the previous verse, the decree was issued on the thirteenth day of the first month, roughly the end of March. The Jewish people were eleven months away from a holocaust.

**The decree included an additional feature not mentioned before: the plunder of Jewish goods. Why do you think this phrase was added?**

_____

_____

_____

If Haman wanted to draw an empire of minority groups into the commission of genocide, it might help to offer to share the plunder!

Finally, one might wonder why the decree was actually issued so many months in advance. We find the answer in the next verse.

> _A copy of the text of the edict was to be issued as law in every province and made known to the people of every nationality so they would be ready for that day._ (3:14)

Issuing the decree right away gave local officials plenty of time to make their preparations. But are we to understand by the phrase _made known to the people of every nationality_ that the decree was made public? If so, what would have prevented the Jews from making preparations of their own? Were Jews throughout the empire to be arrested at once to await execution or would they be allowed to flee? The phrase could be translated _made known to all peoples,_ meaning perhaps the leaders of all nationalities, but the sense of the text seems to be that the decree was announced publicly.

But think of it this way: Even if the Jews were allowed to flee, where would they go?

**Put yourself in their position, as marked men and women in the middle of a vast empire, with their meager resources, lack of transportation, and primitive knowledge of world geography. What could you have done to save your family?**

_____

_____

Do you see the problem? The Jews very likely knew what was coming, but from a legal, military, and even practical standpoint, there was nothing they could do to prevent it.

> _Spurred on by the king's command, the couriers went out, and the edict was issued in the citadel of Susa. The king and Haman sat down to drink, but the city of Susa was bewildered._ (3:15)

The decree went out both throughout the empire and in the citadel of Susa, while Haman and Xerxes sat down to drink. Herodotus wrote of an odd Persian custom in which a decision made while one was sober was considered again while one was drunk. Conversely, a decision made while one was drunk was considered again while one was sober.[14] The idea, apparently, was that if the decision made sense both while one was drunk and while one was sober, it must have been a good decision. If this custom was being practiced here, it was likely just a formality. The decision had been made, and the couriers had been dispatched.

**If Xerxes and Haman were enjoying a drink, the city of Susa, by contrast, was bewildered and confused. Why would non-Jews have been concerned? What do you think?**

_____

_____

_____

Remember that the Persians were a ruling minority that ruled an empire of conquered minorities. There was no "Persian majority" — only other minority groups. Moreover, these other groups would have known the Jews to be good, decent, law-abiding people, deserving of nothing like this. The decree was transparently arbitrary and no doubt terribly alarming to other equally defenseless minorities. Keep in mind that these other groups had no way of knowing that Haman, not Xerxes, was behind it, let alone that it was motivated by a personal vendetta fueled by antisemitism. After all, even Xerxes himself didn't know that. All that these other groups would have seen was a new and terrifying imperial policy. It is not surprising, then, that the city of Susa was bewildered.

> When Mordecai learned of all that had been done, he tore his clothes, put on sackcloth
> and ashes, and went out into the city, wailing loudly and bitterly. (4:1)

Finally, the crisis hit home. Prior to this, all Mordecai knew was that his fellow officials were concerned about his refusal to bow down in honor of Haman. He might not even have been aware that Haman had investigated the matter. Then Mordecai heard of the decree and he was desolate. What had he brought upon his people?

Mordecai may have been completely blindsided and helpless, but God wasn't! Mordecai didn't see it coming, but God did. More than that, God had been preparing for this very moment for at least a decade. Although Mordecai felt utterly helpless, God's solution to the crisis was already in place and ready to be implemented.

Mordecai's reaction was completely understandable, even legitimate, given what he knew. But imagine for a moment that Mordecai knew that God had been at work all along. He might not have understood the significance of every event, but imagine that he was fully convinced that God had been on the job for over a decade arranging a perfect outcome for this crisis. How might Mordecai's reaction have been different had he known that God had already provided not just the solution, but the victory? How might your reaction to your crisis be different if you knew exactly the same thing?

**Reread Esther 4:1. Rewrite the verse as if Mordecai knew that God had been at work for at least a decade — that all the pieces were in place to deliver the Jews from this crisis.**

_____

_____

_____

_____

_____

**What would your reaction be to your current crisis if you knew that God had prearranged your deliverance?**

_____

_____

_____

_____

_____

**PRAYER SUGGESTION**

Ask God to help you react to your circumstances as if you truly believed that He was in control. Thank Him that He said, _Never will I leave you, never will I forsake you_ (Hebrews 13:5), and that _in all things God works for the good of those who love Him_ (Romans 8:28). Then ask Him to give you the ability to express that hope and confidence through your actions. Ask Him to help you to rejoice in Him always (Philippians 4:4), even in the tough times, because you know that He is hard at work on your behalf.

# The Christian and Civil Disobedience

**PASSAGES: Selected passages**

The third chapter of Esther is short, containing only fifteen verses, and we were able to study these verses in four days. That gives us the opportunity to examine an important issue raised in this week's study: the question of the Christian and civil disobedience.

The crisis of Esther 3 was triggered by Mordecai's refusal to obey the king. Mordecai seems to have felt that to bow down to Haman would be a violation of his religious convictions as a Jew. Was Mordecai right or was he wrong? Should he have stood his ground as a principled Jew, or should he have obeyed the king as a good citizen?

Where do we draw the line in our own lives? As moral consensus and "freedom of religion" increasingly give way to moral relativism and "freedom from religion," how should the Christian balance obedience to government with obedience to God?

**READING ASSIGNMENT: Selected passages**

The Word of God admonishes us to obey governing authorities. Read the following key passages carefully, marking significant points as you read. When you've completed your reading, try to summarize what you learned into a clear principle regarding the Christian's responsibility to governmental authority.

**Read Proverbs 24:21-22; Ecclesiastes 8:2-6; Romans 13:1-7; and 1 Peter 2:13-17.**

**Do you detect any consistent principles running through these passages? Summarize what you believe these passages teach us about our responsibility to obey human government. Don't worry now about exceptions or "what ifs."**

_____

_____

_____

_____

We learned from this first set of passages that God commands us to obey human government. Yet other passages show us that there are times when disobedience against human authorities is required. Study the instances of disobedience against government in the following passages, noting the points that you find significant, then try to discern what they have in common.

**Read Exodus 1:15-20; Joshua 2:1-6; 1 Kings 18:3-4; Daniel 6:5-10; Acts 4:16-20; and Revelation 13:4-8.**

**Based on these passages, what circumstances constitute an exception to the general rule, and what should we do under those exceptional circumstances?**

_____

_____

_____

_____

_____

**PRAYER SUGGESTION**

Bring before God your attitude toward government and consider what it says about your attitude toward Him. Confess whatever sins you may have committed against the governing authorities and acknowledge to God that sin against human government is sin against Him. Ask God to guide you as you seek to be both an obedient citizen and an obedient Christian. Finally, ask Him to give you discernment, courage, and faith should the time ever come for you to take a stand.

✝

## WEEK THREE
## WHEN THE CRISIS HITS
# Small Group Discussion Guide

The crises we face in life can be a lot like earthquakes in California. We know they're coming — we're just not sure when or how bad they will be. And when they do come there isn't a thing we can do to prevent them. Even so, there is something we can and must do to get through it and find a solution with a lot less heartache. Today we are going to learn what that something is.

In Esther 3, we have seen how Mordecai was blindsided by the biggest crisis of his life. And we have seen how he responded the wrong way — in other words, pretty much the way any of us would. But by looking at what he did in his crisis, we can discover what we should do when a crisis hits in our own lives.

**TODAY: Esther 3:1-4:1**

**I. Don't depend on your GOOD DEEDS to prevent DISASTERS. They won't.**
**KEY PASSAGE:** Esther 3:1-5 (read it aloud)

**DISCUSSION QUESTIONS:** What godly and courageous action did Mordecai take in this passage? Did his action prevent or contribute to the unfolding crisis?

_____

_____

**PRINCIPLE:** We like to think that if we do enough good things in life God will prevent bad things from happening to us. It doesn't work that way. In fact, sometimes God actually allows the good things we do to trigger things that may seem at first to be bad.

**APPLICATION:** What godly action have you taken that actually seemed to cause rather than prevent problems?

_____

_____

_____

**II. Don't depend on things being BETTER THAN they seem. They may be worse.**

**KEY PASSAGE:** Esther 3:6 (read it aloud)

**DISCUSSION QUESTION:** Mordecai knew that by refusing to bow down in honor of Haman he was taking a risk. In what way was the situation far worse than he feared?

_____

_____

**PRINCIPLE:** We like to think that if we just look on the bright side, we might discover that the crisis isn't as bad as it seems. But unfortunately, sometimes it is. And while there may be some power in positive thinking, there isn't nearly enough.

**APPLICATION:** Have you ever tried to convince yourself that a situation wasn't as bad as it seemed, only to discover that it was far worse? Explain.

_____

_____

_____

**III. Don't depend on "the system" to SET THINGS RIGHT. It may not.**

**KEY PASSAGE:** Esther 3:8-11 (read it aloud)

**DISCUSSION QUESTIONS:** What did "the system" do to thwart Haman's plan?

How can you explain that?

_____

**PRINCIPLE:** We would like to think that if we just hang in there, somebody will eventually see our situation, stop the "bad guys," and come to our rescue. They might, but then again, they might not.

**APPLICATION:** Has "the system," at whatever level, ever failed to protect you? Explain.

_____

_____

_____

_____

**IV. If you believe that God has already solved your problem, ACT LIKE IT.**

**KEY PASSAGE:** Esther 4:1 (read it aloud)

**DISCUSSION QUESTION:** Although Mordecai's actions were justifiable, how might his actions have been different if he had been confident that God was already way ahead of Haman?

_____

_____

**PRINCIPLE:** The loving protection of God doesn't mean that bad things won't happen, but it does mean that you are safe in God's care and that in the end you will be okay. If we believe that God cares, we ought to act like God cares.

**SUPPORT PASSAGES:** Deuteronomy 31:6; Isaiah 41:10-13; Philippians 4:6-7; and 1 Peter 5:7 (read them aloud)

**APPLICATION:** If you believe — if you are absolutely convinced — that God has already arranged your deliverance, what is preventing you from reacting that way right now?

_____

_____

_____

# What to Do in a Crisis

Day 1 — Just Doing Something

Day 2 — Just Avoiding the Wrong Thing

Day 3 — Just Doing Nothing

Day 4 —Just Opting Out

Day 5 — Preparing for Courageous Faith

Mordecai and Esther were both about to learn about Haman's plan. But what could they have done? What should they have done? Like Jews throughout the empire, Mordecai had seen the king's decree, and he couldn't imagine just sitting around and waiting to be executed. But what could he do? Esther was the queen of the Persian Empire, but would her position — less powerful than it sounded — really be useful? The situation was desperate, but what, if anything, should Mordecai and Esther have done about it?

We have all been in this position: We finally have a clear view of the problem; it's the solution that we can't see. What do we do? At times like that, we usually have five options, four of which are not recommended. These four options include: "just doing something," "just avoiding the wrong thing," "just doing nothing," or "just opting out." Unfortunately these options rarely solve the problem. The only constructive option is one that, at first, may not seem very attractive: getting ready to trust God. That's what we are going to look at this week — how to recognize and bypass the bad options and prepare instead for courageous faith.

# Just Doing Something

**PASSAGE: Esther 4:1-3**

A crisis can leave us feeling pretty helpless. A problem forces its way in and there is little we can do about it. Sometimes instead of sitting around feeling helpless, it just feels good to do something, *anything*. As the old saying goes, "Don't just stand there, *do* something!" But just doing something is no guarantee that that something is the right thing to do. When the pressure is on, how can we tell the difference between doing something and doing the right thing?

**READING ASSIGNMENT: Esther 4:1-3**

**FOCUS FOR TODAY: Esther 4:1-3**

> *When Mordecai learned of all that had been done, he tore his clothes, put on sackcloth and ashes, and went out into the city, wailing loudly and bitterly.* (4:1)

Mordecai had not only heard about the decree to annihilate the Jews, he had obtained a copy of the decree itself, as we shall see. His reaction was understandable. Because of his refusal to bow down in honor of Haman, the entire Jewish people had been marked for genocide. Mordecai was devastated. What had he done? What had he brought upon his people?

To express his grief and protest the injustice, Mordecai tore off his usual clothes, put on sackcloth and ashes, and went out into the streets of Susa. We will see in verse six that Mordecai spent at least some of his time in the plaza, or *town square*, immediately in front of the palace gate. What was Mordecai doing there? He was *wailing loudly and bitterly*. The word translated *wailing* has the nuance of crying out against or protesting.[1] In fact, the Greek version of the Old Testament in use in Jesus' day adds that Mordecai said, *A nation that has done no wrong is going to be destroyed.*[2] Mordecai was not only grieving — he was crying out against the injustice, and he was doing it *loudly and bitterly*.

**What do you make of Mordecai's actions? Do you approve or disapprove? Why?**

_____

_____

**What do you think Mordecai could reasonably hope to accomplish? How likely was it that his protest would do any good?**

_____

_____

**What effect might Mordecai's actions have had on the mood in the city?**

_____

_____

We know from the last verse of chapter three that the people of Susa were already bewildered by the king's decree to annihilate the Jews. After all, they too were nothing more than conquered minorities. How long would it be before this new and arbitrary imperial policy would single them out for destruction? And how might this loud and bitter protester named Mordecai test imperial patience? Mordecai's actions must certainly have heightened the tension in an already tense situation.

> _He went only as far as the king's gate, because no one clothed in sackcloth was allowed to enter it._ (4:2)

Mordecai worked in the palace, but he wasn't allowed to come in wearing sackcloth and ashes. The issue might simply have been one of appropriate attire, but there is reason to suggest otherwise. The book of Nehemiah gives us helpful insight into the Persian court.

**Read Nehemiah 2:1-3. What does Nehemiah's experience before King Artaxerxes, the son of Xerxes, tell us about the risk involved in displaying sorrow before the king?**

_____

_____

> _In every province to which the edict and order of the king came, there was great mourning among the Jews, with fasting, weeping and wailing. Many lay in sackcloth and ashes._ (4:3)

Mordecai was not alone in his actions. In every province, Jews were mourning, fasting, weeping, and wailing, indicating that the decree had not only been distributed, but publicized throughout the empire. Like Mordecai, many were in sackcloth and ashes, suggesting that their demonstrations of grief were public. The entire Jewish race was desolate with grief. Although prayer was not mentioned, at least not explicitly, we can assume that it is implied. Surely some of their *mourning...fasting, weeping, and wailing* was directed to God.

How would God respond to these pleas from His people? It's hard to say, but indulge your imagination.

**What would you like to see God do at this point?**

_____

_____

_____

This would have been a wonderful time for God to step in with a great miracle of deliverance. Perhaps a prophet of God like Moses could step forward warning Xerxes of divine retribution if his decree were not revoked. Perhaps a series of plagues through the intervening months would demonstrate that the God of Israel was greater than the gods of Babylon and Persia. God had defeated Pharaoh; surely He could defeat Xerxes.

But there would be no prophet. There would be no plagues. No sea would open up to provide a way of escape. There would, for a time, seem to be only weeping and wailing. And heaven, it seemed, would remain silent.

Mordecai and his fellow Jews throughout the empire were desperate. From the human point of view, there was nothing they could do; there was no recourse. Yet because they felt they should do something, they cried out in desperation to both God and men. It might do no good. It might even put them at more immediate risk. But at least they were doing *something*.

How can we tell if the "something" we are doing is the right thing to do? When faced with a crisis, it is only natural to want to do something about it. But what? Sometimes the crisis is just too big for us. We rack our brains for a plan of action, but nothing looks very promising. We could just cry out in protest or in prayer, but what happens when we do? Will help come? And if it does, will it come in time?

**Have you ever felt that the actions you took during a crisis didn't help the situation at all? Explain.**

_____

_____

_____

**What new difficulties might your actions have created?**

_____

_____

_____

**Sometimes we do things not because they are safe or because we get immediate results, but simply because they are the right thing to do. What biblical truth or principle gives you confidence that your actions in the crisis were the right thing to do?**

_____

_____

_____

_____

**Based on your answer to the previous question, should your plan of action have been continued, modified, or abandoned?**

_____

_____

_____

## PRAYER SUGGESTION

Ask God to give you the wisdom to know the difference between "just doing something" and doing the right thing. Ask Him to help you look past immediate results and even immediate risks to discern whether your actions are based on God-honoring principles. Then ask Him to give you the courage to do the right thing, leaving the results to Him.

Here is a suggested prayer: _Father, I'm facing a crisis. I'm feeling desperate, and I really want to do something, but the truth is, I don't know what to do. I don't want to be so intent on results that I get ahead of You, but I don't want to be paralyzed with fear either. God, please show me the principles that should be guiding my actions. Show me the right thing to do based on those principles. Then help me do it, and I will trust You with the results. Amen._

# Just Avoiding the Wrong Thing

**PASSAGE: Esther 4:4-7**

Word of Mordecai's activities was about to reach Esther. She had not received word of the decree, but whatever the reason for these very public protests, Esther knew that Mordecai was putting himself at risk. Whatever the situation was, a public demonstration would likely only make matters worse. *That,* she reasoned, *had to stop.*

Often when a crisis hits, our first reaction is to try to stop the bleeding, to minimize further damage. We feel vulnerable, so it is only natural that we would want to protect ourselves, to limit our vulnerability. But that's not always the right reaction. After all, there is a difference between avoiding doing the wrong thing and actually doing the right thing, as we will see in today's study.

**READING ASSIGNMENT: Esther 4:1-7**

**FOCUS FOR TODAY: Esther 4:4-7**

> *When Esther's maids and eunuchs came and told her about Mordecai, she was in great distress. She sent clothes for him to put on instead of his sackcloth, but he would not accept them.* (4:4)

Word of the king's decree had spread throughout the empire, yet it had not made its way down the hall and into the king's harem. This is another reminder of how extraordinarily isolated these women were. Esther did hear, however, of Mordecai's demonstration in the plaza in front of the palace gate. Apparently her maids and eunuchs either saw or heard reports about his activities. They told Esther, and *she was in great distress.*

Why? Had she heard of the decree to annihilate the Jews? No; we will learn in the next verse that she was unaware of the decree. Did she feel concern over the obvious grief of her cousin and adoptive father, whatever its cause? No doubt. But think about what you have learned about Persian culture, about authority, and about prejudice.

**What other reasons might there have been for Esther's concern?**

_____

_____

_____

In a totalitarian regime, protest is more than risky; it is virtually suicidal. Moreover, with antisemitism an ongoing concern, it is possible that Esther wanted Mordecai, a Jew, to follow his own advice and stay inconspicuous. (See Esther 2:10.)

Mordecai's actions were no doubt courageous, yet by grieving and even protesting so publicly, he was taking an enormous risk. Esther must have felt that, for the sake of his safety, she had to put a stop to this right away. So Esther sent Mordecai clothes, with the implicit — and perhaps even explicit — advice to stop the demonstrations at once. Mordecai refused.

**Mordecai would not back down. Why? What does this tell you about his character?**

_____

_____

Despite Esther's concerns, Mordecai remained in a state of public mourning and protest.

> *Then Esther summoned Hathach, one of the king's eunuchs assigned to attend her, and*
> *ordered him to find out what was troubling Mordecai and why.* (4:5)

Mordecai was reacting very strongly to something and Esther wanted to know what it was all about. So Hathach was assigned to discover, putting the Hebrew literally, *what this was and why this was.*[3] She wanted the whole story. Notice that Hathach was called the king's eunuch. Mordecai was about to be confronted by a personal servant of the king. Where were Hathach's loyalties? Would he report Mordecai's protests to Esther or to the king?

> *Hathach went out to Mordecai in the open square of the city in front of the king's gate.* (4:6)

Hathach found Mordecai grieving and protesting in the plaza right in front of the palace entrance. Put yourself in Hathach's position. You are a royal official, a representative of the king. You are about to confront a man who is publicly protesting imperial policy. And you are about to do it in the middle of the plaza right in front of the palace gate.

**What would your concerns be?**

_____

_____

_____

He may have been doing this at the queen's request, but would he risk being guilty of divided loyalties? Hathach was in a precarious position.

> *Mordecai told him everything that had happened to him, including the exact amount of money Haman had promised to pay into the royal treasury for the destruction of the Jews. (4:7)*

Now put yourself in Mordecai's position. A representative of the royal household, a servant of the king, is asking you to explain your actions. Here is your chance. What will you say? Will you tell him very candidly that you are protesting the unjust and arbitrary decree of the king to annihilate your entire race? Will you expose the duplicity of Haman, the prime minister, who had offered to spend his own money to fund his antisemitic rampage? If the servant is loyal to the king and to the prime minister, you have in all likelihood just signed your own death warrant.

**What would you say?**

_____

_____

_____

Most of us, I suspect, might be tempted to soft-pedal our accusations at this point in the interest of "living to fight another day." After all, you have eleven months. Why call the question and sacrifice your own life so quickly?

But this was not Mordecai's approach. With amazing boldness, Mordecai told Hathach everything. He spoke of the decree to bow down in honor of Haman. He spoke of his own disobedience to that decree. He spoke of Haman's plan to annihilate the Jewish race. And he spoke of Haman's willingness to pay for it.

Notice something interesting here: Mordecai knew not only that Haman had offered to pay for the annihilation of the Jews; Mordecai knew the exact amount that Haman had offered. It seems unlikely that the decree sent throughout the empire would have included this detail. How did Mordecai know about it? It would appear that Mordecai had inside information. So Mordecai was lodging a protest against the most powerful man in the world, King Xerxes, and he was leveling an accusation against the second most powerful man in the world, Haman, the prime minister. And he was basing this, at least in part, on hearsay. Mordecai was going out on a limb.

Esther was concerned that Mordecai was putting himself at risk, and indeed he was. Mordecai was concerned, too, not with avoiding additional mistakes, but rather with avoiding the consequences for others of what he had already done. When a crisis hits, we can easily fall back into a defensive position. Our concern can quickly become an internal reproach: "Don't make any more mistakes!" But that's not always the best approach.

**Have you ever responded to a crisis simply by being cautious or by trying to avoid further mistakes? Did this cautious approach help resolve your crisis? Why or why not?**

_____

_____

_____

**How would you explain the proper relationship between caution and faith?**

_____

_____

_____

**PRAYER SUGGESTION**

Ask God to show you the difference between caution and real confidence in Him. Confess to Him the times that you have crawled forward cautiously rather than advanced in bold faith. Use your answer to the first question so that you can be specific. Admit that sometimes you use caution to avoid the solution. Finally, ask God to teach you the proper relationship between wise and godly caution on the one hand and outright faithlessness on the other.

Pray something like this: *Father, I need to admit to You that sometimes I use caution as a way of refusing to trust You. I know that faith sometimes calls me to do uncomfortable things and to trust the invisible. But I also know from Hebrews 11:6 that without faith it is impossible to please You. Please open my eyes and let me see my caution for what it is. Show me what it looks like to trust You wisely. Give me godly examples, people who get it right, so that I will know how to combine prudence and faith as I follow You. Amen.*

✦

# Just Doing Nothing

**PASSAGE: Esther 4:8-11**

The pieces are coming together. It is now easy to see how strategic Esther's appointment to the position of queen had been some five years earlier. Easy to see, yes. But was it easy for Esther to act on? That is another question entirely. God's plan was about to challenge Esther's courage.

One way to respond to a crisis is to "play it safe" and do nothing. This is especially appealing when the crisis is happening to someone else. Even if we can see the strategic role that we ourselves could play in the solution, the risk might keep us sidelined. The fact is that there is an enormous difference between knowing and doing. There is an even greater distance between doing nothing and doing the right thing.

**READING ASSIGNMENT: Esther 4:1-11**

**FOCUS FOR TODAY: Esther 4:8-11**

> He [Mordecai] *also gave him* [Hathach, the king's representative] *a copy of the text
> of the edict for their annihilation, which had been published in Susa, to show to Esther
> and explain it to her, and he told him to urge her to go into the king's presence to beg
> for mercy and plead with him for her people.* (4:8)

Mordecai had a copy of the decree on hand, and he gave it to Hathach. The phrase translated as *to show to Esther and explain it to her* could be understood to imply that Esther did not know how to read or perhaps that she didn't know how to read that particular script. It could also mean that Hathach was not simply to show Esther the decree, but he was also to place it in the context of the events as Mordecai had related them. This is probably the better interpretation. But there was something more in Mordecai's request.

**What else was Mordecai asking Hathach to do?**

_____

_____

_____

Mordecai was asking Hathach to plead with Esther not merely to intervene, but to appeal to the king on behalf of *her people,* the Jews. Mordecai had just revealed to a representative of the royal household that the queen was a Jew! The very man who had encouraged her to conceal her identity had just revealed the secret, and he did it in connection with a decree that all Jews be killed. Needless to say, this put Esther at enormous personal risk since even the king was limited in his authority to repeal royal decrees.

Not only had Mordecai identified Esther as one of the condemned, but his request that she approach the king uninvited would have placed her at risk of immediate death, as we shall see. It is remarkable that Mordecai had placed the fate of his people, as well as of his own cousin and adopted daughter, entirely in the hands of a servant of the king. Was Mordecai demonstrating courageous faith or sheer recklessness? What would Hathach do?

> *Hathach went back and reported to Esther what Mordecai had said.* (4:9)

Although Hathach was a servant of the king, he took the report to Esther. It is amazing that Hathach would keep such a report from the king. Mordecai had opposed the king's decree and challenged the integrity of the prime minister, and now he was trying to involve the queen. This would no doubt have been of considerable interest both to Xerxes and Haman. Yet Hathach returned to Esther with the report. The next two verses indicate that he even pleaded with Esther to intervene just as Mordecai had requested.

> *Then she instructed him to say to Mordecai...* (4:10)

Esther had been asked to reveal her ethnicity to the king, then *to beg for mercy and plead with him for her people* (verse 8). If you were in Esther's position, how would you have responded to Mordecai? Remember that although you were chosen for your beauty and your charm, you were under no delusions that the king's interest in you went beyond that. You seldom saw the king, and your uncle had revealed to one of the king's servants that you were among the condemned. He was asking you to reveal that fact directly to the king, and to do so uninvited, which as we shall see was a very serious issue in itself.

**What would you be feeling?** _____
**What would you do?** _____

What message, then, did Esther send back to Mordecai?

*"All the king's officials and the people of the royal provinces know that for any man or woman who approaches the king in the inner court without being summoned the king has but one law: that he be put to death. The only exception to this is for the king to extend the gold scepter to him and spare his life. But thirty days have passed since I was called to go to the king." (4:11)*

**In a word, Esther declined. Why?** _____

We might suppose that, as queen, Esther would have had great access and influence. Yet she did not and she knew it. In fact, she was not even permitted to approach the king without having been summoned. Apparently it was common knowledge that to approach the king uninvited meant certain death. Josephus, the first century Jewish historian, tells us that King Xerxes had guards armed with battleaxes posted on either side of the throne. If someone attempted to approach the throne unbidden, they were executed on the spot.[4] In this respect, Esther was no different from anyone else. Moreover, even though she was the king's favorite concubine, the fact was that he hadn't summoned her in a month — something Mordecai could not have known. If she approached the king unbidden, he might have chosen to extend his scepter, allowing her to live. But even if her life were spared in this way, it would only have been to allow her to identify herself with a condemned people.

Some have wondered why Esther would have to go in uninvited. Why couldn't she simply have made an appointment?

**How would you respond to this question?**

_____

_____

_____

Perhaps Esther could have sought an appointment, but through whom? Haman? What reason would she have given him for wanting to see the king? Would you have expected her to lie? What might the consequences have been if she did? It is no surprise, then, that Esther found the plan unattractive. As far as she was concerned, the safer course of action would have been to decline Mordecai's request and perhaps hope that Hathach would keep her ethnicity a secret. Mordecai would have to look for another solution.

General Eddie Rickenbacker, an American aviator and a hero of two world wars, defined courage as "doing what you are afraid to do." There is no courage, he said, without fear.[5] Esther was afraid — anyone in her shoes would have been. She just hadn't reached the point of acting against those fears. However, in time, she would. Consider the times when you allow fear to paralyze you into refusing to follow God.

**Have you ever faced a crisis, been presented with an opportunity to be part of the solution, yet been paralyzed by fear? Explain.**

_____

_____

_____

_____

_____

_____

**What regrets did you later feel about having missed an opportunity to trust God?**

_____

_____

_____

**What opportunities are you declining right now because of fear?**

_____

_____

_____

**PRAYER SUGGESTION**

Confess to God how you may have allowed important spiritual opportunities — opportunities that could have meant deliverance for you or someone else — to pass you by because of your fear. Ask Him to show you any opportunities that you are overlooking right now and give you the courage to follow through.

Here is a suggested prayer: _Father, I first want to thank You for including me in Your plan, for giving me mountains to climb, and battles to fight and win. Thank You for not leaving me out of the action, but instead giving me many opportunities to trust You and watch You come through in the situation. But I also want to ask Your forgiveness because, the truth is, I haven't always taken advantage of those opportunities. Too often I have allowed fear to paralyze me. I watch the opportunity to trust You come and I watch it go, and I don't do a thing. Lord, I'm tired of doing nothing. I want to do something for You and for Your kingdom. Show me what that is, and when You do, give me a good hard shove. Amen._

# Just Opting Out

**PASSAGE: Esther 4:12-14**

Esther was about to come to a crossroads, a point of crisis in her life. She would have to choose between putting herself at risk for the sake of her people, and keeping her identity a secret in the hope that the executioners would not come for her. There was no avoiding a decision. Despite all that God had done — even because of it — Esther would have to decide and then act.

At some point in every crisis, God calls on all of us to act. Every crisis includes a crossroad, and when we reach that crossroad, the next move is ours. How will we respond when faced with the crossroads in our crises?

**READING ASSIGNMENT: Esther 4:1-14**

**FOCUS FOR TODAY: Esther 4:12-14**

> *When Esther's words were reported to Mordecai… (4:12)*

Hathach delivered Esther's message to Mordecai who presumably had been continuing his demonstration outside of the palace gate. Hathach's willingness to take risks on behalf of Esther is once again both surprising and delightful.

> *…he sent back this answer: "Do not think that because you are in the king's house you alone of all the Jews will escape. (4:13)*

Mordecai listened and then shot back a reply. His answer was almost shocking in its directness.

**What did Mordecai's answer suggest about Esther's motives?**

_____

Mordecai saw what was in Esther's mind: She was trying to save herself, plain and simple. Esther was afraid to speak with the king because it would put her own life at risk. But Mordecai pointed out that, as a Jew, her life was already at risk. Was Esther afraid to die? Mordecai reminded her that she would in all likelihood die anyway. The decree stated that all the Jews would be killed. Nowhere did the decree exclude members of the king's household.

We have to ask the obvious question here: What made Mordecai so sure that Esther's ethnicity would ever be discovered? Was Mordecai assuming that Hathach couldn't be trusted? Not necessarily.

**In what other way might Esther's Jewish identity have become known?**

_____

_____

It occurs to me that since Mordecai was putting his Jewish identity on public display, Esther was at risk from anyone who knew of their relationship. As we have seen, this would include at the very least the local official who conducted the search for young girls in Susa (Esther 2:3-7), the people who carried news of Esther to Mordecai during her year of preparation (Esther 2:11), and perhaps others. Esther was at risk. There was no avoiding it.

> "For if you remain silent at this time, relief and deliverance for the Jews will arise from another place, but you and your father's family will perish. And who knows but that you have come to royal position for such a time as this?" (4:14)

This verse is fascinating for several reasons. First of all, Mordecai seems very confident, at least on one level, that God would deliver His people. Assuming that Mordecai's confidence was genuine, what might have been behind it?

**What do you suppose might have been the basis for his confidence?**

_____

_____

_____

It could simply be that the thought of a holocaust actually being carried out was, frankly, inconceivable. It just couldn't happen. God wouldn't let it happen — would He? It might also have been that Mordecai was familiar with God's covenant promises to Abraham, Isaac, and Jacob, and he realized that those covenant promises could not be kept if the Jews were all killed. Or it could simply have been that Mordecai's statement reflected his hope more than it did his confidence. In any event, Mordecai was counting on some Jews somewhere to escape this holocaust and survive as the remnant of God's covenant people.

Mordecai was also speaking less to the survival of the race than to Esther's naiveté in thinking that she would survive. Mordecai was confident that both he and Esther would die. Why was he so confident of this? It is easy to see why Haman might be able to guarantee the death of Mordecai. But why would Mordecai be so certain of Esther's death? Was he convinced that Hathach would not, in the long run, be able to keep this secret to himself? That seems like a stretch. Was Mordecai threatening to expose Esther as a Jew if she refused to cooperate? That is inconceivable. She was, after all, both his flesh-and-blood cousin and adopted daughter.

**What do you think?**

_____

_____

_____

Some commentators have suggested that Mordecai was alluding to divine discipline.[6] It is as though Mordecai were saying, "Esther, it is clear how God wants to use you. It is equally clear that He will not allow you to get away with telling Him no." God had been setting up the deliverance of His people for almost ten years. It was not all the same to God whether Esther followed through on the role that He had assigned her. His plan included her taking this risk. "So whatever the fate of the Jewish nation," Mordecai reminded her, "you and I will die unless something happens."

That something would seem to include action from Esther, and that is the most fascinating point in this passage.

**Write out what Mordecai told Esther at the end of verse fourteen – the most famous line in the entire book.**

_____

_____

This was so significant because for the first time someone was seeing beneath the surface!

Mordecai called Esther's attention to how the hand of God had been at work all along and how His plan for the deliverance of His people now depended on her. God had begun working ten years in advance to deliver His people from one of the greatest threats they would ever face. He superintended the circumstances down to the smallest detail — in ways Mordecai still could not grasp — so that when this historic moment of crisis came…Esther could say no? Mordecai was not giving up. He was telling her the truth, and he was telling it straight. But would he be able to convince her to trust God?

We know that God is powerful. But too often we would prefer that He be powerful through someone else! If it were up to us, we would stay safely on the sidelines "waiting on the Lord" while someone else actually took the risks. But what if God chooses to put us right in the middle of His plan? What happens when the deliverance God has been preparing comes down to an act of faith and trust on our part, and we say no? The words *no* and *Lord* just don't go together very well — either you are obeying what He tells you to do, or He is not the Lord of your life.

Every crisis includes a crossroad. Making the right choice at such a crossroads often depends on our sensitivity to God's leading. How has God been working in your life? How has He prepared you? What experiences and insights has He given you that have equipped you for *such a time as this*? What is His unique call on your life right now? And, above all, how are you answering that call? Here are some questions that should help you interpret your recent spiritual journey and discern the path that God is calling you to take.

**How does the Bible speak to your situation? What instruction or guidance does God give? If you don't know, what will you do to find out?**

_____

_____

_____

_____

**Whom should you consult about your situation? Who are the wise and godly "Mordecais" in your life, and what are they advising you to do?**

_____

_____

_____

_____

**How intensely are you praying about your situation? Are you asking God for wisdom and guidance? What do you sense that He is leading you to do?**

_____

_____

_____

_____

## PRAYER SUGGESTION

Confess your fear and label it for what it is: a lack of faith. Ask God to convict you deeply about your desire to "play it safe" and your refusal to trust Him.

Next, ask Him very specifically to show you the path He is calling you to take. Tell Him that you do not want to "just do something," simply avoid "doing the wrong thing," or retreat and do nothing at all. You want to do the *right thing*. Ask Him to use His Word, wise counselors, or answered prayer to lead you to a conviction about the path that He is calling you to take. Finally, ask Him to give you the courage to follow through.

Because this is a very important point in our study, I would like you to do something different today: Write out your own prayer to God, expressing these thoughts in your own words. Refer back to your answers to the questions above and use those answers to make your prayer personal and specific.

_____

_____

_____

_____

_____

_____

_____

_____

_____

_____

_____

_____

_____

_____

# Preparing for Courageous Faith

**PASSAGE: Esther 4:15-17**

Esther could finally see what God had been doing in her life, how He had brought her and her people to this crossroad. She could see what was at stake and what God was calling her to do. But seeing is one thing, doing is another. It was clear that God had been at work — Mordecai was right about that — but would Esther have the courage to act on what she knew was right?

God never brings you to a crossroad to just leave you standing there. He brings you to a crossroad so that you will discern the path He is calling you to take and then move forward. Moving forward almost always involves risk — there is no getting around that. So you face a difficult choice: Will you remain in your crisis, or will you do what God is calling you to do?

**READING ASSIGNMENT: Esther 4:1-17**

**FOCUS FOR TODAY: Esther 4:15-17**

> *Esther sent this reply to Mordecai…* (4:15)

Once again, Hathach delivered the message. This man was an unsung hero. Think about it: He was part of a plot that would challenge a royal decree and expose the duplicity of the prime minister. But instead of revealing the plot, he chose to become a participant. He was taking a huge risk. It would have been far safer for Hathach if he had turned these people in. Yet despite the risk, he was delivering the messages faithfully and accurately. The fact that Esther and Mordecai trusted him to do so suggests that Esther at least knew the kind of man he was.

> *"Go, gather together all the Jews who are in Susa, and fast for me. Do not eat or drink for three days, night or day. I and my maids will fast as you do. When this is done, I will go to the king, even though it is against the law. And if I perish, I perish."* (4:16)

Esther had made her decision. She would go to the king.

**But first, what did she request?**

_____

Esther asked Mordecai to gather all the Jews living in the capital city, perhaps thousands of people, to join her and her maids in several days of fasting. The spiritual component is unmistakable. By calling her kinsmen to join her in three days of fasting, Esther was calling them to three days of mourning and prayer.[7]

**Why was this necessary? Was Esther still afraid?** _____

You bet she was! Wouldn't you be? Esther demonstrated amazing courage, but remember: There is no courage without fear. Esther was willing to do what God had called her to do, but she did not feel ready. She would do it, but she was going to need a lot of spiritual support.

**What does this call to prayer and fasting tell us about where Esther was turning for strength?**

_____

Esther hadn't asked for this duty, but God had assigned it to her anyway. She recognized the call of God on her life, and she was saying, _Yes, Lord._ But to do what God had called her to do, she was going to need strength to act against her fear. And for that strength, she turned to the Lord. For three days she and her people cried out to Him. What would happen after those three days? She would risk death and go to the king.

**Read the last line in verse sixteen. Write it out word for word.**

_____

**Look carefully at those words. What did they imply? As Esther and her people turned to God, what were they trusting Him to do?**

_____

_____

Esther wanted to be delivered, certainly. But more than that, she was asking to be prepared. She was asking for the strength to do whatever God called her to do — to stand unbidden before the king, to reveal herself as a condemned Jew, to plead for mercy for herself and for her people. She was not praying, _God, get me out of this,_ or even, _God, get me through this._ She was praying, _God, help me step into this if it is what You want me to do._ She wanted to step forward, but to do that she would need His strength. Where would it lead? What would become of her? She left that up to God.

*Mordecai went away and carried out all of Esther's instructions.* (4:17)

Mordecai had done all that he could, protesting the decree in the public square, but his protest was not to be the key to the deliverance of his people. It played a part, surely. Had he not been wailing in sackcloth and ashes before the palace gate, the decree might not have come to Esther's attention until it was too late. The crucial action, however, would have to be taken by Esther.

Picture Mordecai getting these instructions from Hathach, ever the faithful messenger. Picture him fleeing the plaza before the palace — suddenly, without explanation, and to the confusion of those who had grown accustomed to his wailing — to call the Jews of Susa to prayer. As Esther's cousin and adoptive father, Mordecai would eagerly have taken her place. But that was not an option. She would have to approach the king herself. Esther would have to do what God had called her to do. And Mordecai? He would do what God had called Him to do. He would carry out Esther's instructions, spreading the word among the Jews. And he would pray as he had never prayed before.

Fear is paralyzing American Christianity. We've been presented with great challenges and opportunities, and we have said, "Not yet." We have been provided with vast resources and responsibilities, and we have said, "It's too risky." We have encountered open doors to the Gospel both here at home and around the world, and we've said, "Not now. Maybe later." We've told ourselves for too long that if everything isn't just right, if there is any risk at all, then "it must not be God's timing." Instead of obeying the Lord, we tell ourselves that we are "waiting on the Lord."

We would love to think of ourselves as people of faith without ever actually having to trust God. But that's not the kind of spiritual life God has called us to live. God wants us to trust Him even when — especially when — it involves risk. But just think of what God might do through us if we could learn to trust Him when He calls.

**What is God calling you to do that you might be hesitating to do because of the risk?**

_____

_____

_____

_____

**What might God accomplish through you if you adopted Esther's attitude of "If I perish, I perish?"**

_____

_____

_____

_____

**What will you and the Christians around you do to prepare yourselves for the spiritual challenge?**

_____

_____

_____

_____

## PRAYER SUGGESTION

Ask God to give you a team of supporters and fellow warriors. Ask Him to help all of you be committed to the task and to prepare for it together. Ask Him to give each and every one of you the boldness to say, _Yes, Lord,_ despite your fears.

You might pray something like this: _Lord, that's just what You are — my Lord, my Master, my King. I am Your child, so I can trust You with my safety. But I am also Your servant and Your warrior, so I can trust You boldly and bravely as You do great things through me. Lord, as I do Your will, as I go forward to fight Your battles and give You glory, provide me with companions along the way. Give me fellow warriors who commit with me, prepare with me, and then proceed with me into battle. Give each and every one of us the boldness to say yes to You and no to our fears. And may we all have the great privilege of seeing You powerfully at work through us. Amen._

✠

# Small Group Discussion Guide

We may not have seen the crisis coming, but God did and He was prepared. The question is, are we? Every crisis includes a crossroad, a moment of truth when the next move is ours. Although God has brought us to this crossroad, the path we now take is up to us. How can we know which path to choose? In today's study we will see Esther at the most important crossroad of her life. To choose the right path, she must begin to understand the significance of what God has been doing in her life. She must begin to look beneath the surface of the circumstances.

**TODAY: Esther 4:1-17**

**I. Don't choose to "JUST DO SOMETHING!"**
**KEY PASSAGE:** Esther 4:1-3 (read it aloud)

**DISCUSSION QUESTIONS:** What action did Mordecai take? What was the basis for his action?
_____

In what way did it prove to be significant?
_____


**PRINCIPLE:** Attacking the problem might make us feel better, but how do we know that what we're doing is right? There is a difference between doing something and doing the right thing.

**APPLICATION:** What basis do you have for the action you have taken? Why do you believe that the "something" you are doing is the right thing?
_____
_____


**II. Don't choose simply to AVOID doing the WRONG THING.**
**KEY PASSAGE:** Esther 4:4 (read it aloud)

**DISCUSSION QUESTION:** How does Esther give Mordecai the opportunity to, as she would see it, avoid doing the wrong thing?
_____


**PRINCIPLE:** Caution has its place, but caution alone is rarely the solution. There is a difference between not doing the wrong thing and actually doing the right thing.

**APPLICATION:** What action are you taking that amounts to little more than avoidance of
_____

further risk?

_____

### III. Don't choose to PLAY IT SAFE by doing NOTHING.
**KEY PASSAGE:** Esther 4:5-11 (read it aloud)

**DISCUSSION QUESTION:** How did Esther try to play it safe?

_____

_____

**PRINCIPLE:** Sometimes "waiting on the Lord" is spiritual jargon that actually means "bailing out." There is a difference between doing nothing and doing the right thing.

**APPLICATION:** In what way are you choosing to do nothing as a way of playing it safe?

_____

_____

### IV. Choose instead to do what GOD WANTS YOU TO DO.
**KEY PASSAGE:** Esther 4:12-17 (read it aloud)

**DISCUSSION QUESTION:** How did Esther finally become convinced of God's call to action?

_____

_____

**PRINCIPLE:** To discover God's will, turn to the Word (Psalm 119:105), the wisdom of others (Proverbs 15:22), and prayer (James 1:5). Then do it!

**SUPPORT PASSAGES:** Psalm 119:105; Proverbs 15:22; James 1:5 (read them aloud)

**APPLICATION:** How does the Bible speak to your situation? What instruction or guidance does God give? If you don't know, what will you do to find out?

_____

_____

Whom should you consult about your situation? Who are the wise and godly counselors in your life — and what are they advising you to do?

_____

_____

How intensely are you praying about your situation, asking God for His wisdom and guidance? What do you sense that He is leading you to do?

_____

_____

✝

WEEK FIVE

# Open Doors, Timid Hearts

Day 1 — A Step of Faith

Day 2 — From Stepping to Stumbling

Day 3 — Blind to the Consequences

Day 4 — How to Prevent a Miracle, Part 1

Day 5 — How to Prevent a Miracle, Part 2

Esther had come to the most terrifying moment of her life. She could be the instrument of deliverance for her entire race, or she could be executed at once. She had no way of knowing, let alone controlling, the outcome. God had opened the door for her, but going through that door was going to require enormous faith and courage.

We often find ourselves facing a crisis and standing at a crossroad. We've prayed and studied the Word and sought wise counsel, and we are reasonably confident of the direction that God wants us to take. And we know that it's time to step forward. There is only one problem: We are scared to death! God may have opened a door, but open doors often reveal timid hearts. Where can we find the courage to go through those doors, to do what God is calling us to do?

# A Step of Faith

**PASSAGE: Esther 5:1-3**

Esther had been preparing herself for this moment for the past three days, but God had been preparing her throughout her entire life. Her fellow Jews were praying and fasting on her behalf, crying out to God for strength and protection. Yet those faithful supporters could not join her in the step that she must take. The time had come for one young woman to face her fears and, all alone, step forward in faith. The door was open, but would her heart be strong enough to do what she needed to do?

**READING ASSIGNMENT: Esther 5:1-3**

**FOCUS FOR TODAY: Esther 5:1-3**

*On the third day Esther put on her royal robes and stood in the inner court of the palace, in front of the king's hall. The king was sitting on his royal throne in the hall, facing the entrance.* (5:1)

The third day had arrived. The Persians counted days just as the Jews did: Any part of a day counted as a whole day. It was likely that Esther's decision to speak with Xerxes had been made in the middle of the first day. So the Jews would have fasted for the remainder of that first day, for the entirety of the second day, and into the third day. The time had come for Esther to appear before the king.

Remember that Esther would be going to see the king without having been summoned, and that such an act was punishable by immediate death. Guards bearing battleaxes were posted on either side of Xerxes' throne ready to execute anyone who would presume to approach the king uninvited. The king had the option of accepting the unannounced visitor, yet Esther was little more than a concubine, and even then she had not seen the king in a month. There was no guarantee that the king would intervene to prevent her execution. Esther simply had to take that risk.

Late in the morning of the third day, after she and the Jews had fasted for perhaps as many as forty-five hours, Esther put on her royal robes and entered the *inner court,* or foyer, in front of the king's hall.[1] Typical of structures in that time period, the hall of King Xerxes was a long room lined with columns. The king's throne was placed at one end of the room with the entrance to the hall located at the opposite end. Outside of the entrance was a foyer visible from the throne. Unbidden, Esther appeared in this foyer and waited to speak with the king.

**What does the final sentence of verse one tell us?**

_____

**How would this have served to heighten Esther's level of anxiety?**

_____

_____

_____

> *When he saw Queen Esther standing in the court...* (5:2a)

How long did Esther stand there before the king acknowledged her presence? We don't know. The Hebrew has the nuance of *finally saw,* so Esther might actually have been waiting some time before being recognized. Supposing that there was some delay, imagine what Esther must have been thinking.

**What might have been going through Esther's mind as she stood in plain view, wondering whether she would be recognized or executed?**

_____

_____

_____

_____

We can easily imagine the kinds of things that would be going through Esther's mind at this point: Was the king refusing to recognize her so that she would have the opportunity to reconsider her actions and leave? Was he waiting for the guards to act? Or was he so distracted by other business that he had not noticed her at all? There was no way Esther could have known. The temptation to turn and walk away must have been enormous.

> *...he was pleased with her and held out to her the gold scepter that was in his hand.*
> *So Esther approached and touched the tip of the scepter.* (5:2b)

The king extended his scepter to Esther, indicating that she would be permitted to approach.[2]

**Why did the king allow her to approach? What does the verse say?**

_____

**What do you suppose this means? In what way might he have been pleased?**

_____

**What evidence is there for this in the passage?**

_____

The contrast is interesting: Mordecai met the crisis by wearing sackcloth and ashes, while Esther met the crisis in magnificent royal robes, yet both were correct in their actions.

**What do you make of this? Is there a lesson here?**

_____

_____

God calls each of us to play a unique part in His plan. God's call on one person's life might be very different from God's call on another, even in the very same situation. We should be careful, then, not to judge another person's response to God's leading.

The text tells us that Esther approached the throne and touched the tip of the scepter. What kind of touch did she use? Actually, it was traditional for the supplicant to approach the throne and kiss the tip of the extended scepter.[3]

**What might the significance have been of this gesture? What was the supplicant communicating by kissing the scepter?**

_____

_____

> The king asked, "What is it, Queen Esther? What is your request? Even up to half the kingdom, it will be given you." (5:3)

That's interesting: The king seemed to know that Esther had come with a request. How could this have been?

**What do you think?**

_____

_____

The king might well have been hearing from supplicants at that moment. It would have been natural, then, for him to assume that Esther, too, had come before him with a request. But there is another hint. As Esther had indicated to Mordecai, everyone knew that to appear before the king uninvited was to risk immediate execution. The very fact that Esther would take such a risk told the king that something very important was on her mind. So without knowing what her request might have been, he put her at ease by granting it in advance.

Look again at what he said. We've all had warm welcomes, but this was remarkable! Was the king really willing to give Esther up to half his kingdom? No, probably not. This was a polite exaggeration intended to put the uninvited supplicant at ease. After all, just moments before, this person would have been fearing for his or her very life. The king's exaggerated greeting would have removed all fear. So was the offer insincere? Well, yes and no. Although no one was expected to take the king up on such an offer, recall the Persian emphasis on telling the truth. Herodotus tells of one occasion when a mistress of Xerxes — yes, a man with a harem also had a mistress — appeared before him uninvited. When she was offered anything in the kingdom, she asked for a scarf that had been made by Queen Vashti (Herodotus calls her Amestris). Although Xerxes was fearful of angering his volatile queen, he had no choice but to keep his word and give the woman the scarf.[4]

Even if Esther did not see the king's generosity as anything more than a sign of his acceptance of her presence, imagine her relief! This demonstrates God's power and provision: He had not only put Esther in the right place at the right time to deliver the Jews, but He had also gone ahead of her to give her favor in the eyes of the king. Apart from her courage and obedience, Esther would never have been a part of this amazing deliverance.

Esther was able to act because she saw how faithfully God had provided for His people. He put her in a position of access and influence, He provided her with a timely warning of the king's decree, and then He protected her from execution. Her faith in Him no doubt grew stronger as she prepared to answer the king's question.

God asks us to follow Him, but He doesn't ask us to follow Him blindly. His record of faithfulness ought to have earned Him our confidence many times over. All we have to do is think back on the times that God has provided for us, protected us, and cared for us. By recalling such times of provision from the past, we will find it easier to trust God as we step into the future.

**Have you taken any "steps of faith" — large or small — in your life? If so, what were they?**

_____

**What open doors have you gone through, even though you were scared to death?**

_____

_____

**What did God do in response to your act of faith? What reassurance did He provide that He was with you all the way?**

_____

_____

_____

**How will you use that initial victory to build your confidence in God for the victories to come?**

_____

_____

_____

_____

**PRAYER SUGGESTION**

Thank God for how He has been with you in your current crisis. Talk to Him about that initial step of faith, small though it may have seemed, when you faced your fears and did His will. Ask Him to show you how He rewarded that step of faith. (He always does, although sometimes it may not be obvious at first.) Finally, ask Him to use that victory to build your confidence and boldness for victories to come.

Here is a suggested prayer: *Father, I know that You are with me through my current crisis — and not only because You said You would be, but also because I can see how You are challenging and blessing me. I remember how You impressed upon me to trust You.* Recount the story that you mentioned in the first question above. *Even though I was scared, I went forward. I did what I believed You wanted me to do. And You were faithful. You came through for me.* Now tell Him what you wrote in response to the second question. *Father, please use that victory to build my faith, to help me trust You for the next step and for the step after that. And as I follow You, keep my eyes wide open so that I won't miss a thing that You are doing in response. Amen.*

# From Stepping to Stumbling

**PASSAGE: Esther 5:4-8**

Esther had survived her uninvited appearance before the king. Now the time had come to reveal Haman's plot, and in so doing to reveal herself as one of the condemned. Esther was not out of trouble just yet. God had demonstrated His faithfulness in an amazing way, but could Esther trust Him with her next step?

God often proves Himself faithful — just before He asks us to trust Him one more time! Those who accept that God can be trusted move ahead with confidence. But those who doubt Him find themselves paralyzed by fear, unable to move, unable to obey. We need to remember God's faithfulness in the past so that we can trust Him with our future and do what He asks us to do without question or hesitation.

**READING ASSIGNMENT: Esther 5:1-8**

**FOCUS FOR TODAY: Esther 5:4-8**

*"If it pleases the king," replied Esther…* (5:4a)

The king asked Esther why she had come before him. He even assured her in advance that whatever her request might be, it would be granted. Here, then, was her chance. It was the perfect opportunity to expose Haman's duplicity and request the deliverance of her people.

*"…let the king, together with Haman, come today to a banquet I have prepared for him."* (5:4b)

What? Instead of exposing Haman and requesting the deliverance of her people, Esther invited both the king and Haman to lunch. What was Esther up to? Esther had both the king's attention and his favor. He had promised to grant her request, whatever it might have been. It seems that the situation couldn't have been any better. Yet Esther postponed the actual request and invited the king to join her for lunch. Why did Esther delay?

**The passage gives no clue, but what do you think?**

_____

_____

_____

Some have suggested that Esther wanted to reveal the plot in Haman's presence so that she would have a chance to respond to his inevitable protests and objections. Others have suggested that Esther wanted Xerxes to have a few drinks before she made her request. Still others wonder whether God might simply have laid out the plan for her, including the luncheon. Again, it is impossible to speculate with any certainty.

> *"Bring Haman at once," the king said, "so that we may do what Esther asks." So the king and Haman went to the banquet Esther had prepared. (5:5)*

Regardless of Esther's motivation, the king accepted the invitation, and since the banquet was prepared, he summoned Haman at once. We will learn in verse twelve that the king, the queen, and Haman were the only people present at this banquet.

**How must this invitation have struck Haman? What do you think?**

_____

_____

With no knowledge of Esther's relationship to Mordecai, Haman had no reason to be suspicious of the queen's intentions. On the contrary, Haman was probably flattered by this invitation.

> *As they were drinking wine, the king again asked Esther, "Now what is your petition? It will be given you. And what is your request? Even up to half the kingdom, it will be granted." (5:6)*

Recall from chapter one that the word translated *banquet* suggests that alcohol would be present in abundance. Although food was certainly served, wine was served as well, particularly after the meal. It is probable, then, that at this point, the meal had been served and consumed and that the king and Haman were enjoying a few after-dinner drinks. No doubt the king's mood, already warm toward his queen, had improved even more.

Yet the king felt that the time had come for Esther to come to the point. What made the king so sure that Esther had a request? How did the king know that Esther had something more than a luncheon on her mind?

**What might have tipped him off?**

_____

_____

_____

Xerxes would have understood that, as pleasant as this meal must have been, Esther would not have risked her life for the sake of an impromptu dinner party. She must have had something else on her mind. So once again the king asked her to make her request, even repeating the assurances he had given her before.

> Esther replied, *"My petition and my request is this:... (5:7)*

Here it comes...

> *"If the king regards me with favor and if it pleases the king to grant my petition and fulfill my request... (5:8a)*

This is it...

> *"...let the king and Haman come tomorrow to the banquet I will prepare for them. Then I will answer the king's question." (5:8b)*

What? She did it again! She delayed making her request for another twenty-four hours. But why? We can scarcely imagine greater openness on Xerxes' part. And if she wanted to reveal the plot in Haman's presence, he was right there. The opportunity seemed to be perfect. All the pieces seem to be in place, yet she hesitated hoping that...what? That the next day the pieces would be arranged in an even better scenario?

**Why did Esther delay? What reason might you suggest?**

_____

_____

_____

_____

It may well be that God had told Esther precisely what He wanted her to do, that she was following His revealed will to the letter. We have to be open to that possibility.

The fact is, however, that there is no indication that Esther had any special leading from God. We seem to see someone with the perfect opportunity to do what God had called her to do, but who chose instead to delay. Was Esther concerned about revealing her Jewish heritage? Was she hesitant to reveal her relationship with Mordecai, a condemned man? We don't know. True, she had just witnessed the faithfulness of God in allowing her to approach the king unbidden. But even so, she may well have been uneasy about actually making her request.

We can't be sure whether Esther was delaying out of fear. But if she were, I could certainly understand. I can almost hear Esther saying to herself, *Slow down, girl! You have eleven months. What difference will twenty-four hours make? Sure, the king looks open, but isn't that just a formality? You've seen him when he is mad; his anger can flare up in an instant. What will he think when you tell him that you are one of the people that he has condemned to death? Besides, Mordecai may think that the whole idea was Haman's, but are you really sure? Maybe the king is as much of an antisemite as Haman is. Obviously the king trusts this man. Look at how well they are getting along! Why would he believe you anyway? Don't rush this. Take it one step at a time.*

If I find this easy to imagine, it is because I've done it myself more times than I would like to remember! No matter how many times God shows Himself faithful, I can still manage to be fearful. Each step of faith presents new challenges, and Esther could have been facing those challenges at this point in her crisis. After all, when we walk by faith, we are walking one step at a time.

It's impossible to know why Esther delayed, but if she were delaying out of fear, each one of us can sympathize. We've all given ourselves little speeches like the one we just speculated about in Esther's situation. We know what God wants us to do, but we convince ourselves that there is a "problem with the timing"! We may have every intention of doing what God has told us to do. We don't know when, but we are going to do it. Why aren't we doing it right now? Well, we're not sure. Something feels wrong. The timing isn't right. But we will do it! Absolutely! Or so we tell ourselves.

Granted, there are times when the timing genuinely isn't right. We may look at the situation as wisely and as prayerfully as we can, but something is still wrong. We know that God wants us to take that step of faith, but in all honesty before Him, we do not feel that it is the right time. But what about all those times when the door was wide open, when the opportunity was right there, and we still said, "No, not now. I'm going to wait." Everything was ready — everything, that is, except us.

The funny thing about courageous faith is that it is often immediately preceded by timidity and fear. Let's try to identify our primary areas of fear so that we can begin to release them to God and then start moving forward in faith.

**Have you ever had a moment of great faith that was followed immediately by a moment of paralyzing fear? Explain.**

_____  _____

_____

_____

**If there is something right now that you are hesitating to do — some step of faith that you are reluctant to take — chances are you've worked up a pretty good rationalization. If so, what is it?**

_____

_____

_____

**Now critique your rationalization. Pick it apart. Look at it from God's point of view and tell yourself what He thinks of it.**

_____

_____

_____

**PRAYER SUGGESTION**

Acknowledge to God the things that you are hesitant to do. Ask Him to help you see your hesitation through His eyes. Ask Him to show you your rationalization for what it is, then confess it as sin.

You might pray something like this: _Father, I know that You want my faith to show itself in my actions. I even know what You want me to do. The sad thing is, I've got all sorts of reasons for not doing what You want me to do when You want me to do it._ Tell Him what you wrote in response to the second question. _But Lord, the truth is, I'm just scared. I know that sounds ridiculous with the victories You've given me recently._ Mention to Him what you wrote under the first question. _Please remind me of those victories and use them to increase my faith. Amen._

# Blind to the Consequences

**PASSAGE: Esther 5:9-14**

God gave Esther two opportunities to make her request, and both times she hesitated. She had every intention of doing what God expected of her, yet she seems to have been struggling a little with the timing. Then again, Esther could hardly be blamed if she believed that, with the slaughter eleven months away, twenty-four hours could not possibly make a difference. But if that is what she believed, she was terribly mistaken.

God cares about timing, almost always for reasons that we can neither see nor anticipate. We would like to think that we can examine the situation, gather the data, weigh the various factors, calculate the cost of delay, and then make an informed decision on our own. We can't. We're not nearly that intelligent or that informed. We need to trust God not only for what to do, but also for when to do it. That lesson will begin to unfold in today's brief passage.

**READING ASSIGNMENT: Esther 5:1-14**

**FOCUS FOR TODAY: Esther 5:9-14**

> *Haman went out that day happy and in high spirits. But when he saw Mordecai at the king's gate and observed that he neither rose nor showed fear in his presence, he was filled with rage against Mordecai.* (5:9)

Haman began his day in a terrific mood. Why?

**What reasons can you suggest for Haman's *high spirits*?**

_____

_____

_____

_____

_____

Haman was on top of the world! His career had taken off. He had been promoted to a position of unprecedented power. He was, in effect, the chief executive officer of the most powerful empire in the world. Now he was dining alone with the king and queen, indicating a level of personal intimacy and familiarity that few, if any, officials would ever have known. For Haman, life was good — until he got out to the main gate of the palace.

**As Haman was leaving the palace, what did he see?**

_____

Haman passed Mordecai. What was Mordecai doing?

**Was he back on the job _at the king's gate,_ or was he in sackcloth and ashes demonstrating at the palace gate? (Hint: What had he been doing the past few days?)**

_____

Like me, you might have pictured Mordecai fasting and praying in private. What were we thinking? This was Mordecai! If he were going to fast and pray, he was going to do it right in front of the palace gate, which was exactly where Haman encountered him.

When Mordecai suddenly found himself face to face with Haman, he refused to rise. No matter what else he might have been, Mordecai was consistent! If Haman were around, and Mordecai were seated, he wouldn't rise. If he were standing, he wouldn't bow. Worse still, Mordecai showed no fear. He wouldn't yield an inch.

**How did Haman react?**

_____

By refusing to yield, Mordecai was depriving Haman of the enjoyment of his position and power, and he was driving Haman wild with rage. What did Haman do with his rage?

_Nevertheless, Haman restrained himself and went home._ (5:10a)

Despite his rage, Haman did nothing, at least for the moment. Keep in mind that Haman could have had Mordecai killed at once for his refusal to obey the king's command. Instead, he restrained himself and went home.

**Why do you think Haman held back?**

_____

_____

It's impossible to be sure, but consider this: Why had Haman decreed the death of the entire Jewish race rather than just Mordecai? Simply executing Mordecai hadn't seemed satisfying then, and it didn't seem satisfying now. Why not? Whatever the reason, the incident at the gate had triggered something in Haman. His thirst for Mordecai's blood had risen to such a level that a wait of eleven months seemed intolerable to him.

Where was Esther at this moment? No doubt back in the palace planning the next day's luncheon, unconcerned about a twenty-four hour delay. Esther could not have anticipated it, but by choosing to delay, she had opened the door to a new and more immediate threat to Mordecai. What form would that threat take? Even Haman didn't know. He needed advice.

> *Calling together his friends and Zeresh, his wife...* (5:10b)

The phrase translated *calling together* includes the same word that was translated as *invite* in verse twelve. It suggests that Haman sent out servants to bring these people in. Haman was not simply coming home from a hard day at the office and sharing his frustrations with his wife. He had reached a point of crisis and he needed advice, so he was calling a meeting.

> *...Haman boasted to them about his vast wealth, his many sons, and all the ways the king had honored him and how he had elevated him above the other nobles and officials.* (5:11)

Haman began with a review of his accomplishments, and although it may have looked like simple bragging, it really wasn't. He seems genuinely perplexed. Consider what he said. He was a man of vast wealth — recall the staggering amount he was able to pay to fund his holocaust. He had many sons, ten as we will learn later, and according to Herodotus, that was something that the Persians esteemed second only to prowess in battle.[5] He had been honored by the king in many ways, the greatest of which was his elevation to a post of unprecedented power. No other noble or official enjoyed the power and prestige that he did.

> *"And that's not all," Haman added. "I'm the only person Queen Esther invited to accompany the king to the banquet she gave. And she has invited me along with the king tomorrow.* (5:12)

**More than that, Haman was now dining privately with the king and queen. Why might this be significant? What do you think?**

_____

_____

_____

To dine privately with the king and queen was an extraordinary expression of friendship and intimacy, particularly given the way Persian monarchs isolated their concubines, and especially their queens, from contact with other men.

Haman had it all: money, power, prestige, and influence. What more did the world have to offer?

> *"But all this gives me no satisfaction as long as I see that Jew Mordecai sitting at the king's gate."* (5:13)

Everything that he had achieved in the world gave Haman no satisfaction. The Hebrew literally says, *This is not equal to me.* Haman had it all, but it wasn't enough. Why not? Certainly, Mordecai didn't hold him in awe. Certainly, Mordecai didn't fear him. But the passage suggests something further might have been going on.

**What was really keeping Haman from enjoying his accomplishments?**

_____

_____

Haman revealed his own heart. He wasn't angry with Mordecai. He was angry with *"that Jew Mordecai."* Haman was driven by racism. We can almost hear him saying, "If Mordecai won't respect me, let him fear me. If he won't fear me, let him…what?" His wife and friends answered the question.

> *His wife Zeresh and all his friends said to him, "Have a gallows built, seventy-five feet high, and ask the king in the morning to have Mordecai hanged on it. Then go with the king to the dinner and be happy." This suggestion delighted Haman, and he had the gallows built.* (5:14)

"If Mordecai won't fear you, kill him" was the suggestion. "And don't wait. Kill him now!" The word translated *gallows* might refer to a structure built for hanging, but it is just as likely a stake on which Mordecai would be impaled, with his body left on display. They suggested that Haman have the gallows constructed overnight — he could do that, being the prime minister — and that with the king's permission, he hang or impale Mordecai the next morning.

This advice seems almost predictable, if gruesome. One point, though, seems odd, and it is really the key to their advice: Why would they specify not simply a gallows or stake but one that was seventy-five feet high?

**What do you think?**

_____

_____

_____

The message was this: "While you are at it, Haman, make an example of this Jew." Remember that very likely the root of Haman's anger was racism. Sure, he could have killed Mordecai. That would have been easy. But how could he do it in a way that would feed his antisemitism? The answer: Execute Mordecai in a very public, very humiliating way. After all, a Jewish body suspended seventy-five feet above the ground would have made quite a statement.

"Do that," they advise him, "and you can go to Queen Esther's dinner with peace of mind." Their advice delighted Haman. He ordered that the gallows be built.

Even before the second luncheon would have started, Mordecai's lifeless body would be suspended seventy-five feet above the streets of Susa. As far as Esther knew, a twenty-four hour delay would have been completely harmless. But in fact, it could very well have cost Mordecai his life.

We think our delays are harmless. We say to ourselves, *What difference could a day make...or a year? None, surely! The opportunity will still be there, only by then I will be ready.* The truth is, like Esther, we have absolutely no way of knowing what problems our delays might create. We just do not have the ability to get a clear and comprehensive view of our present situation, let alone get a look into the future. But even so, we tell ourselves, *What harm could it do?* and we delay.

**Think back. What price have you or others paid in the past for your delayed obedience?**

_____

_____

_____

_____

**Is there an act of obedience that are you delaying right now? If so, what are you telling yourself might be the consequences of your delay?**

---

---

---

**Why are you so certain that these and these alone are the possible consequences of your delay?**

---

---

---

**Why do you presume to delay obedience based upon your assessment of the consequences?**

---

---

---

## PRAYER SUGGESTION

Ask God to remind you of the price that you and others have paid for your delayed obedience, and ask Him to impress upon you the importance of His timing. Confess the times that you have delayed and especially the presumptuous attitude that allowed you to do so. Finally, ask Him for the strength and the courage to obey Him promptly.

Here is a suggested prayer: *Father, I understand now that delayed obedience is just another word for disobedience. For some reason I told myself that delay was all right if I had weighed all the consequences. But I had no right to do that. Only You know the consequences, and knowing those consequences, You told me to act. Lord, remind me of the price I've paid for delay, and of the price I've forced others to pay as well. And give me the strength and confidence in You that I will need to go forward the next time. Amen.*

# A Special Introduction to Days 4 and 5

So far this week we have learned that God opens doors and that going through those doors requires faith. We have also learned that when we fail to go through those doors there may be serious and unforeseeable consequences.

But do you realize that the consequences of our timid hearts affect not only us, but also the people who are looking to us for spiritual leadership?

For the next two days we will explore the devastating influence of spiritual leaders who are afraid to trust God. To do this, we will take advantage of a natural break in the story of Esther to look at an incredible story found in the Old Testament book of Numbers. We will see God keep a centuries-old promise as He opens one of the biggest doors of all time — and we will watch in horror as the so-called "leaders" frighten God's people into refusing to go in. I have entitled this special two-day study, "How to Prevent a Miracle."

✝
## WEEK FIVE  DAY FOUR
# How to Prevent a Miracle
## PART 1

**PASSAGE: Numbers 13:1-14:10**

Ever since Abraham was called by God as recorded in Genesis 12, God had promised His people a land of their own, a land of great beauty and abundance, a land flowing with milk and honey. That promise was about to be fulfilled. The people of God had just been released from four hundred years of bondage in Egypt, and after a short trip through the wilderness, they were standing on the threshold of the Land of Promise. The door was open, but did they and their leaders have the courage to trust God? Or would their timid hearts prevent a miracle?

**READING ASSIGNMENT: Numbers 13:1-14:10**

**FOCUS FOR TODAY: Selected passages**

> The LORD said to Moses, "Send some men to explore the land of Canaan, which I am giving to the Israelites. From each ancestral tribe send one of its leaders." So at the LORD's command Moses sent them out from the Desert of Paran. All of them were leaders of the Israelites. (13:1-3)

Before entering the land, the Lord allowed Moses to send scouts in ahead of the people to determine the geography and demography of the land. By sending in scouts, was Moses demonstrating a lack of faith?

**What do you think?**

_____

_____

_____

To follow God is faith. To follow God without a plan is foolishness. By sending in scouts, Moses was simply being a good leader.

The key to these first few verses, however, is found at the end of verse three.

**Whom did Moses send to explore the land?**

_____

**Why was this so important?**

_____

_____

What did these leaders discover? Let's take a look at their report.

> *At the end of forty days they returned from exploring the land. They came back to*
> *Moses and Aaron and the whole Israelite community at Kadesh in the Desert of Paran.*
> *There they reported to them and to the whole assembly and showed them the fruit of*
> *the land. They gave Moses this account: "We went into the land to which you sent us,*
> *and it does flow with milk and honey! Here is its fruit. (13:25-27)*

In other words, these leaders had discovered that everything was just as God had promised. God could be trusted! So far, so good.

> *"But the people who live there are powerful, and the cities are fortified and very large.*
> *We even saw descendants of Anak there. The Amalekites live in the Negev; the Hittites,*
> *Jebusites and Amorites live in the hill country; and the Canaanites live near the sea*
> *and along the Jordan." (13:28-29)*

Suddenly the report took a terrible turn. What concern were these "leaders" expressing?

**Looking past all the Amalekites, and Hittites and so forth, what were they really saying?**

_____

_____

These so-called leaders were sending a simple and unmistakable message to God's people: We've seen the challenge, and God can't handle it.

**Were they right?**

_____

**How do you know?**

_____

_____

**Why didn't these so-called leaders know that? What was the problem here?**

_____

_____

We're calling this lesson "How to Prevent a Miracle," so if you want to prevent a miracle of God in your life, here is the first thing you have to do:

## 1. DOUBT THE POWER OF GOD.

Were there no godly leaders in Israel? Was there no one willing to trust God?

> *Caleb silenced the people before Moses and said, "We should go up and take possession of the land, for we can certainly do it." (13:30)*

Praise God for leaders like Caleb! But wait — Caleb saw the same cities and inhabitants that the others had seen.

**Why was he so confident?**

_____

_____

> *The men who had gone up with him said, "We can't attack those people; they are stronger than we are." (13:31)*

Unfortunately Caleb was not the only one who was trying to influence God's people. Rather than helping the people trust God, the other leaders created doubt.

**How were they creating that doubt? Where were they putting their focus?**

_____

**Where should they have been putting their focus?**

_____

Spiritual leadership involves getting people to follow you as you follow God. When we refuse to trust God — when we focus on human limitations rather than divine power and promises — we are refusing to lead. And that brings us to the second thing you must do to prevent a miracle of God in your life:

## 2. REFUSE TO LEAD.

Unfortunately, these nonleaders didn't stop there.

> *And they spread among the Israelites a bad report about the land they had explored.* (13:32a)

> *That night all the people of the community raised their voices and wept aloud. All the Israelites grumbled against Moses and Aaron, and the whole assembly said to them, "If only we had died in Egypt! Or in this desert! Why is the LORD bringing us to this land only to let us fall by the sword? Our wives and children will be taken as plunder. Wouldn't it be better for us to go back to Egypt?" And they said to each other, "We should choose a leader and go back to Egypt."* (14:1-4)

**What were these leaders doing? What were they trying to accomplish here?**

_____

_____

_____

Not only did these nonleaders refuse to trust God, they encouraged others to join them. Were they successful? Of course they were! Unbelief is easy. It's our spiritual default mode. Convincing us not to trust God is simply convincing us to do what comes naturally — to do what we're already doing. That's not leadership. That's jumping out in front of the parade of spiritual mediocrity. So if you want to prevent a miracle, there is a third thing you have to do:

## 3. CREATE DISUNITY.

How did the godly leaders respond? They appealed directly to the people.

> *Then Moses and Aaron fell facedown in front of the whole Israelite assembly gathered there. Joshua son of Nun and Caleb son of Jephunneh, who were among those who had explored the land, tore their clothes and said to the entire Israelite assembly, "The land we passed through and explored is exceedingly good. If the LORD is pleased with us, he*

*will lead us into that land, a land flowing with milk and honey, and will give it to us. Only do not rebel against the* LORD. *And do not be afraid of the people of the land, because we will swallow them up. Their protection is gone, but the* LORD *is with us. Do not be afraid of them."* (14:5-9)

**How would you summarize this message to the people? What were Moses, Aaron, Joshua, and Caleb saying?**

_____

_____

Their message was a good one. Yet in an important sense the battle for leadership was already over. Moses and the others had already lost.

**How can we tell? What indication do these verses give us that the godly leaders were, in fact, no longer leading the people?**

_____

_____

That's a tough question. Let me tell you what I see in this appeal to the people. I see the decision of whether or not to trust God being left to the whiners. I see leadership being turned over to the critics. When a situation deteriorates to that point, leaders can be certain of one thing: They are no longer the leaders. So there is a fourth thing we need to do if we are to prevent a miracle of God in our lives:

## 4. LET THE NAYSAYERS DECIDE.

Moses and the others had made their appeal as clearly and as passionately as they possibly could. How would the people respond?

> *The whole assembly talked about stoning them.* (14:10a)

Such is the influence of faithless leaders. Why did the people want to stone Moses and the others?

**What did they probably give as their reason?**

_____

_____

_____

**Assuming that you would find that reason unconvincing, what in your view would be the real reason?**

_____

_____

It's tough for spiritual leaders to remember that the opposition is often not directed against them personally, but against God. Faithless people usually won't acknowledge that; it's too convicting. But the leader has to keep that in mind. This brings us to a fifth thing that we must do if we are to prevent a miracle:

## 5. THROW ROCKS AT THE LEADERS.

The leaders were struggling. They were quite literally facing down an angry mob. Where was God?

> Then the glory of the LORD appeared at the Tent of Meeting to all the Israelites. (14:10b)

God stepped down to intervene. We'll see what He did in tomorrow's study.

✝

In one way or another, we have all been under the spiritual leadership of others. Whether they were our parents, pastors, elders, or leaders of some other kind, each one of us has been called by God to be good spiritual followers. What we often fail to realize is that many of us are also spiritual leaders. It might be in a role as obvious as a parent or as unexpected as the "only Christian at your office." Whatever the case, we all face the challenges of leadership and the challenges of following.

In today's application section, let's ask ourselves what we, or those we are called upon to lead, might be doing to prevent a miracle of God in our lives. Look again at the "five ways to prevent a miracle" that we've discussed today, then answer the following questions.

**Which of these "miracle-preventing" behaviors have you seen in the people you are called upon to lead?**

_____

_____

_____

**Which of these "miracle-preventing" behaviors have you yourself been guilty of as a follower?**

_____

_____

_____

_____

**PRAYER SUGGESTION**

Ask God to make you a faithful leader. Tell Him about the challenges you are facing from those He has called you to lead, then give those burdens and frustrations to Him. Ask Him to give you so much love for His people that you would willingly put yourself on the line, even at risk, for their sake.

Then ask God to make you a faithful follower. Refer to your answer to the preceding question and confess the times that you may have prevented a miracle of God. Repent of the arrogance that may have kept you from being a good follower. Finally, read Hebrews 13:17, and pray a prayer such as this: _Lord, help me to obey my leaders and submit to their authority. They keep watch over me as men who must give an account. Give me the humility to obey them so that their work will be a joy, not a burden, for that would be of no advantage to me. Thank you for their faithfulness. Amen._

# How to Prevent a Miracle
## PART 2

**PASSAGES: Numbers 14:10b-45; Deuteronomy 1:19-2:1**

Yesterday in part one of our special two-day study, "How to Prevent a Miracle," we saw the importance of both good spiritual leadership and the ability to follow. God's purpose and plan often depends on both leaders who are willing to trust God and people who are willing to follow those leaders.

In today's study, we will witness the consequences that occur when God's people won't trust Him. We will see how God really feels about leaders who won't lead and people who won't follow. Along the way we will pick up the sixth and most surprising key to preventing a miracle.

**READING ASSIGNMENT: Numbers 14:10b-45; Deuteronomy 1:19-2:1**

**FOCUS FOR TODAY: Selected passages**

> *The glory of the LORD appeared at the Tent of Meeting to all the Israelites.* (14:10b)

Key leaders were refusing to lead. Worse still, they were stirring up dissension. The people were demanding to go back to Egypt and were threatening to enforce their will by stoning Moses and the others. Rather than experiencing the victory and blessing of entering the Land of Promise, the people of God were in rebellion. The situation was close to a meltdown.

Then God showed up.

The Hebrew word for *glory* is terrific in this context. The root word means *heavy* or *weighty*.[6] When used as a description of God it emphasizes, metaphorically, the "weightiness" of His presence. The holiness of God is not just felt; it lands like a blow — it has impact.

**Why was this such an appropriate word to use in this context? Why did the presence of God need to be felt in just this way at just this moment?**

_____

_____

_____

God is overwhelming simply in the glory of His presence. Yet at that moment, overwhelming glory alone could not adequately express what was on the heart and mind of God. He would speak to His people as well.

> The LORD said to Moses, "How long will these people treat me with contempt? How long will they refuse to believe in me, in spite of all the miraculous signs I have performed among them? (14:11)

God's reaction speaks for itself. When we see the word LORD written in just that way, with the O-R-D in small capital letters, it tells us that the Hebrew writer is expressing the covenant name of God, _Yahweh_.[7] The emphasis in these contexts tends to be on God as the covenant God, God as both Promise Maker and Promise Keeper. Why would that have been such an appropriate emphasis here? Why was God so angry? More specifically, why did He characterize their behavior as contempt?

**What do you think?**

_____

_____

_____

_____

What did God do in response to the faithlessness of His people?

> "I will strike them down with a plague and destroy them, but I will make you into a nation greater and stronger than they." (14:12)

God's response had two components: The first dealt with the faithless people and their faithless leaders; the second addressed God's larger purpose and plan in light of this rebellion.

**What did God say that He would do to these rebellious people?**

_____

_____

**Again, why did God feel this way? Was it simply because His orders had not been carried out, or was a more personal affront involved?**

_____

_____

God — the covenant God of Abraham, Isaac, and Jacob — had just had His offer of a Promised Land rejected. Worse still, His offer had been rejected by the very people He had just delivered from slavery in Egypt.

**What did God propose to do instead?**

_____

_____

Recall that all of this was taking place before the Tent of Meeting in full view — and, for those close by, within earshot — of the offenders themselves.

**How do you think they would have been reacting at this point?**

_____

_____

_____

_____

We will not examine Numbers 14:13-19 in detail, but as you recall from today's reading, Moses appealed to God on the basis of His promises and His character.

What did God do?

> The LORD replied, "I have forgiven them, as you asked. Nevertheless, as surely as I live and as surely as the glory of the LORD fills the whole earth, not one of the men who saw my glory and the miraculous signs I performed in Egypt and in the desert but who disobeyed me and tested me ten times — not one of them will ever see the land I promised on oath to their forefathers. No one who has treated me with contempt will ever see it." (14:20-23)

Although God relented, He assured that generation that they would pay for their timidity of heart. How would the people pay for their refusal to trust God and go forward?

**Summarize what the consequences of their timidity would be.**

_____

_____

_____

_____

The offense had been identified, the judgment passed, and the sentence specified. But had God said all that He wanted to say? Not yet.

> *"How long will this wicked community grumble against me? I have heard the complaints of these grumbling Israelites. So tell them, 'As surely as I live, declares the LORD, I will do to you the very things I heard you say: In this desert your bodies will fall — every one of you twenty years old or more who was counted in the census and who has grumbled against me. (14:27-29)*

Let's pause for a moment. This appears to be a restatement of what God had just said.

**What does that, in itself, suggest to you about God's heart at this moment?**

_____

_____

**But look again, a bit more closely this time. What additional detail do we see and why do you think it might be significant?**

_____

_____

_____

_____

I am struck by the line, *"I will do to you the very things I heard you say."* It was ironic and somehow fitting that their fears would end up being their punishment.

> *"'Not one of you will enter the land I swore with uplifted hand to make your home, except Caleb son of Jephunneh and Joshua son of Nun. As for your children that you said would be taken as plunder, I will bring them in to enjoy the land you have rejected. But you — your bodies will fall in this desert. Your children will be shepherds here for forty years, suffering for your unfaithfulness, until the last of your bodies lies in the desert. For forty years — one year for each of the forty days you explored the land — you will suffer for your sins and know what it is like to have me against you.'"* (14:30-31)

**Again, what additional details do you see here, and why do you think they might be significant?**

_____

_____

_____

_____

I can't help but note the emphasis on the children and the consequences they would face.

**What would ultimately become of them?** _____

God would keep His promise to His people. Although the ones who rebelled against Him would not enter the land, their children would. Yet they would still pay a price.

**What price did their children have to pay?**

_____

_____

Sin has consequences, even for the innocent.

God then made His final statement on the fate of that generation:

> "I, the LORD, have spoken, and I will surely do these things to this whole wicked community, which has banded together against me. They will meet their end in this desert; here they will die." (14:35)

**Can you think of any way that God could have been more emphatic?** _____

**Do you see any offer of a "second chance?"** _____

**Is there any hint at all that God might reconsider?** _____

Keep your answers in mind. We will come back to them.

> So the men Moses had sent to explore the land, who returned and made the whole community grumble against him by spreading a bad report about it — these men responsible for spreading the bad report about the land were struck down and died of a plague before the LORD. Of the men who went to explore the land, only Joshua son of Nun and Caleb son of Jephunneh survived. (14:36-38)

**What became of the men who led the people into rebellion and faithlessness?**

_____

_____

**Note the timing of their punishment. Why did God move their death sentence up on His calendar?**

_____

_____

_____

**Among those who had explored the land, who alone survived and why?**

_____

_____

This is pretty dramatic!

**What impact do you think all this would have had on the people? What would you predict would have been their response?**

_____

_____

> _When Moses reported this to all the Israelites, they mourned bitterly._ (14:39)

**Why did they mourn? What do you suppose was going on in their minds and hearts?**

_____

_____

_____

_____

Confronted with the consequences, the people deeply regretted their rebellion. What did they do about it?

> _Early the next morning they went up toward the high hill country. "We have sinned,"_
> _they said. "We will go up to the place the LORD promised." (14:40)_

This may be perfectly understandable, but there was a problem.

**What would you have said if you were in Moses' position?**

_____

_____

_____

*But Moses said, "Why are you disobeying the LORD's command? This will not succeed!*
*Do not go up, because the LORD is not with you. You will be defeated by your enemies,*
*for the Amalekites and Canaanites will face you there. Because you have turned away*
*from the LORD, he will not be with you and you will fall by the sword." (14:41-43)*

The people of Israel wanted a second chance — in fact they intended to take one, whether it was offered to them or not. But Moses warned them that they would fail because God would not go with them.

### Why wouldn't He? Had God abandoned His people?

_____

_____

_____

Would the people heed Moses' warning?

*Nevertheless, in their presumption they went up toward the high hill country, though*
*neither Moses nor the ark of the LORD's covenant moved from the camp. Then the*
*Amalekites and Canaanites who lived in that hill country came down and attacked*
*them and beat them down all the way to Hormah. (14:44-45)*

Once again, God had shown His people that He could be trusted — although not in the way they had expected. He can be trusted when He tells you that He will be with you, and He can be trusted when He tells you that He won't.

### What would you identify as the key word in this verse? _____

For me, it would be the word *presumption*. Why do we think that timing doesn't matter to God? That it's all the same to Him whether we obey now or at our own convenience?

Many years later, Moses told the story to the children, then grown, of that generation just as they were about to enter the Promised Land. We join him near the end of Deuteronomy 1. It provides a fitting, though bitter end to our lesson today.

*"The Amorites who lived in those hills came out against you; they chased you like a*
*swarm of bees and beat you down from Seir all the way to Hormah. You came back*
*and wept before the LORD, but he paid no attention to your weeping and turned a deaf*
*ear to you. And so you stayed in Kadesh many days — all the time you spent there.*
*Then we turned back and set out toward the desert along the route to the Red Sea, as*

*the LORD had directed me. For a long time we made our way around the hill country*
*of Seir." (Deuteronomy 1:44-2:1)*

One can only imagine the weeping and wailing as the nation stood at the door of the Promised Land, only to find that the door had been shut to them because of their own disobedience.

This brings us to the sixth and final thing that we must do if we are to prevent a miracle:

## 6. MISS GOD'S TIMING.

Let's get this firmly in our minds: God will deliver us from our crises, but our deliverance often depends on obedience to His timing. The cost of delayed obedience can be terrifyingly high. That's why it is best to view delayed obedience for what it really is: disobedience.

**Have you ever missed God's blessing because you missed His timing? What consequences did you face for your "delayed obedience?"**

_____

_____

_____

_____

_____

**Have you ever suffered consequences for the "delayed obedience" of a spiritual leader in your life? Explain.**

_____

_____

_____

### PRAYER SUGGESTION

Ask God to teach you the importance of His timing. Ask Him to remind you that delayed obedience is actually disobedience. You might pray something like this: *Father, I can see in this passage from Numbers as well as from my own life that timing matters. I realize that doing what You tell me to do is only one part of obedience. The other part is doing it when You tell me to do it. God, I don't want to miss either Your deliverance or Your blessing, so please stay after me on the issue of timing. Amen.*

✠

## WEEK FIVE
## OPEN DOORS, TIMID HEARTS
# Small Group Discussion Guide

You are facing a crisis and you are at a crossroad. You are confident of the direction that God wants you to take. You know that it's time to step forward. There is only one problem: You are scared to death! God has opened a door, but open doors often reveal timid hearts. Where can we find the courage to go through those doors, to do what God is calling us to do?

**TODAY: Esther 5:1-14**

**I. Remember God's FAITHFULNESS.**
**KEY PASSAGE:** Esther 5:1-3 (read it aloud)

**DISCUSSION QUESTIONS:** Esther took a bold step of faith and once again God came through. How did He do it? How did God demonstrate His faithfulness in a way that should have given Esther growing confidence?

_____

_____


**PRINCIPLE:** God is asking you to follow Him, but not blindly. Just look at His record! Has He been faithful to you in the past? If so, why do you doubt Him now?

**APPLICATION:** God deserves your trust. What demonstrations of His faithfulness to you in the past should embolden you to trust Him today?

_____

_____

_____

_____

## II. Trust God's TIMING.

**KEY PASSAGE:** Esther 5:4-8 (read it aloud)

**DISCUSSION QUESTION:** Esther knew what to do, yet she seemed to delay in doing it. Why?

_____

_____

_____

**PRINCIPLE:** When God is asking you to follow Him, He is asking you to follow Him right then. Waiting is not following. Waiting is doing nothing.

**APPLICATION:** Refusal to trust God's timing is refusal to trust God. Is there something that God wants you to do, some step He wants you to take, that you keep putting off?

_____

_____

Why do you delay?

_____

_____

## III. Recognize the danger of DELAY.

**KEY PASSAGE:** Esther 5:9-14 (read it aloud)

**DISCUSSION QUESTION:** Apart from a direct leading from God, and none is mentioned in the text, was Esther in a position to know that following God tomorrow is as good as following Him today?

_____

_____

**PRINCIPLE:** We often tell ourselves, *Sure, I'm going to obey God, just not right now. Now doesn't seem to be quite the right time for some reason. I'll do it tomorrow, or later, no harm done.* But how can we say that? How do we know that no harm will be done? Our life principle should be: "God knows everything. I know nothing."

**APPLICATION:** We can't predict the price of delayed obedience. Have there been times in your past when your delay in following God's leading created a crisis in His plan?

_____

_____

_____

_____

_____

_____

✝

WEEK SIX

# The Invincible God

One of the most encouraging truths from the story of Esther is that our God is invincible. Nothing intimidates Him. No one can outmaneuver Him. Even our greatest challenges present no challenge to Him. Sure, there are times when we may feel overmatched and overwhelmed. There are times when it seems that everything is against us and we are out of options. But God specializes in times like that. Just when we are feeling the most helpless and hopeless, God takes action. Months, perhaps years, of preparation on His part suddenly come together. And the result is often something we never could have imagined, let alone foreseen. As we look on in wonder, we find ourselves smiling, shaking our heads, and saying, "Only God could have done that!" There are few places in Scripture that demonstrate this truth as startlingly as Esther 6.

Before we get started, however, there is something else in this week's passage I want you to notice, something very significant: When God acts, He does so entirely on His own. We won't see any remarkable "demonstrations of faith" from either Esther or Mordecai. True, Esther's great step of faith was now only hours away, but it was a step she had not yet taken. And while Mordecai had trusted God with great boldness, all God would ask in this week's passage was that Mordecai, quite literally, just go along for the ride. This chapter is all about our invincible God — about how thoroughly He cares for His people and how effortlessly He overwhelms His enemies. Let's watch Him work!

# The God of the Details

**PASSAGE: Esther 6:1-6a**

Esther had delayed, and in delaying she had put Mordecai's life at risk. Within a few short hours, Mordecai was to be executed at the hands of Haman. Had God's own people succeeded in doing what His enemies could not do — had they thwarted God's plan? Or could His plan somehow accommodate, even use, this delay?

In today's passage we are going to see the sovereignty of God, or more precisely His providence, displayed with effortless effectiveness. The providence of God is His sovereignty over the events and circumstances of life. God is God, even of the details. And nowhere is that providential oversight of the details of life better demonstrated than in today's passage.

**READING ASSIGNMENT: Esther 6:1-6a**

**FOCUS FOR TODAY: Esther 6:1-6a**

> *That night the king could not sleep; so he ordered the book of the chronicles, the record of his reign, to be brought in and read to him.* (6:1)

As it happened, on the very night that Haman was having the gallows constructed for Mordecai, King Xerxes was having trouble sleeping. The Hebrew says that sleep *fled* the king. Is a reason given? No.

**What, then, should we assume?**

_____


Xerxes' sleeplessness doubtless had nothing whatever to do with Mordecai or Haman or the crisis facing the Jews. He knew nothing of the subterfuge surrounding his recent decree and he certainly had not heard that anyone was about to be executed. During the day he was the king, but at the moment he was just a guy who couldn't sleep. This is the first of several remarkable coincidences that we will see in this chapter.

Xerxes ordered his attendants to bring in the *book of the chronicles*, which was the official record of daily events in the royal court. These scrolls contained a meticulous daily record of events, visitors, decisions, and anything else of significance that happened during the king's reign. By the way, this was the same record referred to in Esther 2:23 as the *book of the annals*.

**Take a moment and reread Esther 2:21-23. What was recorded in this *book of the chronicles*?**

_____

_____

To while away the sleepless hours, Xerxes had his servants read aloud the events of his reign. This reading perhaps went on for most of the night. Of all the recorded details of Xerxes' reign, what would be the chances of this particular event about Mordecai being read to the king? But just before dawn the readers came to the record of an event that caught the king's attention.

> *It was found recorded there that Mordecai had exposed Bigthana and Teresh, two of the king's officers who guarded the doorway, who had conspired to assassinate King Xerxes.* (6:2)

Sure enough, sometime very early in the morning, the readers came across the account recorded five years earlier of a plot to assassinate the king. What made this threat particularly serious, as this verse reminds us, was that the conspirators were the king's personal bodyguards. Somehow Mordecai found out about the plot and reported it to Esther who in turn reported it to the king. The king investigated the report, the plot was exposed, and the conspirators were executed.

**What had the king done to reward Mordecai for saving his life?**

_____

_____

Although the court record would reflect that it was Mordecai who had saved the life of the king, Mordecai had, for some unexplained reason, never been rewarded.

Now five years have passed and late one night, or rather early one morning, in yet another amazing coincidence, the sleepless king was reminded of this event and of the loyalty of a man named Mordecai. He stopped the reader with a question.

> *"What honor and recognition has Mordecai received for this?" the king asked. "Nothing has been done for him," his attendants answered.* (6:3)

The king recalled the event, certainly, but he did not recall whether anything had been done to reward Mordecai. Persian kings were careful, as a matter of honor, to reward those who had done them a particular service. Herodotus mentions an Order of Benefactors, membership in which was similar to a knighthood.[1] Who could be worthier of such an honor than one who had saved the life of the king? Yet Xerxes could not recall if anything at all had been done to reward him. So he asked his attendants what honor and recognition had been bestowed on Mordecai.

In fact, nothing at all had been done. We are not told how the king's attendants knew this. It seems unlikely that they were operating purely on memory, because if they had been aware of the oversight they would in all likelihood have corrected it. It is possible that they simply looked ahead in the court records and discovered that there was no record of any honor or recognition having been bestowed. Needless to say, this terrible oversight would have to be corrected immediately — another wonderful coincidence.

Before we move on, and since we looked at chapter five early last week, let's review what Haman had been up to.

**On the previous day, what advice had Haman decided to take?**

_____

_____

**What was to happen later that morning?**

_____

_____

The king, of course, was completely unaware that any of this was happening. He had his own problems to deal with, specifically, deciding how best to reward a loyal yet neglected servant. It was the king's turn to seek advice.

> The king said, "Who is in the court?" Now Haman had just entered the outer court of the palace to speak to the king about hanging Mordecai on the gallows he had erected for him. (6:4)

As Persian officials seem to have done so often, when there was a question to be answered, a meeting would be called. But it was probably about five o'clock in the morning. Who would have been in the court at that hour? In fact, it wouldn't have been too surprising if several people had already arrived for the day's work. Ancient Near Eastern afternoons were terribly hot, so it was not at all unusual for people to begin their work very early in the day, even before dawn, get their work done, and then rest through the heat of the afternoon.[2] So even at that early hour it was not unlikely that someone would have been available to discuss with the king the matter of Mordecai's reward. The king asked, *"Who is in the court?"*

> His attendants answered, *"Haman is standing in the court." "Bring him in," the king ordered.* (6:5)

The king had asked who might be available in the court to give him some advice. The servant stepped outside for a moment to have a look around, and who should be standing in the court at that moment but Haman? Another stunning coincidence! The king ordered that Haman be brought in.

> When Haman entered, the king asked him, *"What should be done for the man the king delights to honor?"* (6:6a)

**Why had Haman come to see the king?**

_____

**What happened the instant he stepped into the king's presence?**

_____

**What might have happened had Haman asked his question first, particularly given that he might not have mentioned Mordecai by name?**

_____

**If the king had decreed execution for the nameless offender, could that decree have been revoked?**

_____

Haman had no opportunity to ask for permission to execute Mordecai. Yet another coincidence.

As soon as Haman stepped through the door, the king asked him a question: *"What should be done for the man the king delights to honor?"* Haman was probably not the best person to ask about gift ideas for Mordecai, but look again at what the king actually said.

**What do you notice?**

_____

_____

_____

In yet another amazing coincidence, the king asked Haman the question in a way that failed to mention Mordecai by name. This omission had to be unintentional. Xerxes had no knowledge of Haman's dispute with Mordecai. He had heard nothing of their encounter the previous afternoon. He had no idea that Mordecai was a member of the supposedly disloyal minority group whose execution he had recently authorized. Xerxes had no reason to keep Mordecai's identity a secret. He simply failed to mention the name. Even the greatest skeptic would have to admit that all of these coincidences were not looking very coincidental. Someone was behind all this.

✝

We can choose to believe in coincidences. We get a timely phone call. We get a welcome reassignment at work. We run into an old friend and have an unplanned but encouraging conversation. We follow up on a hunch about our teenager, and we are glad we did. We can view these things, and countless others like them, as coincidences if we really want to.

Or we can choose to believe that God really does care and that He really does keep His promises to love and protect us.

Many of the things that we call coincidences are really just God's being faithful. These wonderful and timely things happen because we have a loving God who pays fantastic attention to detail. In fact, when we look at the proofs of God's faithfulness and call them coincidences, we are not only insulting God, we are robbing ourselves of the joy of recognizing His hand at work in our lives.

**Think back on a crisis in your past. What amazing coincidences did God use to encourage you, strengthen you, or even deliver you from that crisis?**

_____

_____

_____

_____

**What coincidences has God used in your current crisis?**

_____

_____

_____

_____

## PRAYER SUGGESTION

Ask God to help you trust Him with the details of your life, to give you the confidence that He is hard at work, caring for you even when you cannot see it. Ask Him to open your eyes so that you see His work as it becomes evident. But more importantly, ask Him to open your heart so that you can trust Him even when you cannot see what He is doing. Remember what Jesus told Thomas: _Because you have seen me, you have believed; blessed are those who have not seen and yet have believed_ (John 20:29).

Pray this prayer: _God, what You did for Mordecai was amazing. The way You arranged all the events so far in advance and the way You brought them together with perfect timing — only You could have done that. I know that You are working in my life too. Help me trust You with that. And when that work comes together and becomes visible, help me see that it was You all along — loving me and caring for me just the way You said You would. But also, Lord, help me trust You even when I can't see You at work. Use the times when I can see You to build my faith for the times when I can't. Amen._

# ✝

WEEK SIX ✝ DAY TWO

# Victory Laps

**PASSAGE: Esther 6:6b-11**

Xerxes discovered that Mordecai was never rewarded for exposing the plot to assassinate the king. It was high time for this oversight to be corrected. But what should be done? The king was unsure, so he asked the only other official present in the palace at that early hour: Haman. What happened next? Something Haman could never have imagined, even in his worst nightmares; and something Mordecai would never forget.

We've all seen it: An athlete, often an Olympian, wins a race, but before heading to the bench, they run one more lap in celebration. We call it a victory lap. That is what happens next in our story: God gave Mordecai a victory lap, and He used Haman to do it. After all, the race might not have been over, but the outcome was certain. So God gave His faithful servant Mordecai an opportunity to enjoy, in advance, the victory that was just around the corner. And while He was at it, He allowed Haman to experience the greatest humiliation of his life. Our God is a mighty God, who gives us victory over those who stand against Him.

**READING ASSIGNMENT: Esther 6:1-11**

**FOCUS FOR TODAY: Esther 6:6b-11**

> *Now Haman thought to himself, "Who is there that the king would rather honor than me?"* (6:6b)

When Xerxes asked the question, *"What should be done for the man the king delights to honor?"* he failed to mention just who that man was.

**What does Haman assume?**

_____

_____

_____

Being the self-centered man that he was, Haman assumed that the king was asking how best to honor *him*.

**What do you think might have happened if the king had mentioned Mordecai by name?**

_____

_____

**But what was likely to happen now that Haman thought that the king wanted to honor him?**

_____

_____

_____

Notice that Haman was just thinking this — he didn't say it out loud — so the king had no chance to correct him. When he did open his mouth he gave us a clear view of how firmly the hook had been set.

> *So he answered the king, "For the man the king delights to honor... (6:7)*

Notice how Haman's answer began: not with the usual formalities, such as "if it please the king," but with a dreamy reverie. He was entranced. He was relishing the moment. What was it he had come to the palace for? Oh yes, to ask permission to execute Mordecai; but that could wait. For now he was completely intoxicated with imagining how Xerxes might show him honor. He visualized one possibility, then another, and then he had it!

> *"...have them bring a royal robe the king has worn and a horse the king has ridden,*
> *one with a royal crest placed on its head... (6:8)*

Haman was just getting started, but let's pause for a moment. Why would Haman have proposed a royal robe and a royal horse? Why might he have thought that this would be such an appropriate way to show him honor?

**What do you think?**

_____

_____

I'm sure the idea made perfect sense to Haman. After all, how could one honor the second most powerful man in the empire, except by bestowing upon him the trappings of the first most powerful man in the empire? So he suggested a royal robe and a royal horse. The *crest* placed on the head of the king's horse was actually a royal headdress or crown, a custom depicted in numerous engravings.[3] But Haman was just warming up. There was more!

> *"…then let the robe and horse be entrusted to one of the king's most noble princes. Let them robe the man the king delights to honor, and lead him on the horse through the city streets, proclaiming before him, `This is what is done for the man the king delights to honor!'"* (6:9)

This is interesting — not at all what we might have suggested. Why would Haman make this specific request? True, he had all the wealth he could ever want, so it makes sense that he wouldn't ask for cash. Yet something more was going on here. Recall that seven Persian families ruled the Persian Empire. Recall further that Haman was an Agagite, not a Persian, and certainly not a member of these aristocratic families.

**With this in mind, why might Haman have suggested being robed and led around by a Persian aristocrat?**

_____

_____

_____

Despite his position as prime minister, Haman's second-class background must have gnawed at him. Such a man must have resented the aristocrats who, in Haman's mind at least, would have considered themselves his social superiors.

So as Haman imagined how he ought to be honored, he saw one of these Persian aristocrats placing the robe on him, holding the horse as he mounted it, and leading horse and rider through the city streets while proclaiming repeatedly in a loud voice for all to hear, *"This is what is done for the man the king delights to honor!"* Ah, the bliss!

That, Haman proposed, was what the king should do.

> *"Go at once," the king commanded Haman. "Get the robe and the horse and do just as you have suggested for Mordecai the Jew, who sits at the king's gate. Do not neglect anything you have recommended."* (6:10)

The king loved the idea, so he commanded Haman to do the very things he has suggested — for Mordecai the Jew! The verse doesn't record whether Haman actually passed out, but the shock must have been immense. That the honoree was not Haman was disappointing and embarrassing. That the honoree was Mordecai was unimaginable. That Haman would be the *noble prince* who would lead Mordecai through the city was sickening. But actually having to shout, *"This is what is done for the man the king delights to honor"* — that would surely be the most degrading, the most humiliating experience of Haman's life.

It had to have been especially grating for Haman that the king should refer to Mordecai as *"Mordecai the Jew."* How did the king know of Mordecai's heritage? We can only speculate. While it seems certain that the controversy over Mordecai had escaped the king's attention, word of his Jewish ancestry somehow had not. But why would the king bother to mention Mordecai's ancestry in this situation? Again, we can only speculate, but consider this: Although it would have been difficult for Haman to keep his feelings off his face in the presence of the king, it would have been important that he do so, because demonstrating one's disapproval of the king's command was dangerous. So we can imagine the blank look that must have come on Haman's face at the mention of Mordecai's name. Perhaps the king, misreading the blank expression, thought that Haman didn't know who Mordecai was, so the king added, in effect, "You know, the Jew, who sits at the king's gate."

Xerxes concluded with, *"Do not neglect anything you have recommended."* Haman's ideas now had the force of a royal decree. What about Haman's request? He probably figured that this wouldn't be a good time to bring it up. What could he say? "By the way, Your Majesty, after I honor Mordecai, can I hang him?" Haman had no choice but to honor Mordecai precisely as he had described.

**What had God done to prepare for this threat to Mordecai's life and, just as importantly, when had He done it? Be specific.**

_____

_____

_____

_____

_____

_____

> So Haman got the robe and the horse. He robed Mordecai, and led him on horseback
> through the city streets, proclaiming before him, "This is what is done for the man the
> king delights to honor!" (6:11)

As we have seen, the interview between Xerxes and Haman likely took place just before dawn. As we shall see in tomorrow's study, the upcoming conversation between Haman, his wife, and his friends would take place just before the midday meal. This means that Haman probably had to lead Mordecai, robed and mounted in royal fashion, through the city streets for five hours or more. How many times during those five interminable hours did Haman repeat the phrase, "*This is what is done for the man the king delights to honor?*" It was not exactly the morning that Haman had planned.

**As we conclude our study today, describe very briefly the morning Haman had originally planned.**

_____

_____

**And, once again, how did he end up spending his morning?**

_____

_____

**How difficult was it for God to rescue Mordecai?**

_____

_____

Enough of Haman's humiliation! Imagine with me Mordecai's being led about in royal robes on a royal horse. As I contemplate that picture, I can't help but think of 2 Corinthians 2:14, where the apostle Paul reminds us that God *always leads us in triumphal procession in Christ.* Mordecai had never heard that verse; it was written centuries after he died. But he surely would have understood what it meant. What an amazing moment for a faithful servant of God.

Have you ever experienced a moment like that? You were in the race, but just barely. Winning was out of the question. Even finishing seemed doubtful. Then God showed up. He took the baton from your hand. He sped on ahead. And He finished your race. More than that, He won it. Then He did something truly wonderful: He handed you the gold medal so that you could run the victory lap.

I remember one such "victory lap" in my life. It was my final commencement, the one for my Ph.D. As a husband, the father of two teenagers, and a full-time pastor, there were times when

I wondered if that day would ever come. In particular, one of the language requirements, Latin, had me thoroughly overwhelmed. I honestly wondered whether I had the ability to finish the course. But several months before I was scheduled to graduate, the lights began to come on. Suddenly I was absorbing grammar and vocabulary as never before. Whole sentences began leaping off the page at me. In what seemed like no time at all I had passed the Latin exam, defended my dissertation, and was ready to graduate. I know what I'm good at and I know what I'm not good at, and I can tell you — that was God! When I walked across the stage to receive my degree, I was running the victory lap even though God had won the race for me.

**Tell the story of a "victory lap" in your life.**

_____

_____

_____

**How do you see God giving you victory in the crisis you are facing right now?**

_____

_____

_____

_____

**PRAYER SUGGESTION**

Read 2 Corinthians 2:14 aloud: _But thanks be to God, who always leads us in triumphal procession in Christ and through us spreads everywhere the fragrance of the knowledge of him._ Make the details of that verse your prayer for today, and make it personal: _God, I want to thank You for always leading me in triumphal procession in Christ. Even when I am fearful and faithless, I am never defeated because You have given me victory in Your Son. I also want to thank You that through me You are spreading everywhere the fragrance of the knowledge of Him. When I experience and celebrate the victory that is mine in Christ, it makes Him look good. The people around me can see that being Yours pays off and they want to know Him too. Lord, I want to live my life as a victorious, attractive Christian. When tough times come, as I know they will, I want to rejoice because I know that You are there for me. More than that, I want my response to the tough times to attract others to You because our relationship is so beautifully evident. Thank You for the victory laps, Lord, and please use them for Your glory. Amen._

# No Match for God

**PASSAGE: Esther 6:12-14**

The trap had been sprung, and Haman was caught. A day that, for Haman, had dawned with the promise of victory had instead become a day of humiliation. What happened? What went wrong? Or, from Mordecai's point of view, what went right? How had the situation changed so dramatically and so suddenly? The answer is God's intervention. Although Haman was oblivious to the workings of God in the situation, Haman's friends could see it clearly. Haman was no match for God, and even though he couldn't see that, others could.

Today we will see God at work as He delivers us in the everyday crises in our lives. More than that, we will learn how to see God at work in our lives through the eyes of the people around us. Often we are too close to the situation, too overwhelmed, to see what God is doing. His actions might be clear and out in the open, but even so, we can't see them. At times like that, we need help. We need perspective. We need to see God at work through the eyes of others.

**READING ASSIGNMENT: Esther 6:1-14**

**FOCUS FOR TODAY: Esther 6:12-14**

> *Afterward Mordecai returned to the king's gate. But Haman rushed home, with his head covered in grief…* (6:12)

What must have seemed like an eternity to Haman no doubt flew by for the perplexed but amused Mordecai. Yet all good things must come to an end, and the procession around the city of Susa concluded shortly before midday. When it did, Mordecai returned *to the king's gate.* Are we to understand that he returned to work, or are we to assume that he returned to his demonstration? Based upon all we have seen of Mordecai, a return to the demonstration seems more likely.

Haman's day, indeed Haman's life, had taken a serious and unexpected turn. Instead of returning to the palace and to his duties as prime minister, Haman covered his head and rushed home in shame and grief. What did he do when he got there? He called another meeting.

**If Haman had asked your advice at this point, what would you have said to him? What counsel would you have given?**

_____

_____

_____

Consider what his wife and friends told him.

> ...and told Zeresh his wife and all his friends everything that had happened to him. His advisers and his wife Zeresh said to him, "Since Mordecai, before whom your downfall has started, is of Jewish origin, you cannot stand against him — you will surely come to ruin!" (6:13)

Haman explained to his wife and friends — the Hebrew words carry the nuance of _advisers_[4] — what had happened that morning. How much Haman could explain would have depended, of course, on how much Xerxes had told him.

**How much do you think Xerxes might have explained to Haman and why?**

_____

_____

_____

How much did he know about the king's sleepless night, about the reading of the court records, about the incident five years earlier with Mordecai, or about the fact that no reward had been given? The text doesn't say, although it would be a little surprising if Xerxes had failed to mention to Haman just what it was that Mordecai had done to be deemed worthy of such an honor. It is probably safe to assume that Haman had heard all about the assassination plot, about Mordecai's role in exposing it, and so forth, and that he explained all of this to his wife and friends.

Their reaction was wonderful: "Haman, if you oppose Mordecai, your life will surely be ruined!" Why did they draw this conclusion?

**What do you think?**

_____

_____

_____

Why didn't they reassure Haman that, as the prime minister, the situation would soon turn to his favor? Because they had no such assurance to give! Hearing how the events unfolded, it seemed clear that Haman was up against something even more powerful than his status as prime minister.

Notice, though, how they put it: *"Since Mordecai...is of Jewish origin, you cannot stand against him."* In other words, it was Mordecai's Jewish ancestry that would ultimately be Haman's undoing.

**Why might they have concluded that the key to Mordecai's victory was his Jewish ancestry?**

_____

_____

_____

These people had connected the dots between this series of coincidences and the fact that Mordecai was a Jew. Although the unnamed writer of the book of Esther was careful to leave God's name off of the surface of the book, it was clear to Haman's friends that something supernatural was going on. They could not bring themselves to explain away the events of the past twelve hours as mere coincidence. Someone was behind these events, carefully orchestrating them in a way that even the prime minister was completely powerless to resist. It must have been God. Note their certainty: *"before whom your downfall has started."* Haman was doomed. After all, even a prime minister could not stand against the power of God.

> *While they were still talking with him, the king's eunuchs arrived and hurried Haman*
> *away to the banquet Esther had prepared.* (6:14)

**What was this all about? Where were they taking him?** _____

Things had been going so badly for Haman that we might be inclined to see this as an arrest. But it wasn't. These servants had arrived to escort the prime minister to his luncheon appointment with the king and queen. With all that had happened, it's hard to imagine that only twenty-four hours have passed since the previous luncheon. Haman probably remembered how confident he had felt just one day ago. With the arrival of these escorts, things seemed to be looking up again. Maybe things would work out for Haman after all.

Although Haman couldn't see it himself, his wife and friends quite readily recognized in these events the unmistakable hand of God. God might not have been working on Haman's behalf, but He was certainly working — clearly, unmistakably, and irresistibly. Nevertheless, Haman needed someone else to help him to see the obvious.

It is strange, isn't it? We often overlook the clear demonstrations of God's power in the circumstances of our lives, even though others can see them clearly. Why are we so blind? Are we just too close, or perhaps too overcome by our personal crises, to see the hand of God moving in our lives? I don't know. But I do know that when I am in the middle of a crisis, I need to hear from others. I need their input. I need them to tell me what they are seeing that I may be missing, especially when it comes to the work of God on my behalf.

**Make a list of the people in your life who have been close to you during your current crisis. If you've been an active participant in your small group times, include the group members; their insights will be especially valuable.**

_____

_____

_____

**Have they seen God working in your crisis in ways that you have missed? What have they been telling you?**

_____

_____

_____

**Speak with two or three of these people and ask them these questions: "What have you seen God doing in my current situation? How have you seen Him working, whether in my life or in the circumstances themselves, to bring me through?" Record their responses here.**

_____

_____

_____

_____

**PRAYER SUGGESTION**

Acknowledge to God that even though you know that He is there for you and that He is hard at work behind the scenes, your crisis is obscuring your spiritual vision, making it hard for you to see. Ask Him to open your eyes by allowing you to see through the eyes of others. Ask Him to use the people around you to show you how He is working faithfully in your crisis. Pray this prayer: *Lord, I know that You love me and that You are always there for me. I know that You care about my current situation and that You are hard at work on my behalf. And I know that You want me to trust You even when I can't see what You're doing. But I also know that sometimes I miss what You're showing me. I can't see the things You want me to see. At times like that, please give me the boldness to go to others. Let them be my eyes. Let me see through them what I was missing on my own. Make your work obvious to them so that it can be obvious to me. Thank You, Lord, that You are at work and that I know that. Even when I can't see You helping me, I know that You're there doing wonderful things for me. Amen.*

# A Special Introduction to Days 4 and 5

Once again, we have completed our study of this chapter of the book of Esther a bit early. Rather than move on, however, I want to take this opportunity for another two-day side trip through God's Word. More specifically, I want to bring God out on stage. For weeks now we have seen God's work behind the scenes. It would be refreshing to spend the next two days focusing on God Himself.

But brace yourself, because the God we are about to see will take your breath away. Remember the wonderful scene in *The Wizard of Oz* when Dorothy and the others spot the little old man behind the curtain? Although they had been transfixed by the fire, the smoke, and the disembodied head hovering above the throne, they were disappointed, even angry, when they saw who was actually behind the curtain. Well, we are about to have the opposite experience. If you have been impressed by what God has been doing in the story of Esther, wait until you see God Himself!

# The Glory of God

**PASSAGE: Selected passages**

Last week on Day Five, we looked briefly at the Hebrew word for *glory*. We saw that the root word means *heavy* or *weighty*. When used to describe God, it emphasizes that His presence is not simply seen — it is felt. His holiness lands like a blow. It has impact. Have you ever wondered what it would be like to come face to face with God? What would you experience? How would you react?

In today's study, we are going to share the experience of God's presence with some of the leading figures in Scripture. Each one of them had a moment — a brief but unforgettable and life-changing moment — when they encountered God's glory, the *weightiness* of His holiness. What is it like when this God of wonders steps out from behind the curtain and takes His rightful place on center stage?

**READING ASSIGNMENT: Read all three accounts of the Transfiguration of Christ: Matthew 17:1-8; Mark 9:2-8; and Luke 9:28-36.**

**FOCUS FOR TODAY: Selected passages**

The glory of God was glimpsed several times in Scripture. Today we are going to look briefly at three examples from the Old Testament and three from the New. The Old Testament examples will include the appearance to Moses in Exodus 33, the appearance to Isaiah in Isaiah 6, and the appearance to Ezekiel in Ezekiel 1. In the New Testament, we will witness the appearance of Christ at the Transfiguration as reported by Matthew, Mark, and Luke; the appearance of Christ to Paul on the road to Damascus; and the appearance of Christ to John in Revelation 1. As we look at these passages, take careful note of two things: how God's glory is described and how the eyewitnesses reacted to it.

**Moses' Glimpse of God's Glory (Exodus 33:18-23)**

*Moses said, "Now show me your glory." And the LORD said, "I will cause all my goodness to pass in front of you, and I will proclaim my name, the LORD, in your presence…. But," he said, "you cannot see my face, for no one may see me and live." Then the LORD said, "There is a place near me where you may stand on a rock. When my glory passes by, I will put you in a cleft in the rock and cover you with my hand until I have passed by. Then I will remove my hand and you will see my back; but my face must not be seen."*

**What do you learn about the appearance of God's glory in this passage?**

_____

_____

**What do you learn about the risk to an eyewitness?**

_____

_____

I've often wondered how Moses responded to this glimpse of God's glory, but unfortunately we are not told.

**Isaiah's Glimpse of God's Glory (Isaiah 6:1-5)**

*In the year that King Uzziah died, I saw the Lord seated on a throne, high and exalted, and the train of his robe filled the temple. Above him were seraphs, each with six wings: With two wings they covered their faces, with two they covered their feet, and with two they were flying. And they were calling to one another: "Holy, holy, holy is the LORD Almighty; the whole earth is full of his glory." At the sound of their voices the doorposts and thresholds shook and the temple was filled with smoke. "Woe to me!" I cried. "I am ruined! For I am a man of unclean lips, and I live among a people of unclean lips, and my eyes have seen the King, the LORD Almighty."*

**How is the glory of God expressed in this passage?**

_____

_____

**How did Isaiah, an eyewitness to God's glory, respond?**

_____

_____

A quick side note before we move on: If you compare Isaiah 6:10 with John 12:39-41, you will discover that Isaiah was actually seeing the glory of the preincarnate Christ.

## Ezekiel's Glimpse of God's Glory (Ezekiel 1:4a, 26-28)

*I looked, and I saw a windstorm coming out of the north — an immense cloud with flashing lightning and surrounded by brilliant light. Above the expanse...was what looked like a throne of sapphire, and high above on the throne was a figure like that of a man. I saw that from what appeared to be his waist up he looked like glowing metal, as if full of fire, and that from there down he looked like fire; and brilliant light surrounded him. Like the appearance of a rainbow in the clouds on a rainy day, so was the radiance around him. This was the appearance of the likeness of the glory of the LORD. When I saw it, I fell facedown, and I heard the voice of one speaking.*

## How is God's glory described in this passage?

_____

_____

## How did Ezekiel respond?

_____

_____

This glory was also seen in the New Testament. Here are three examples.

## Peter, James, and John at the Transfiguration (Matthew 17:1-8; Mark 9:2-8; and Luke 9:28-36)

*There he was transfigured before them. His face shone like the sun, and his clothes became as white as the light....the disciples...fell facedown to the ground, terrified.* (Matthew 17:2, 6)

*He took Peter, John and James with him and went up onto a mountain to pray. As he was praying, the appearance of his face changed, and his clothes became as bright as a flash of lightning. Peter and his companions were very sleepy, but when they became fully awake, they saw His glory.* (Luke 9:28-29, 32)

*There he was transfigured before them. His clothes became dazzling white, whiter than anyone in the world could bleach them.* (Mark 9:2b-3)

**How is the glory of Christ described in these passages?**

_____

_____

**How did Peter and the others respond?**

_____

_____

### Paul's Glimpse of Christ's Glory (Acts 9:3-8)

_As he neared Damascus on his journey, suddenly a light from heaven flashed around him. He fell to the ground and heard a voice say to him, "Saul, Saul, why do you persecute me?" "Who are you, Lord?" Saul asked. "I am Jesus, whom you are persecuting," he replied. "Now get up and go into the city, and you will be told what you must do." The men traveling with Saul stood there speechless; they heard the sound but did not see anyone. Saul got up from the ground, but when he opened his eyes he could see nothing. So they led him by the hand into Damascus._

**How is the glory of Christ described in this passage?**

_____

_____

**How did Saul [or Paul] respond?**

_____

_____

### John's Glimpse of Christ's Glory (Revelation 1:10, 12-18)

_On the Lord's Day I was in the Spirit, and I heard behind me a loud voice like a trumpet...I turned around to see the voice that was speaking to me. And when I turned I saw... someone "like a son of man," dressed in a robe reaching down to his feet and with a golden sash around his chest. His head and hair were white like wool, as white as snow, and his eyes were like blazing fire. His feet were like bronze glowing in a furnace, and his voice was like the sound of rushing waters. In his right hand he held seven stars, and out of his mouth came a sharp double-edged sword. His face was like the sun shining in all its brilliance. When I saw him, I fell at his feet as though dead. Then he placed his right hand on me and said: "Do not be afraid. I am the First and the Last. I am the Living One; I was dead, and behold I am alive for ever and ever! And I hold the keys of death and Hades."_

**How is the glory of Christ described in this passage?**

_____

_____

**How did John respond?**

_____

_____

✟

How do people respond when they are given a glimpse of the glory of God? They cry out in terror or fall paralyzed on their faces — and this in response to a mere glimpse of the glory and splendor of God. Although God hides His glory from our direct view, He reveals His glory in the person and work of Christ (John 1:14), including the work He does through us.

**Where has God's glory been most visible in your life and experience? What has He done to display His splendor around you, through you, and in you?**

_____

_____

_____

**What have today's passages taught you that can enrich and deepen your response to God's glory? (Read Psalm 29, Psalm 63, and Psalm 66 for inspiration.)**

_____

_____

_____

### PRAYER SUGGESTION

Let's do something different today — something simple, yet meaningful. Get a hymnal and look up the wonderful old hymn, "Immortal Invisible." If you know the tune or if you can read music, sing it to the Lord. If you can't sing it, just read it aloud as a prayer of tribute. And be sure to include all the verses!

If you would like, close your prayer time with this request: _Lord, thank You for the glimpse You have given me today of Your glory. Please open the eyes of my heart to see Your glory more consistently. Let me feel the weightiness, the crushing reality, of Your holiness. Let it land like a blow. Let me be overwhelmed. Let me truly be in awe of You. Amen._

✦

# The Humility of God

**PASSAGE: Philippians 2:3-8**

Yesterday we looked at the glory of God. Today we will look at His humility. Why humility? Because it is in the voluntary laying aside of His glory that the humility of Christ is most wondrously displayed. In today's passage, the apostle Paul compares the humility of Christ with the arrogance of man. In a shocking and deeply convicting contrast, we will see ourselves glorying in our emptiness while we see Christ emptying Himself of His glory.

**READING ASSIGNMENT: Philippians 2:1-8**

**FOCUS FOR TODAY: Philippians 2:3-8**

*Do nothing out of selfish ambition or vain conceit, but in humility consider others better than yourselves.* (2:3)

In this passage, the apostle Paul was concerned with the selfish and arrogant way we treat each other. Part of the problem, he wrote, is our *vain conceit*, from the Greek word *kenodoxian*. The word does mean *vain conceit*, but the literal meaning is even more helpful. The word literally means *empty glory*.[5] The apostle Paul was telling us that we operate out of vain conceit, or *empty glory.*

**Why did Paul consider all of our glorying in ourselves *empty*?**

_____

_____

_____

Our egos get all puffed up. We develop a false view of our own importance, and we begin to assert ourselves over others. We take glory in ourselves, but it is empty glory. We exalt ourselves, but without justification. How should we treat one another?

*Each of you should look not only to your own interests, but also to the interests of others.* (2:4)

Instead of letting selfish ambition or *empty glory* guide our actions, we should care about and be concerned for one another. The great example of such concern is, of course, Christ Himself.

*Your attitude should be the same as that of Christ Jesus.* (2:5)

What did Paul have in mind?

**What was Christ's attitude toward others and how was that attitude demonstrated?**

_____

_____

_____

_____

Now let's see what Paul said.

> *...Who, being in very nature God, did not consider equality with God something to be grasped...* (2:6)

Before we can fully appreciate what Jesus did, we have to remind ourselves of who Jesus is. Notice where Paul began: with the nature of Christ. What does it mean that Jesus is in *very nature God*? The Greek word here is *morphe,* and it indicated not His nature itself, but the outward expression of His nature.[6] Jesus was God, certainly; but more than that, His deity showed. His external form manifested the reality of His nature. It was the radiance we saw in our study yesterday. It was deity on display. Paul was reminding us not simply that Jesus was God, but that, as God, Jesus glowed with the full and unveiled glory of His deity.

Or at least He did before His birth, and that brings us to Paul's point: Jesus' humility in setting that glory aside. The passage was built around three key Greek verbs, translated by the *New International Version* (and with a bit of context) as, *did not consider, made Himself nothing,* and *taking the very nature.*

Despite the fact that Jesus had, throughout eternity past, shone with the glory of His pure deity; despite the fact that He had forever freely radiated His glory as God Himself; despite this He *did not consider equality with God something to be grasped.* Despite the fact that His glory had remained unveiled for all eternity past, He did not consider that glory something to be selfishly retained. He did not regard the outward expression of His deity as a prize to be jealously guarded, a possession that He was unwilling to relinquish. He did not hesitate to abandon the external manifestation of His person. As someone once put it, Christ willingly surrendered His right to manifest Himself visibly as the God of all splendor and glory.[7] Why? Because He did not regard that glory as something to be selfishly grasped.

Why is it so important for us that Jesus was willing to give up His external glory?

**What do you think?**

_____

_____

_____

If Jesus did not selfishly grasp His external glory, what did He do?

> _He made himself nothing, taking the very nature of a servant, being made in human likeness._ (2:7)

Christ _made Himself nothing_. This is what theologians call the _kenosis_ or _self-emptying_ of Christ, and it is a difficult concept.[8] How are we to understand this phrase? What does it mean? First of all, it does not mean that Christ gave up any attributes of deity.

**Look up the following passages. In what way does each passage suggest that Jesus could not have given up any aspects of His deity when He became a man?**

**John 14:9**

_____

_____

**Colossians 2:9**

_____

_____

**Hebrews 13:8**

_____

_____

What, then, does it mean? Look at the context: The Greek word, from which we get the expression _kenosis_, is _keno_, which simply means _to empty_.[9] But of what did Christ _empty Himself_? The key here is a word play that takes us back to something Paul said in a previous verse. Recall that verse three speaks of our *vain conceit,* or more literally, *empty glory,* from the Greek word *kenodoxian.* Now verse six tells us that Christ, who has true glory, *emptied Himself.*

It is this word play that brings out the crucial contrast between our attitude and the attitude of Christ: What do we do? Although we are empty, we glory. What does Christ do? Although He is glorious, He empties. How different we are from our Savior! Christ has true and infinite glory, but does He exalt Himself? Never! He who has true glory does not exalt Himself, but *empties* Himself, humbles Himself. What a contrast! We who are empty, glory; He who is glory, empties.

**What, then, did Christ give up when He became one of us? Of what did He empty Himself? (Hint: What was emphasized at the beginning of verse six?)**

_____

_____

When He became a human being, Christ gave up the external manifestation of His divine glory. He veiled His divine splendor. He forfeited the external glory of His deity.

Now we are ready for the next question: How did Christ do this? By ceasing to be fully God? Not at all! We see how He did it in verse seven: *taking the very nature of a servant.* The phrase *very nature* is the same phrase we saw at the beginning of verse six; it is an outward expression of an attribute, this time, the outward expression of Christ's humanity.

In becoming a man, however, Christ did not cease to be God. As it is used here, the Greek word *labone,* translated *taking,* means *taking on* or *putting on.*[10] When a man puts on clothing he does not cease to be a man; likewise, when Christ put on human nature, He did not cease to be God. Christ did not replace His deity with humanity. He added humanity. He took on human nature and allowed that nature, rather than the deity, to express itself outwardly. In other words, the God-man looked nothing like God and everything like man. He took on the nature and with it the outward form of a humble servant.

But His selflessness didn't end there. His humility had not, even then, found its limit.

> *And being found in appearance as a man, he humbled himself and became obedient to death — even death on a cross!* (2:8)

Note that Christ's outward appearance was an expression of His humanity rather than His deity. But beyond simply manifesting His humanity, Christ humbled Himself even further. How? By becoming *obedient to death*; but not just any death, *a cross death.*

There has never been a more humiliating or more degrading way to die than by death on a cross. Yet this Lord of glory — in whose magnificent presence men fall to their faces in terror, blinded by His dazzling brightness — this Jesus willingly traded His infinite, preincarnate splendor for total humiliation. But the point is not the humiliation of Christ; the point is the humility of Christ. The Lord of Glory is humble. This One who when He spoke, the galaxies leaped into existence, this Creator of the universe, is humble.

And we are proud.

I hope this "glimpse behind the curtain" has given you a deeper appreciation of God's glory — and of His humility in setting aside that glory for our sake. Your small group discussion this week will bring the focus back to the story of Esther. But before we move on, let's consider some applications of what we have seen today in the person and character of Christ. Rather than base the application on Paul's purpose in writing Philippians 2, let's explore the implications of Christ's humility in how we deal with the crises of life.

**We've seen in today's passage the lengths to which God will go to personally meet us at our point of need. How does this encourage you to trust God in your current crisis?**

_____

_____

_____

_____

**How does Christ's example encourage you to be available to someone else in need?**

_____

_____

_____

**PRAYER SUGGESTION**

Thank God for His humility. Thank Him that He willingly gave up the external manifestation of His glory in order to meet you at your point of need. And thank Him that He still loves you and cares about you today — that His heart of self-giving is as much a part of who He is as it was when Christ came to earth. Ask Him to remind you of that fact, especially in the tough times. Ask Him to help you remember His loving, caring, giving heart so that you will trust Him more readily. Finally, ask Him to give you that same heart for others. Ask Him to give you that same eagerness to set aside self-interest in order to meet others at their point of need.

✝

WEEK SIX
THE INVINCIBLE GOD

# Small Group Discussion Guide

We've faced our crisis, we've determined God's will, and we've stepped boldly forward. Despite our fears, we've done what God expected of us. Now what can we expect of Him? What will God do, and how will we know when He does it? How can we see the invisible God at work? In today's passage we will see God act in a way that is powerful and unmistakable — and very much like the way He acts in our lives today.

**TODAY: Esther 6:1-14**

**I. God may be invisible, but His ACTIONS aren't. Look for His ACTIONS!**
**KEY PASSAGE:** Esther 6:1-6a (read it aloud)

**DISCUSSION QUESTION:** What act of God is evident in this passage?

_____

_____

**PRINCIPLE:** God is at work in your life. Are you going to believe in coincidences, or are you going to believe in God?

**SUPPORT PASSAGES:** Ephesians 1:11; Romans 8:28 (read it aloud)

**APPLICATION:** How has God been at work in your crisis? What people, events, or circumstances has He used to encourage you, strengthen you, or carry you through?

_____

_____

_____

**II. God may be invisible, but His VICTORIES aren't. Look for VICTORY!**

**KEY PASSAGE:** Esther 6:6b-11 (read it aloud)

**DISCUSSION QUESTION:** What victory of God do we see here?

_____

_____

**PRINCIPLE:** God is delivering you daily. Are you going to stay mired in your defeats, or are you going to rejoice in God's deliverance?

**SUPPORT PASSAGE:** 2 Corinthians 2:14 (read it aloud)

**APPLICATION:** What victories, large or small, has God already given you in your crisis?

_____

_____

How has He spared you by keeping your crisis from getting worse?

_____

_____

**III. God may be invisible, but His power is INVINCIBLE. Be CONFIDENT!**

**KEY PASSAGE:** Esther 6:12-14 (read it aloud)

**DISCUSSION QUESTION:** How does God reveal His invincible power in this passage?

_____

_____

**PRINCIPLE:** God is protecting you. Are you going to depend on your ingenuity and resourcefulness, or are you going to find refuge and rest in Him?

**SUPPORT PASSAGE:** Psalm 121:7-8 (read it aloud)

**APPLICATION:** How has God displayed His power either in your crisis or in you personally? How has He shown Himself invincible?

_____

_____

How can this display of His power give you greater confidence?

_____

_____

_____

# How to See God in Action

It has been said, "Don't be afraid to go out on a limb, because that's where the fruit is."[1] That is also where the power of God is! We all long to see God powerfully at work in our lives, doing the things that only He can do. But if too few of us fail to experience the evidence of His power, it might be because so few of us ever give Him the opportunity. We are so busy either avoiding risk or depending only on ourselves that God can't get a miracle in edgewise. Why do we do this? Have we forgotten that *without faith, it is impossible to please God* (Hebrews 11:6)?

In this week's passage, Esther joined the ranks of the faithful. She stepped out from behind her fears and trusted God with amazing boldness. We will see courageous faith at its best. And God will come through! As you study this week's passage, watch Esther carefully. Pay attention to what she says, what she does, and even what she is feeling. Learn everything you can from her. Then, when you see what God does in response, ask yourself, *Isn't it time that I stepped forward with courageous faith of my own?*

# The Moment of Trust

**PASSAGE: Esther 7:1-2**

As the story resumes, Esther had another opportunity to expose Haman's plot. Did she come through? Twice before she was presented with the same opportunity and both times, she let it go by. She wanted desperately for God to save her and her people, yet she seemed to be struggling to do the very thing that would reveal the incredible deliverance God had already provided. Esther had to realize that in order to see God, she had to look for opportunities to trust God. After all, moments of truth are often "moments of trust."

**READING ASSIGNMENT: Esther 7:1-2**

**FOCUS FOR TODAY: Esther 7:1-2**

*The king and Haman went to dine with Queen Esther…* (7:1)

For the second day in a row, Esther welcomed King Xerxes and Haman, the prime minister, to an intimate luncheon. Much had happened since the previous day's luncheon, especially in Haman's life and circumstances. But keep in mind that as incredible as these events were, they did not expose, let alone overturn, Haman's plot. Mordecai had enjoyed an unforgettable morning at Haman's expense, but the Jews were still a condemned people.

Before we join Esther, Xerxes, and Haman at the luncheon, consider the king's position. Xerxes had no idea that the supposedly disloyal group of people whose annihilation he had authorized were the Jews, and that in condemning the Jews he had condemned Mordecai, the very man who had saved his life. Neither did Xerxes have any notion that his own queen was numbered among the condemned. All Xerxes knew was that a benefactor, whose loyalty had gone unrewarded for five years, had finally received the honor and recognition that he was due. It was also extremely unlikely that Xerxes was even the least bit aware of the humiliation that Haman had endured, since any show of opposition to the king's command would have put Haman at grave personal risk.

Also, consider Esther. How much would she have known about the events that had transpired since their visit the previous day?

**What do you think?**

_____

_____

_____

How would Esther have known that Mordecai had offended Haman or that Haman, under the advice of his wife and friends, had plotted to kill Mordecai? How would she have known of the incredible chain of coincidences that had turned Haman's plans against him, resulting in his complete humiliation? How, indeed, would she have known about the honor that had been accorded Mordecai that very morning? Recall that women in the harem lived in complete isolation.

**How do you think Esther might have responded if she had heard the news?**

_____

_____

_____

_____

As it happens, however, Esther hadn't heard. God does a lot of amazing things, including many things that we never hear about. That's one reason it is so important to allow the things we do know about to build our faith.

While we are at it, consider Haman. He was, in all likelihood, the only one who knew everything that had gone on over the past twenty-four hours. Yet there are some things — some very important things — that even Haman didn't know, at least not yet.

So Xerxes and Haman arrived for their midday banquet with the queen. Haman was probably trying to feel encouraged at this moment.

**What do you think Haman might have been saying to himself? How might he have been trying to lift his mood?**

_____

_____

_____

From one point of view things didn't look so bad for Haman. He was, after all, enjoying a private luncheon with the king and queen. And despite the personal humiliation of the morning, he was still the prime minister, second only to the king himself in power and influence. Yet that haunting warning from his wife and friends was no doubt still ringing in his ears: "*Since Mordecai, before whom your downfall has started, is of Jewish origin, you cannot stand against him — you will surely come to ruin!*"

> *As they were drinking wine on that second day, the king again asked, "Queen Esther, what is your petition? It will be given you. What is your request? Even up to half the kingdom, it will be granted." (7:2)*

The meal was complete and the men were enjoying their wine. Whatever the small talk had been during the meal, the king was ready for Esther to get to the point. He repeated his question of the previous day, and he did so with the same warmth and openness he had shown before. Again, the offer of half the kingdom was a polite exaggeration intended to put her at ease. After all, the Persian king was fiercely autocratic, so it took boldness for someone — even the queen — to trouble him with one's personal concerns. Naturally, then, it took some exaggeration on the king's part to put at ease anyone who had taken such a risk.

The king's words certainly sounded reassuring, but put yourself in Esther's position for a moment.

**What was she about to do, and why would the prospect of doing it have been so frightening?**

_____

_____

_____

Keep in mind that Esther was about to identify herself, before the king and the prime minister, as a member of a condemned race. She was about to challenge a royal decree that could not be reversed. She was about to challenge the integrity of the man that the king trusted more than anyone else in the world. And she was going to do this as a concubine. The risk of Esther's overplaying her hand was immense.

Yet her moment of opportunity had come. Esther must act.

God had brought Esther to her "moment of trust" and the next step was hers. That morning God had done something for Mordecai that was truly amazing, and He had done it entirely on His own. But Esther's situation was different. Yes, God had assembled the pieces, and they were all in place. And yes, God was standing right in the wings, ready and waiting to send in a miracle. But if Esther wanted to see that miracle, if she wanted to see God in action, she was going to have to make the first move. She was going to have to exercise courageous faith.

We often find ourselves in just that kind of situation. God has assembled the pieces and they are all in place — or at least we're hoping they are. We are trusting that God is there, ready to act on our behalf. So what's the holdup? Why doesn't He just go ahead and do it? Because He has decided that the next move will be ours. He is waiting for us to exercise some courageous faith.

If we want to *see* God in our crises, we must look for opportunities to *trust* God in our crises. And you can depend on it — those opportunities abound. God often chooses to act only when somebody trusts Him. Are you beginning to suspect that, in your current crisis, that somebody is probably *you*?

**Take an "up-to-the-moment" look at your current crisis. What has God done to bring you to this moment? How has He prepared you for this moment? What has He done on His own? How has He put the pieces in place?**

_____

_____

_____

**Now that your moment of trust has arrived, what opportunities is God giving you to trust Him — not simply to trust Him *passively* by doing nothing, but to trust Him *actively* by obeying Him?**

_____

_____

**Chances are, there is a part of you that is scared to death, begging for delay. How has God prepared you and emboldened you to face your fears?**

_____

_____

### PRAYER SUGGESTION

Tell God what you wrote in response to today's first application question, then thank Him for it. Thank Him for taking such good care of you, for going ahead of you and preparing your way. Thank Him for putting all the pieces in place. Then acknowledge that the next move is yours. Ask Him to help you see as clearly as possible what He wants you to do — and then, just as important, make a commitment to do it. If you are struggling with fear — and we all do — thank Him for all the ways that He has shown Himself trustworthy. Finally, close your prayer time by reading Psalm 23, the one that begins, *The Lord is my shepherd....* Chances are, you already know it by heart.

# Seizing the Moment

**PASSAGE: Esther 7:3-6**

The moment of trust had arrived, and Esther seized that moment. She had been presented with a third opportunity to expose Haman, and this time she did not hesitate. Despite the enormous risk, Esther boldly revealed her petition to the king. Trusting God had become anything but passive. Faith and trust now seem to be all about taking risks and taking action.

**READING ASSIGNMENT: Esther 7:1-6**

**FOCUS FOR TODAY: Esther 7:3-6**

> *Queen Esther answered, "If I have found favor with you, O king, and if it pleases your majesty, grant me my life — this is my petition. And spare my people — this is my request.* (7:3)

Esther finally presented her request, and it must have stunned the king. Look at how Esther put it.

**Why would these words have come as such a shock to the king?**

_____

_____

_____

*"Grant me my life,"* she said. Who could possibly have been threatening the life of the queen? Just that morning Xerxes had been reminded of an attempt on his own life. Now he heard that someone was threatening the life of his queen. What was going on? Was there a larger conspiracy at work?

And what did she mean by *"spare my people?"* Had the king ever considered the question of Esther's ethnic background? The Scriptures give no hint of that. Even if he had, there is no reason to think that he would have considered it of any consequence.

**What hints do we have of Xerxes' attitude on the issue of race?**

_____

_____

_____

Remember, the Persian Empire was, to say the least, culturally diverse, so it would not have been the least bit unusual for the king to interact with people from a wide range of cultural backgrounds. Notice that when his order went out as recorded in chapter two to scour the empire for the most beautiful young women, there were no restrictions regarding race. The king even promoted Haman to the position of prime minister, despite the fact that Haman was not Persian. It is probably safe to say that Xerxes did not consider the question of a person's ethnicity particularly important. If he did know of Esther's Jewish heritage, it was apparently of no concern to him. That is, until now.

Someone was threatening the queen's people. How wide-ranging was this conspiracy that it should include even the queen's relatives? Moreover, Xerxes alone had the authority to order mass executions. Who could possibly have been behind such a far-reaching conspiracy?

Remember that Haman was sitting right there listening to the conversation. We have to ask ourselves what he must have been thinking at that moment.

**What do you suppose Haman would be making of all this?**

_____

_____

_____

When did Haman begin to realize what Esther was saying? We don't know. It was highly unlikely that he knew of Esther's Jewish heritage. Was there an assassination plot that had escaped his notice? Possibly. But the phrase _"spare my people"_ might well have given Haman pause. Esther was reporting a plot to murder an entire ethnic group, the very thing Haman had been plotting against the Jews. Were the pieces starting to come together? If they weren't, they would very soon!

> _"For I and my people have been sold for destruction and slaughter and annihilation._
> _If we had merely been sold as male and female slaves, I would have kept quiet, because_
> _no such distress would justify disturbing the king."_ (7:4)

Esther continued her request, stating that she and her people had been _"sold for destruction."_ That was an interesting but appropriate way to put it. Recall from chapter three that Haman had offered to pay the price for the annihilation of an unnamed minority group. The king had accepted the offer, and then returned the funds to Haman's control to carry out his plan. In a very real sense, then, the king had sold the Jews for destruction.

Yet they were sold not merely for destruction, but for *"destruction and slaughter and annihilation."*

**Why did Esther put it this way? Where have we heard these words before?**

_____

Recall that this was precisely the way the decree itself, issued only weeks prior, had been worded. (See Esther 3:13.) Would the king have recognized these words? Not necessarily, since the king might never have seen the decree as it had been issued. After all, if Xerxes had seen the decree to commit genocide against the Jews, he would surely have been alarmed if only for the sake of Mordecai, whom, as we learned last week, the king knew to be a Jew. (See Esther 6:10.) So it seems unlikely that Xerxes would have recognized these words as having come from a decree which bore his own seal. Of course Esther would have had no idea of whether Xerxes had seen the decree. Nevertheless, she took the risk and quoted the decree directly.

Which raises the question: Did Haman recognize these words as his own? He knew the decree intimately. He had dictated it. Did he hear in Esther's request a reference to his own decree and hence to his own plot? We can't be sure, but the clues are piling up.

Esther concluded her request with a remarkable statement — remarkable particularly to our ears. Esther said that, had she and her people merely been sold into slavery, she would not have presumed to disturb the king.

**How does this statement strike you?**

_____

_____

**What does it tell you about the Persian culture?**

_____

_____

**What does it tell you about Esther and the risk she was taking?**

_____

_____

We tend to take for granted our First Amendment right to petition the government for a redress of grievances. If we feel that we have been treated unjustly, we speak up. If the injustice is serious, we take legal action. To our way of thinking, all wrongs must be righted, particularly when we are the aggrieved party. Esther's statement reveals that this was not the case in Persian culture, nor indeed has it been the case in totalitarian regimes throughout history. Would it have been morally wrong to enslave Esther and her people? Absolutely. Yet as most people living under most governments throughout history could tell you, the mere fact of a wrong does not imply the right to a remedy. Some governments recognize the rights of the people. Most, including the Persian Empire, do not. Let's be clear, then: Esther was not exercising a right — she was taking a risk.

> King Xerxes asked Queen Esther, "Who is he? Where is the man who has dared to do such a thing?" (7:5)

Esther had taken her courageous step of faith, and God was free to act, specifically through the response of Xerxes. Recall that the king had spent the morning honoring the man who had saved him from assassins, so he was already thinking in terms of plots and conspiracies.

**Why was this significant? How do you see God at work here?**

_____

_____

_____

We can recall from chapter six how God led Xerxes to the record of Mordecai's role in exposing the assassination plot, how He saved Mordecai from the gallows, and how He gave Mordecai an unforgettable "victory lap" at Haman's expense. Yet now we get a hint that something else might have been behind God's timing. Mere hours before Esther revealed Haman's conspiracy, God used a sleepless night to awaken Xerxes to the danger such conspiracies posed to him and to his reign. What amazing timing! Xerxes could hardly have been better prepared to move quickly and forcefully against any threat to himself or those close to him.

Someone was behind this plot, and King Xerxes wanted to know who it was. Why would the king have assumed that Esther knew the identity of her would-be assassin? Presumably because she was asking him to intervene. The time had come to expose Haman.

> Esther said, "The adversary and enemy is this vile Haman." Then Haman was terrified before the king and queen. (7:6)

The moment had arrived, and Esther came through! Did she glance in Haman's direction? Did she point at him accusingly? Or did she simply expose him with her words? We don't know; but whatever she did, it left Haman shocked and terrified.[2] No doubt his mind was racing as the pieces came together: sold, destruction, slaughter, annihilation — the queen was a Jew! Haman had deceived and manipulated the king into decreeing the death of the queen herself! And now he had been exposed.

We can scarcely imagine his horror at such an unexpected turn of events. But was it really unexpected? What was it that his wife and friends had said only hours before? *"Since Mordecai, before whom your downfall has started, is of Jewish origin, you cannot stand against him — you will surely come to ruin!"* (6:13). They were right — absolutely, sickeningly, dizzyingly right. But who could ever have imagined that it would happen like this?

Haman had somehow been outmaneuvered in his plot to execute Mordecai, but this — this was beyond his comprehension. Before the decree to kill the Jews had been issued, before Haman had even been appointed to the position of prime minister, a beautiful young Jewish woman had been made queen. His plot was doomed to failure even before it began. And now he would face the consequences of his plot to murder the queen.

I recall a short poem by J. G. Whittier that introduces a chapter in a wonderful book entitled *Hudson Taylor's Spiritual Secret*, by Howard Taylor. The poem reads:

> *Nothing before, nothing behind:*
> *The steps of faith*
> *Fall on the seeming void, and find*
> *The rock beneath.*[3]

I think Esther would have appreciated that poem. The moment of trust came — and she seized the moment. In a single act of courageous faith, Esther identified herself with a condemned people, challenged the justice of a royal decree, and accused the prime minister of wrongdoing. Any one of these statements would have placed her at grave personal risk. Yet she made all three with boldness.

Esther stepped into the seeming void. What did she find? She found the rock beneath.

Not all moments of courageous faith are affirmed so immediately and dramatically. Some are, but most are not. More often it seems that the affirmation comes slowly, at times even secretly. I'm sure that you have experienced, as I have, both the sudden and dramatic rewards of faith as well as the slower, secret rewards. Sometimes the affirmation is as dramatic as a deliverance from a crisis. Sometimes it is as quiet and gentle as a much-needed hug from a friend. God affirms our faith in so many different ways.

**Have you ever experienced the immediate, dramatic affirmation of your step of courageous faith? Explain.**

_____

_____

_____

**Have you ever experienced the gradual, even secret affirmation of your step of courageous faith? Explain.**

_____

_____

_____

**How did these affirmations of your step of faith make you feel? How did they encourage and strengthen you?**

_____

_____

_____

**If you honestly cannot recall any times when God affirmed your faith, why do you think that is?**

_____

_____

_____

**PRAYER SUGGESTION**

Tell God the stories you just recorded above. I know, He remembers the details better than you do, but it is appropriate to remind Him of what He did simply as a way of praising Him. Be sure to tell Him how His affirmation made you feel, how it lifted you up and carried you forward. Thank Him for the victory and encouragement He gave you. Also, thank Him for the people He used to deliver His message of encouragement and ask Him to use you to encourage those people in return. Finally, thank Him for all the preparation He did to bring you to that moment, and for giving you the courage to seize that moment when the time came.

# Keeping the Faith

**PASSAGE: Esther 7:7-10**

Esther had taken her great step of faith. She had acted selflessly, boldly, courageously — and immediately she was faced with a new challenge: the challenge of keeping the faith. Esther had no idea what was going to happen next. She knew what she was going to do, and she had prepared herself for that. But what would Xerxes do? What would Haman do? And, above all, what would God do? Having done her part, would Esther be able to trust God with the unforeseeable consequences of her actions? We often face this very same challenge: trusting God for the aftermath.

**READING ASSIGNMENT: Esther 7:1-10**

**FOCUS FOR TODAY: Esther 7:7-10**

> *The king got up in a rage, left his wine and went out into the palace garden. But Haman, realizing that the king had already decided his fate, stayed behind to beg Queen Esther for his life. (7:7)*

The king was burning with rage.[4] Not only had his prime minister and his trusted advisor lied to him, he had actually deceived and manipulated him into decreeing the death of his queen. Notice that Xerxes got up and went into the garden.

**Why did Xerxes leave the banquet? What do you think?**

_____

_____

_____

Some have suggested that Xerxes was incapable of making a decision without advisors.[5] I think he was simply struggling to take in the news. Haman — the man he had personally entrusted with the role of prime minister — *Haman* had betrayed him? It was incomprehensible, shattering, dizzying, so much so that he had to step away from the table and into the garden.

Don't worry that the king had left Esther unguarded. Servants, including armed guards, stood all around.

There was no doubt about what had to be done. As the Hebrew puts it, the king had *determined evil against* Haman.[6] And how did Haman react? He was panicking! There was no point in speaking with the king; Haman realized that the king had already decided his fate. His only hope left was to beg the queen for his life. How ironic — and what a difference a few hours can make when God is involved!

**What had Haman intended to ask of the king earlier that morning?**

_____

_____

_____


Only hours before, this same man had stood at the doorway of the king's apartments, waiting to ask permission to take the life of Mordecai — Esther's cousin, adoptive father, and fellow Jew. Did he ever make that request? No, he didn't. But he was making one now, although not at all the one he had planned! Haman was now begging Queen Esther, a Jew, to intervene to save his life.

> *Just as the king returned from the palace garden to the banquet hall, Haman was falling on the couch where Esther was reclining. The king exclaimed, "Will he even molest the queen while she is with me in the house?" As soon as the word left the king's mouth, they covered Haman's face. (7:8)*

When the king returned, he found Haman in a compromising position. When the Persians dined, they didn't sit up in chairs as we do. Instead, they reclined on couches.[7] Apparently Esther had remained in this position throughout the conversation. But as Haman pled for mercy, he got a little too close. The Persians followed the lead of the Assyrians in matters of courtly rules and regulations; their practice was for a man to maintain a distance of at least seven paces between himself and a concubine of the king's.[8] Defying all customary decorum, Haman acted recklessly as he threw himself at the queen in desperation. We might envision him on his knees before the queen, holding Esther's legs to his chest, with his head on her lap as he tearfully begged for mercy.

And just then the king walked in. *"Will he even molest the queen while she is with me in the house?"*

**What do you think Xerxes meant by this?**

_____

_____

Whether he was accusing Haman of physical or sexual assault is not clear. But it would not be surprising, given the circumstances, if Xerxes had actually believed Esther to be under attack.

**How would you describe Xerxes' frame of mind at this point?**

_____

_____

Recall that Xerxes was _burning with anger,_ and that he had already _determined evil_ against Haman. Because he was in this frame of mind, it wouldn't have been at all surprising if the king gave Haman's actions the worst possible interpretation.

At this point the servants who had been standing nearby did something highly symbolic of Haman's fate: They covered his head and face with a cloth. There is little record of the Persians engaging in this practice, but the Greeks and later the Romans would do this to indicate that the accused had received a sentence of death.[9]

> _Then Harbona, one of the eunuchs attending the king, said, "A gallows seventy-five feet high stands by Haman's house. He had it made for Mordecai, who spoke up to help the king." The king said, "Hang him on it!"_ (7:9)

How did Harbona know about the gallows, and how did he know it had been built for Mordecai?

**What do you think?**

_____

_____

_____

Recall from the end of chapter six that several of the king's eunuchs, including quite possibly Harbona himself, had gone to Haman's house to escort him to the luncheon. It is certain that they would not have missed seeing the gallows, impressive as they were. How did Harbona and the other eunuchs find out that the gallows were intended for Mordecai? If they listened to palace gossip, they might have guessed. But they also might have asked. We can easily imagine Harbona walking past the gallows and asking a servant standing nearby, "Who is this for?"

"Mordecai," he would have been told. Of course this eunuch also would have known of the honor that had been bestowed on Mordecai that very morning. Perhaps something told Harbona that the existence of this gallows just might, under the right circumstances, be of interest to the king.

Now that it was clear that Haman was to be executed, Harbona spoke up: *"A gallows seventy-five feet high stands by Haman's house."* How convenient! But he didn't stop there. *"Moreover,"* as the original Hebrew text says, *"he had it made for Mordecai, who spoke up to help the king."*[10]

**Why was this extra detail so significant?**

_____

_____

_____

Still more shocking news for the king! This was the first the king had heard of Haman's personal grudge against Mordecai. So not only had Haman planned to kill Esther, he had also planned to kill the very man who had that very morning been honored for saving the life of the king.

And then the king learned that there was a gallows ready and waiting near Haman's house.

The king's response? *"Hang him on it!"*

Let's not miss a subtle but telling point: Hegai in chapter two, Hathach in chapter four, and now Harbona in chapter seven — these minor characters were continuing to play a major role in God's plan. Moreover, because these men were all eunuchs, they would have been excluded from public worship in Israel (Deuteronomy 23:1); yet God was only too happy to include them in His plan.

> *They hanged Haman on the gallows he had prepared for Mordecai. Then the king's fury subsided.* (7:10)

This passage speaks for itself. Amazingly, some commentators actually take Esther to task for not having intervened on Haman's behalf. But to intervene would have been to step in the way of God's perfect provision. God didn't need Esther to get in the way and second-guess His plan. All He needed was for her to trust Him and then stand aside.

Esther can teach us a lot not only about courageous faith, but also about how to trust God during the aftermath. In one sense, it is not all that complicated: Esther did what she needed to do, and then she let God do what He needed to do. Things tend to get complicated when we get in God's way. But Esther knew better. She spoke out boldly, and then she trusted God to work through the king. Can we do that? Can we trust God boldly, and then keep trusting Him by allowing Him to do His part?

**Have you ever taken a bold step of faith, only to have your faith falter almost immediately? Explain.**

_____

_____

**Why did you stop trusting God? Did you plan to stop trusting Him, or did it "just happen?"**

_____

_____

_____

Sometimes we are so focused on the moment of trust that we aren't prepared for the moment after that. We are thoroughly prepared to trust God one moment, yet have given absolutely no thought to trusting Him the next. Don't allow that to happen again. When the moment of trust comes in your current crisis, be ready to trust God with the aftermath.

**What will you do right now to prepare yourself to keep the faith, to keep trusting God after your moment of trust has passed?**

_____

_____

_____

### PRAYER SUGGESTION

In her crisis, Esther had now taken her step of courageous faith. She had faced her moment of trust and had gone forward. Have you? If you haven't, begin your prayer time today by asking God for the courage and strength to do what He has called you to do.

Next, ask God to prepare you for the time following your moment of trust. Ask Him to remind you that trusting Him and walking with Him is something you have to do one day at a time. Tell Him the story you told in response to today's first question. Admit to Him how you may have stopped trusting Him and how you got in His way, and be specific. Then ask Him to prepare you so that you will do better next time. Ask Him to remind you that each moment of trust is followed by another, and that our work of trusting Him is never done. Finally, thank Him that when each and every one of those moments of trust come, He will be there for you — ever prepared and ever faithful.

# A Special Introduction to Days 4 and 5

Since we have completed our study of chapter seven a bit early, let's take this opportunity to look at another Old Testament hero who knew how to see God in action: Joseph. Like Esther, Joseph learned to see God at work in the midst of the crises of life. And because he learned to trust in God's plan, Joseph was able to avoid the bitterness and resentment that might otherwise have robbed him of the fulfilling life that God had planned for him. Let's spend the next two days benefiting together from some important moments of trust in the life of Joseph.

# Meant for Evil

**PASSAGE: Genesis 37**

The story of Joseph is among the best known in the Old Testament. All of us who grew up attending Sunday school know about the coat of many colors, Joseph's being sold into slavery, his ability to interpret dreams, and his rise to power in Egypt. Yet too few of us, it seems, have taken to heart one of the great lessons of Joseph's life: his complete confidence in the sovereign care of God. In today's passage we are going to see God's sovereign care as a work in progress. Although Joseph's situation may have looked grim, God was already hard at work advancing His purpose and plan for Joseph.

**READING ASSIGNMENT: Genesis 37:2-36**

**FOCUS FOR TODAY: Selected verses from the passage**

> *Joseph had a dream, and when he told it to his brothers, they hated him all the more.*
> *He said to them, "Listen to this dream I had: We were binding sheaves of grain out in*
> *the field when suddenly my sheaf rose and stood upright, while your sheaves gathered*
> *around mine and bowed down to it."...Then he had another dream, and he told it to*
> *his brothers. "Listen," he said, "I had another dream, and this time the sun and moon*
> *and eleven stars were bowing down to me." (37:5-7, 9)*

These dreams suggested that Joseph would one day lead his family. The brothers grasped this meaning at once and were defiant, even incredulous (see verse 8). The Hebrew gives this sense to their reply: *"You can't seriously think that you're going to rule us?"*[11] Even Jacob, Joseph's adoring father, rebuked him for impertinence (verse 10).

**Do you think Joseph was right to reveal these dreams to his family? Why or why not?**

_____

_____

_____

Can we really blame Joseph's family for having been offended? After all, look again at these verses.

**What indication was there that Joseph's dreams were given to him by God?**

_____

_____

Of course, Joseph's dreams didn't reveal his own plans — they revealed God's plans. It would take many years, however, before that would become clear.

In the meantime, Joseph's brothers had had enough. Their opportunity to deal with him came unexpectedly. One day, while the other brothers were out in the fields caring for the sheep, Jacob sent Joseph to check up on them. As Joseph approached his brothers, they decided to take advantage of the situation to take their revenge. What would they do to him?

> They saw him in the distance, and before he reached them, they plotted to kill him…So when Joseph came to his brothers, they stripped him of his robe — the richly ornamented robe he was wearing — and they took him and threw him into the cistern. Now the cistern was empty; there was no water in it. (37:18, 23-24)

**Why was it significant that the brothers stripped Joseph of his robe? (For a hint, reread Genesis 37:3-4.)**

_____

The robe had to go! It was a symbol of Joseph's favored status and perhaps even of Jacob's intention to make Joseph the heir both of the family leadership and the traditional _double portion_.[12] In other words, the robe stood for everything they resented.

One of the brothers, Reuben, had second thoughts about killing Joseph, so he persuaded the others to throw him in a cistern or pit, apparently to let him die of exposure.

**What were the brothers trying to accomplish by killing Joseph?**

_____

**Would it be fair to say that their intention was to thwart the purpose and plan of God?**

_____

Perhaps it wouldn't be fair to go that far. It seems more likely that they were just jealous and were lashing out. They were offended by Joseph's dreams, certainly, but did they really understand them to be God's revealed will? Whatever their reasons for wanting to kill Joseph, Reuben had no intention to let the others follow through with it. But then events took an unexpected turn.

> *As they sat down to eat their meal, they looked up and saw a caravan of Ishmaelites coming from Gilead. Their camels were loaded with spices, balm and myrrh, and they were on their way to take them down to Egypt…So when the Midianite merchants came by, his brothers pulled Joseph up out of the cistern and sold him for twenty shekels of silver to the Ishmaelites, who took him to Egypt.* (37:25, 28)

Instead of killing Joseph, the brothers sold him into slavery. Let's pause for a moment and remind ourselves of who was responsible for things reaching this point.

**First of all, who was responsible for the atmosphere of favoritism that was destroying Joseph's family?**

_____

**Who was responsible for the resentment brought on by the dreams?**

_____

**Who was responsible for the murderous attitude of the brothers?**

_____

**Who was responsible for Joseph's being thrown into the cistern rather than murdered outright?**

_____

**Finally, who was responsible for the caravan coming along at that precise moment, resulting in Joseph's being taken to Egypt rather than being rescued?**

_____

My point is not to spread the blame around, but to remind us of something important:

> *Many are the plans in a man's heart, but it is the LORD's purpose that prevails* (Proverbs 19:21).

So Joseph was on his way to a life of slavery in Egypt — or so it would appear. How did the brothers explain his disappearance to their father? They told Jacob that an animal had killed his favorite son.

*Meanwhile, the Midianites sold Joseph in Egypt to Potiphar, one of Pharaoh's officials, the captain of the guard. (37:36)*

The word *meanwhile* reminds us that God was already at work.[13] As we will see, rather than destroy Joseph, his brothers actually delivered him right to the center of God's will for his life. The plot of the brothers was thwarted, although Joseph could not possibly have understood that at this point.

Our topic this week is, "How to See God in Action." In today's application, let's resist the temptation to talk about how bad some people can be, and talk instead about how good God is. Joseph was in grave danger. Yet, despite the danger, God was able not simply to protect Joseph, but actually to place Joseph right in the middle of His perfect plan.

Sometimes God does more than simply rescue us from a crisis. Sometimes He actually uses the crisis to advance His perfect plan for our lives. Can you remember a time like that? Have you ever been in what you thought was a desperate situation, only to discover that God was using that situation to do something wonderful? Maybe He used a tough situation to open a new door of opportunity or set you on a new course. Perhaps He used that time of difficulty to bring about a deep change in your relationship with a loved one or even with Him. What such crises have in common is not simply that God rescued us, but that He caused us to grow and develop. He didn't just resolve the crisis; He used it for His ends.

**Tell about a time when God used a crisis in your life to advance His purpose and plan for your life.**

_____

_____

_____

**Thinking back on the good things God did through that crisis, how might your life have been different if that crisis had never taken place or if God had rescued you from it prematurely?**

_____

_____

_____

_____

**How should your experience in that and similar crises influence your response to the crises you are facing today?**

_____

_____

_____

_____

## PRAYER SUGGESTION

Tell God about the crisis you discussed above, and then thank Him for it. Thank Him that He didn't answer your prayers right away by rescuing you from the situation before His work was complete. Thank Him for all that you have experienced as a result of His work and that He cared enough to want you to experience all of those things. Finally, ask Him to remind you of that experience as you face new crises today, to allow that experience to temper your prayers for immediate deliverance, and to give you a deeper confidence that His purpose and plan is indeed perfect.

# Meant for Good

**PASSAGE: Genesis 45:1-8; 50:15-21**

We are going to "fast forward" the story of Joseph to the moment years later when he revealed his identity to his brothers. So much had happened in the intervening years. Joseph was sold as a slave, falsely accused and imprisoned, forgotten, and finally delivered from prison and raised to the level of prime minister of Egypt. Throughout each of these experiences, Joseph clung to both his integrity and to his faith. Even as he achieved the position of prime minister, and especially as God used him to prepare for an impending famine, Joseph recognized God's hand at work. Just as importantly, his experiences prepared him to be reunited with the brothers who had sold him into slavery in the first place.

**READING ASSIGNMENT: Genesis 45; 49:29-33; 50:15-21**

**FOCUS FOR TODAY: Genesis 45:1-8; 50:15-21**

> *Joseph said to his brothers, "I am Joseph! Is my father still living?" But his brothers were not able to answer him, because they were terrified at his presence.* (45:3)

Before revealing his identity, Joseph put his brothers through a series of tests designed to determine whether they were ready for reconciliation. Now, deeply moved by the obvious change, Joseph revealed his identity to his family. And they were stricken with panic.

**Why did Joseph's brothers have such a reaction?**

_____

_____

It was only natural for them to be terrified! They had sold Joseph into slavery. Sure, things had worked out brilliantly for Joseph in the end, but that didn't change what they had done. As obvious as their reasons for fear might seem, it is important to emphasize these reasons, because they put Joseph's response in context.

*Joseph said to his brothers, "Come close to me." When they had done so, he said, "I am*
*your brother Joseph, the one you sold into Egypt! And now, do not be distressed and do*
*not be angry with yourselves for selling me here, because it was to save lives that God*
*sent me ahead of you. (45:4-5)*

Joseph reassured them that he was, in fact, the very brother they had sold into Egypt. But he added that they should not be worried or angry with themselves.

**Why did Joseph tell his brothers not to be angry with themselves?**

_____

_____

Notice the three key words near the end of verse five: *"God sent me."* Sure, his brothers had plotted to kill him. Sure, they had decided instead to profit by selling him into slavery. Sure, they had taken the money, gone home, and told their father some outrageous lie. Even so, Joseph told them that *they* weren't the ones who had sent Joseph to Egypt — *God* had. What an amazing perspective! How could Joseph possibly look at the situation this way?

*"For two years now there has been famine in the land, and for the next five years there*
*will not be plowing and reaping. But God sent me ahead of you to preserve for you a*
*remnant on earth and to save your lives by a great deliverance. So then, it was not you*
*who sent me here, but God. He made me father to Pharaoh, lord of his entire household*
*and ruler of all Egypt." (45:6-8)*

**On what basis was Joseph able to forgive his brothers? What did he see that gave him the ability to do that?**

_____

_____

_____

Joseph was able to forgive his brothers because he recognized that God had been directing his life all along. Notice how Joseph used the phrase *"God sent me"* three times (see verses 5, 7, and 8). He recognized that what his brothers had done, although evil, was God's way of bringing about His will in Joseph's life.

Let's "fast forward" again, this time to the events immediately following the death of Jacob. We will pick up the story beginning at Genesis 50:15.

*When Joseph's brothers saw that their father was dead, they said, "What if Joseph holds a grudge against us and pays us back for all the wrongs we did to him?" So they sent word to Joseph, saying, "Your father left these instructions before he died: 'This is what you are to say to Joseph: I ask you to forgive your brothers the sins and the wrongs they committed in treating you so badly.' Now please forgive the sins of the servants of the God of your father." When their message came to him, Joseph wept. His brothers then came and threw themselves down before him. "We are your slaves," they said. (50:15-18)*

Apparently the brothers had never entirely been convinced that Joseph's forgiveness was genuine. They were still afraid that Joseph might have spared them simply for their father's sake. Now, with Jacob dead and buried, the brothers were concerned that Joseph might finally avenge himself.

**What did the brothers do?**

_____

_____

_____

Had their father really left such a message for Joseph? Perhaps not; but whether he had or hadn't is of little consequence. Joseph had forgiven them.

**How did Joseph respond to their message?**

_____

**Why do you think he responded this way?**

_____

_____

_____

There could have been so many reasons for Joseph's tears: the realization that his kindness had been misinterpreted; the discovery that the family relationship was still strained; the notion that his father had died with no real assurance of Joseph's forgiveness and faith; the realization that his brothers were still very far from understanding the workings of God. No doubt there were other possibilities as well.

But with his brothers now on their faces before him, Joseph had yet another opportunity to help them see God's hand in their lives.

*Joseph said to them, "Don't be afraid. Am I in the place of God? You intended to harm me, but God intended it for good to accomplish what is now being done, the saving of many lives. So then, don't be afraid. I will provide for you and your children." And he reassured them and spoke kindly to them. (50:19-21)*

In response, Joseph explained that what they had meant for evil, God meant for good. Did Joseph doubt that their intentions were evil? Not for a moment. What, then, permitted him to overlook their evil intentions?

**What do you think?**

_____

**How might the dreams that Joseph had while still at home have confirmed his understanding of God's will?**

_____

_____

Joseph would not question what God had done. Although the brothers had intended the loss of his one life, it had become plain that God had intended the salvation of many lives. Consequently, Joseph reassured them of his forgiveness and kindness.

One final question: Did Joseph's remarks suggest that he was fully informed about why God had brought the descendants of Israel into Egypt? What did his account leave out?

**What do you think? (Hint: Read Genesis 15:12-14.)**

_____

_____

Joseph might not have seen the entirety of God's purpose and plan, but he understood just enough to trust God with the rest. Ultimately faith in God cannot be based on what we think we understand about the events and circumstances of life. Faith in God must ultimately be based on the trustworthiness of God.

Joseph can teach us a lot about how to see God in action. As we look at his life, we find that he was very good at a simple, four-step process:

1. He looked at the purpose and plan of God;
2. He looked at the circumstances of his life;
3. He saw all the places where they lined up;
4. And he trusted God with the rest.

We may not have revelatory dreams the way Joseph did, but we do have God's promises that are spelled out in His Word — and they can tell us a lot more than any dream ever could.

**What do you know about God's purpose and plan for your life? (If you don't know many specifics, just write down what you do know of a general nature.)**

_____

_____

_____

**Combine steps two and three. What circumstances of your life do you see that line up with your understanding of God's purpose and plan for your life?**

_____

_____

_____

**What circumstances don't seem to line up in your limited understanding? In other words, with what is God asking you to trust Him?**

_____

_____

_____

**PRAYER SUGGESTION**

Thank God that He has a purpose and plan for your life, even if you aren't entirely clear what it is. Ask Him to help you understand His plan as He has revealed it in His written Word, the Bible. Thank Him that He oversees the circumstances of your life for His purposes. Ask Him to show you where those circumstances are already aligned with His plan for your life, and thank Him for those areas of alignment. Finally, ask Him to help you trust Him for the many areas of your life that seem to be confusing at this time.

✝
# Small Group Discussion Guide

The moment had finally come when God delivered Esther and her people from their crisis. What finally caused Him to take action? What do we need to do to see God take action in our own crises?

**TODAY: Esther 7:1-10**

**I. If you want to SEE God, look for an opportunity to TRUST God.**
**KEY PASSAGE:** Esther 7:1-2 (read it aloud)

**DISCUSSION QUESTIONS:** How did God present Esther with a concrete opportunity to trust Him? What was Esther's moment of trust?

_____

_____

**PRINCIPLE:** Nothing happens until someone believes God.[14]

**SUPPORT PASSAGE:** 2 Chronicles 16:9 (read it aloud)

**APPLICATION:** In your present crisis, what opportunities is God giving you to trust Him actively?

_____

_____

What do you need to do — what specific, concrete actions do you need to take — to grab onto the opportunities God is giving you? When will you take those actions?

_____

_____

## II. When you find that opportunity, take THE RISK and take ACTION.

**KEY PASSAGE:** Esther 7:3-6a (read it aloud)

**DISCUSSION QUESTION:** What risks did Esther face as she exposed Haman's plot?

_____

_____

**PRINCIPLE:** God uses people who aren't afraid to take risks.[15]

**SUPPORT PASSAGE:** Acts 15:25-26 (read it aloud)

**APPLICATION:** As you take action, what risks will your actions present?

_____

_____

Why can you trust God with those risks?

_____

_____

## III. Then STEP BACK and give God ROOM TO WORK.

**KEY PASSAGE:** Esther 7:6b-10 (read it aloud)

**DISCUSSION QUESTION:** How did Esther allow God room to work in the aftermath of her "moment of trust?"

_____

_____

**PRINCIPLE:** Don't snatch defeat from the jaws of victory.

**SUPPORT PASSAGE:** Exodus 14:13 (read it aloud)

**APPLICATION:** After you trust God and take action, what opportunities will you have to lose your faith and get in God's way?

_____

_____

Commit now, in writing, to keep your faith.

_____

_____

_____

_____

✦

# New Challenges, New Victories

Day 1 — The Doors We Can See

Day 2 — Welcome Reminders

Day 3 — Be Bold, Be Joyful, Be Attractive

Day 4 — Great Risks, Greater Victories

Day 5 — Victory!

Although Haman was dead, Esther and Mordecai still faced the even greater challenge of rescuing their people from the irrevocable decree that ordered the annihilation of the Jewish people. God was certainly concerned about the welfare of His people and so He was surely involved, but how? What would He do? And what would He call on His people to do? Would this new and greater challenge result in a new and greater victory? In this week's passage, we will discover not only how to survive challenges, but to rejoice in them, trust God through them, and experience victory on the other side.

# The Doors We Can See

**PASSAGE: Esther 8:1-6**

In all of the excitement of Haman's execution, Esther and Mordecai could not afford to overlook one significant fact: the edict concerning the massacre of the Jews still stood. Despite the fact that it was the result of Haman's antisemitism and deceit, the edict still contained the seal of the king and therefore it was irreversible. The Jews were a condemned people. The crisis of the confrontation of Haman had passed, but the greater crisis of the slaughter of the Jews loomed large. What would God do? And what would God ask His people to do? The answer was simple. Look up.

**READING ASSIGNMENT: Esther 8:1-6**

**FOCUS FOR TODAY: Esther 8:1-6**

> *That same day King Xerxes gave Queen Esther the estate of Haman, the enemy of the Jews. And Mordecai came into the presence of the king, for Esther had told how he was related to her.* (8:1)

As Haman's lifeless body hung from the very gallows that he had constructed for Mordecai, the king was awarding Haman's entire estate to Esther. But didn't Haman have sons? (See Esther 5:11.) Why wouldn't the property have gone to them? Because the property of traitors was forfeited to the crown.[1] In this instance the king decided in turn to award Haman's property to Esther. This included not only the house we read about earlier, but also whatever was left of the vast fortune out of which Haman had proposed to fund the annihilation of the Jews. Recall that Haman had offered to contribute a staggering sum to the treasury. If our understanding of the transaction was correct, the king accepted the contribution and then returned the money to Haman for use in carrying out the decree. Those funds would no longer have belonged to Haman, but to the king. It is reasonable to suppose, then, that those funds were lost to the estate. But whatever was left, presumably a vast fortune, went to Esther.

Esther then spoke to the king about Mordecai, her cousin and adoptive father. She revealed not only the nature of their relationship but more literally *what he was to her*, or as we might put it, "the kind of man he was and what he meant to her."

**How do you think Esther described Mordecai? What might she have said about him?**

_____

_____

_____

Although Mordecai had been in the king's service for years and had even saved his life, it is entirely possible that the two men had never met. But having heard what was no doubt a moving tribute to this brave man and loyal servant, the king summoned Mordecai to appear before him — a great honor indeed, but only the beginning of what the king had in mind.

> *The king took off his signet ring, which he had reclaimed from Haman, and presented it to Mordecai. And Esther appointed him over Haman's estate.* (8:2)

Esther's tribute to Mordecai made a remarkable and immediate impression on King Xerxes. Obviously, the king had a very recent opening for a new prime minister! What made Mordecai such a suitable candidate?

**What do you think?**

_____

_____

_____

Trustworthiness was a quality the king had doubtless come to appreciate, so he awarded the position to Mordecai. He even gave Mordecai the signet ring that had been "reclaimed" from Haman — whether before or after the execution, we are not told. Mordecai now had the same power to make laws that the king had entrusted to Haman. But that's not all. Esther appointed Mordecai as the steward over her newly acquired fortune. So to the position and power of prime minister was added the vast resources of Haman's estate.

**How might this new position and these new resources prove to be significant as Mordecai grappled with Haman's decree?**

_____

_____

_____

Would Mordecai have seen this connection?

> *Esther again pleaded with the king, falling at his feet and weeping. She begged him to put an end to the evil plan of Haman the Agagite, which he had devised against the Jews.* (8:3)

Esther realized that her actual request had not been granted. After all, she hadn't requested the execution of Haman; she had requested the reversal of the king's decree ordering the annihilation of the Jews. Haman was dead, yes, but his plot against the Jews was still very much alive. The Jews were still facing execution, so Esther once again appealed to the king. But note her approach.

**Why did Esther fall at the king's feet? Why didn't she simply present her request?**

_____

_____


Despite the exposure and subsequent execution of Haman, the protocols of the court had not changed. Since Esther had not been granted permission to approach the king with a formal request, she fell at his feet, weeping in despair and begging for mercy.

> *The king extended the gold scepter to Esther and she arose and stood before him.* (8:4)

Once again the king indicated his willingness to hear her petition, so Esther stood before him and stated her request in more formal terms.

> *"If it pleases the king," she said, "and if he regards me with favor and thinks it the right thing to do, and if he is pleased with me, let an order be written overruling the dispatches that Haman son of Hammedatha, the Agagite, devised and wrote to destroy the Jews in all the king's provinces.* (8:5)

Note the formality of the request. Before presenting her request, Esther qualified it in four ways.

**Why did she make her request in such guarded and qualified terms?**

_____

_____

_____

Two things were probably influencing Esther's request. First, she had not forgotten her position. Despite the remarkable events of the day, there had been no breakthrough to a new level of intimate familiarity. Esther continued to speak to the king with due regard for his position and authority. Second, Esther understood that her request was based not on her rights as a citizen — she had none — but solely on the mercy of the king. He was under no obligation whatsoever to act in her behalf. It was entirely up to him whether he would make any attempt at all to spare either Esther or her people. Her request continued.

*"For how can I bear to see disaster fall on my people? How can I bear to see the destruction of my family?"* (8:6)

Esther's request seems simple enough: reverse the previous decree. The king had been, after all, manipulated into consenting to the annihilation of a multitude of his own law-abiding subjects. Haman alone had devised it. Moreover, the request to reverse the decree was coming from the queen herself, whose interest was completely understandable.

Despite the queen's concern, however, the situation was anything but simple. What was the problem?

**What do you think?**

_____

_____


As the writer of the book of Esther already explained (see Esther 1:19), a decree of the Persian king could not be reversed, not even by the king himself. Despite the fact that the king had been tricked into issuing the decree, there was nothing Xerxes could do to reverse it. The decree stood.

On a side note, recall that Haman had arranged to pay for the annihilation of the Jews out of his own resources. Why didn't Esther and Mordecai, who now had control of Haman's fortune, simply refuse to fund the decree? The answer is that the funds had been donated to the treasury and were not part of Haman's estate; they were the property of the king. Moreover the king had decreed the authorization of the funds, and that decree could not be reversed. Refusal to fund the decree was not an option. It had already been funded.

Why was Esther appealing to a pagan king to secure the safety of God's people? Hadn't she learned that God could be trusted? Yes, she had, but specifically she had learned that God could be trusted to be sovereign over and to work through the circumstances of everyday life. She had learned that opportunities to trust God were usually opportunities to act with boldness in specific situations. So Esther was trusting God by approaching the king.

Sometimes we ignore the doors we can see in favor of the doors we cannot see. We face a crisis and as we look for a way out or a way through, we see a door. The door may not be standing open — we may see obstacles and difficulties of various kinds — but it is a door nevertheless. How often do we insist upon "trusting God" for another door, a door more to our liking, a door we cannot see? How often do we trust God and try the door we can see?

**In the current or emerging crisis in your life, what doors of opportunity has God presented to you, however unappealing they may be?**

_____

_____

_____

**How are those doors blocked? What is it that might make trying those doors unappealing to you?**

_____

_____

_____

**Are you holding out for some other door of opportunity, a door you cannot see? Describe the door for which you are waiting.**

_____

_____

_____

**Why might you feel justified in passing on the door you can see in favor of a door you cannot see?**

_____

_____

_____

_____

## PRAYER SUGGESTION

Instead of asking God for an open door to take you out of or through your current crisis, ask Him to help you see the doors that He has already provided. Admit to Him that sometimes you see those doors perfectly well, but that you ignore them. Tell Him about the doors you see in your current crisis, and then tell Him why you are struggling to trust Him enough to try those doors. Be honest with Him about the kind of door for which you are waiting, and then ask Him to be honest with you about what He thinks about it. Often trying the door we can see demands more faith of us than we feel we can muster. If that is the case, admit that to Him and ask Him for boldness. At other times, what looks like a door is actually a trap. This is most often and most clearly the case when going through such a door would involve sin on our part. Ask God for wisdom to see the traps for what they are, so that you can avoid them.

# Welcome Reminders

**PASSAGE: Esther 8:7-12**

As Esther approached the king, she was immediately reminded of something wonderful. She was reminded that God had once again gone ahead of her and had already been at work in her new challenge. In today's passage, we will be reminded that God provides for His people even before we ask.

**READING ASSIGNMENT: Esther 8:1-12**

**FOCUS FOR TODAY: Esther 8:7-12**

> *King Xerxes replied to Queen Esther and to Mordecai the Jew, "Because Haman attacked the Jews, I have given his estate to Esther, and they have hanged him on the gallows. (8:7)*

Esther had made her request and now the king responded. But notice that he responded not to Esther alone, but to Mordecai as well.

**Why was this so significant?**

_____

_____

_____

_____

Mordecai was present, of course, having just been installed as the king's new prime minister, but that was not why the king addressed him. In his response to Esther's request, the king began to remind both Esther and Mordecai of something highly significant, of something that had already taken place: the transfer of all necessary power and resources from Haman to Mordecai. King Xerxes was about to remind Mordecai that, as prime minister, he already possessed full authority to do whatever could be done. So, what did the king propose?

*"Now write another decree in the king's name in behalf of the Jews as seems best to you, and seal it with the king's signet ring — for no document written in the king's name and sealed with his ring can be revoked." (8:8)*

Although the first decree could not be repealed, a second decree, equally binding, could be issued that might in some way lessen the impact of the first. What would that second decree say?

**What did the king suggest?**

_____

_____

It seems that the content of such a decree would have to have been determined by the prime minister — *"in behalf of the Jews as seems best to you."* I don't think the king was saying, "Gee, I'm fresh out of ideas. I think I need Mordecai's help to come up with something." The king simply wanted to remind Mordecai that as prime minister he wore on his finger the king's signet ring, so he already had the full authority to compose and issue whatever decree he might deem most helpful under the circumstances. Besides, prime ministers were paid to solve problems, not to pass them along to the king.

We might imagine Mordecai looking at the king, looking at the ring, and then thinking, *Wow, this is great!* Whatever his reaction, once reminded of his power and resources, Mordecai wasted no time in taking action.

*At once the royal secretaries were summoned — on the twenty-third day of the third month, the month of Sivan. They wrote out all Mordecai's orders to the Jews, and to the satraps, governors and nobles of the 127 provinces stretching from India to Cush. These orders were written in the script of each province and the language of each people and also to the Jews in their own script and language. (8:9)*

Reminded of the extent of his new power, Mordecai went to work. Two and one-half months had already passed since the decree to destroy the Jews had been issued. Only eight months remained before the genocide would be carried out. Time was precious. Once again the order was translated into the languages of the people, with copies also prepared for officials at every level of government. But look closely at the end of verse nine and compare it with the similar passage in Esther 1:22.

**What group received special emphasis this time around?**

_____

_____

As before, the decree was translated into every language of the empire, including this time the language of the Jews. What did this second decree say? We will find out in a moment.

> *Mordecai wrote in the name of King Xerxes, sealed the dispatches with the king's signet ring, and sent them by mounted couriers, who rode fast horses especially bred for the king.* (8:10)

Using the full authority of his new office, Mordecai wrote his decree in the name, and hence with the full authority, of the king. As soon as they were written and translated, copies of the decree were sealed with the king's signet ring and sent to every corner of the empire.

> *The king's edict granted the Jews in every city the right to assemble and protect themselves; to destroy, kill and annihilate any armed force of any nationality or province that might attack them and their women and children; and to plunder the property of their enemies.* (8:11)

The content of the decree was now spelled out: The Jews would be permitted to organize in their own defense and to plunder the property of any enemies that they might defeat. It would, of course, have been expected that the Jews would attempt to defend themselves when attacked. What, then, other than allowing them the right of plunder, does this second decree actually accomplish?

**What do you think?**

_____

_____

This second decree accomplished at least two things. First, it allowed the Jews to organize and take up arms against government forces legally, that is, without being considered rebels. This would be especially significant in the days following the attacks, when action might ordinarily have been taken against surviving rebels.

Second, and more importantly, the decree sent a powerful message to those who would take up arms against the Jews that the winds of imperial policy had shifted. While local officials were still under orders to commit genocide against the Jewish people, the second decree had made it clear that in carrying out these orders they would not enjoy the support of the king. It would be surprising, then, if local officials were to make any serious attempt to carry out the first decree. Only virulent antisemites would be likely to seize the opportunity, particularly since it meant they would have been putting their women and children at risk.

In light of this new perspective, why was it so important that the decree be translated into the language not only of the Jews but of the other people groups as well?

_____

_____

_____

> *The day appointed for the Jews to do this in all the provinces of King Xerxes was the thirteenth day of the twelfth month, the month of Adar. (8:12)*

The second decree further specified that the right of self-defense and plunder would be afforded to Jews throughout the empire, but that this right would be theirs only on the day appointed for the attack under the first decree.

**Why was this important?**

_____

_____

The Jews were not being given the right to become the insurrectionists that Haman had accused them of being. They would be allowed to defend themselves, but they were still subjects of the king and as such were expected to live in submission to the governing authorities.

As Esther and Mordecai confronted their newest and greatest challenge, they discovered that God had once again gone ahead of them to provide solutions even before they asked. He even used a pagan king to deliver this welcome reminder!

✝

God does the same thing in our lives: He goes ahead of us, anticipating problems and preparing solutions. Then He uses all kinds of people and circumstances — welcome reminders — to alert us to His provision along the way. And inevitably He calls on us to act on His provision, just as He did Mordecai.

**Consider some of your newest challenges. How has God already gone before you to provide solutions to these problems?**

_____

_____

_____

_____

**What people or circumstances is God using to remind you of that fact? How is He bringing His provision to your attention?**

_____

_____

_____

**What is He asking you to do with that provision?**

_____

_____

_____

## PRAYER SUGGESTION

As you face your newest challenge, thank God that He has already gone ahead of you and that He has been hard at work to provide for you. Thank Him for all the ways He has taught you to trust Him and for the confidence you've gained in Him. Ask Him for the faith to trust Him in this new crisis as well. However, faith almost always requires action on our part, and since it is difficult to take specific action on the basis of generalities, ask Him to help you see the actual provision He has made in your current situation. When you do, thank Him for it specifically, and then ask Him for the strength to take full and faithful advantage of it.

# Be Bold, Be Joyful, Be Attractive

**PASSAGE: Esther 8:13-17**

Mordecai was hard at work implementing his plan to rescue the Jewish people. But as he exercised his new power as the prime minister, the responses were varied. The Jews responded with preparation and celebration. The Gentiles, understandably, responded with fear. Today's passage is about responses, and as we study it, we will discover that recognizing God's provision isn't enough. We must respond to His provision in a way that demonstrates and builds on our faith.

**READING ASSIGNMENT: Esther 8:1-17**

**FOCUS FOR TODAY: Esther 8:13-17**

> *A copy of the text of the edict was to be issued as law in every province and made known to the people of every nationality so that the Jews would be ready on that day to avenge themselves on their enemies.* (8:13)

The second decree was carried throughout the empire, but why? *So that the Jews would be ready on that day.* Yet God had already done so much to show Himself faithful to His people. Did the Jews really need to prepare to defend themselves? Surely God would defend them when the time came. By calling them to prepare for their own defense, was Mordecai failing to trust God?

**How would you respond to this objection?**

_____

_____

There is a principle at work here, one that we encountered earlier: Trusting God is not always a matter of our waiting for God to act; more often it is a matter of God's waiting for us to act. Recall how Mordecai had to remind Esther that God's plan required her to put her life at risk. Later, when Esther finally spoke with the king, she did it with full appreciation of the risks involved.

Now Mordecai was asking the nation to trust God in that same "risk-taking" way. This decree is a call to action — risk-taking, God-trusting action.

> *The couriers, riding the royal horses, raced out, spurred on by the king's command.*
> *And the edict was also issued in the citadel of Susa.* (8:14)

Like the first decree, the second decree was issued throughout the empire, including in the capital city itself. What reaction did it bring in Susa?

> *Mordecai left the king's presence wearing royal garments of blue and white, a large*
> *crown of gold and a purple robe of fine linen. And the city of Susa held a joyous cele-*
> *bration.* (8:15)

Having issued the decree, Mordecai *left the king's presence wearing royal garments.* The blue and white colors remind us of the imperial pavilions (1:6), while the headdress was typical of those worn by Persian nobles.[2] Mordecai left the palace and appeared in public in full royal regalia. A public appearance of some sort was probably taking place at this point. With the second decree in hand and Mordecai standing before them as their new prime minister, the Jews in Susa broke out in celebration of their victory. In fact the suggestion is that the entire city was celebrating. Why would the other ethnic minorities share in the joy of the Jews?

**What do you think?**

_____

_____

Remember that the Persian Empire was made up almost entirely of minorities. Perhaps the people were relieved that the genocidal policies of Haman had been reversed before any other ethnic minorities had been targeted.

> *For the Jews it was a time of happiness and joy, gladness and honor. In every province*
> *and in every city, wherever the edict of the king went, there was joy and gladness*
> *among the Jews, with feasting and celebrating.* (8:16-17a)

For the Jews in particular, the response was celebration. Yet does it strike you that they were celebrating prematurely? After all, they still had to fight for their lives against government forces. How many would come against them and in what strength? Who could say? Even so, this is most certainly the perfect time for celebration.

**Why would this be the perfect time for the Jews to celebrate?**

_____

_____

As they faced the days ahead, God's people would need to remember His faithfulness in the days that had just passed. There is an old World War I song that includes the line, "Praise the Lord and pass the ammunition." The Jews were right to do both. Probably the best time to celebrate the faithfulness of God is when we are facing our next big battle, our next big challenge. So this celebration was anything but premature. On the contrary, it was timed perfectly.

> _Many people of other nationalities became Jews because fear of the Jews had seized them._ (8:17b)

The final response came from the Gentiles, the people of other ethnic backgrounds. What did they do? As the edict went out, many of them began to feel that it just wasn't safe anymore not to be a Jew, so a great number of them decided to convert! But why? True, the passage says that fear of the Jews had seized them, but why would these people have been afraid? The decree authorized the Jews to defend themselves against their attackers, but not to go on the offensive against people who meant them no harm. Why, then, were these people afraid?

**What do you think?**

_____

_____

Think back to what Haman's wife and friends said to him in chapter six. As Haman told the story of the king's sleepless night, of the reading of the annals of the court, and so forth, they realized that there was something very special, even supernatural, about the Jews. There was only one way to account for the incredible protection enjoyed by the Jews: They had a special relationship with God.

Now people of other nationalities were coming to the same conclusion. One month a decree was issued ordering the extermination of the Jewish race. A few months later the man who had been the prime minister and who had issued that decree had been hanged and a new prime minister, this one Jewish, was issuing another decree giving the Jews the right of self-defense and even plunder. As the people of other nationalities watched these events unfold, it dawned on them that their gods never did that sort of thing for them. Just to be on the safe side, people began converting to Judaism.

A lot of people like to trust God passively. "God is sovereign," they may say, "so I don't *have* to do anything." But God calls us to trust Him aggressively. "God is sovereign," we should say, "so I *can* do whatever He asks me to do!"

**How are you trusting God aggressively in your life?**

_____

_____

_____

People who trust God aggressively are still just people. We get scared. We get nervous. We need to remind ourselves that God is faithful, and one very good way to do that is by celebrating the victories He has given us in the past.

**What victories are you celebrating?**

_____

_____

_____

Wouldn't it be exciting to live your life in such a way that non-Christians would realize that it just doesn't make sense not to have Jesus in their lives?

**How are the non-Christians in your life hearing about the amazing things God has done for you?**

_____

_____

_____

**PRAYER SUGGESTION**

Confess the ways in which your responses to God's provision have been inadequate. Begin by telling Him about a time when your trust in Him was too passive — when you knew how you should have acted, but didn't. Next, tell Him about a time when you forgot to celebrate, how the memory of His faithfulness began to fade, and how it cost you the confidence that you needed the next time you faced a challenge. Now mention the people who might have seen something wonderful, had you simply made God's faithfulness known. Finally, ask God for the boldness to trust Him aggressively, to celebrate Him joyfully, and to proclaim His greatness boldly.

# Great Risks, Greater Victories

**PASSAGE: Esther 9:1-10**

As before, the moment for action had come. Once again God had called His people to a bold, risk-taking faith. If they would trust Him and follow His lead, they would experience a victory that was even greater than their victory over Haman had been. But would they take the risk? These final studies for the week will remind us again of the importance of bold, risk-taking faith.

**READING ASSIGNMENT: Esther 8:1-9:10**

**FOCUS FOR TODAY: Esther 9:1-10**

> *On the thirteenth day of the twelfth month, the month of Adar, the edict commanded by the king was to be carried out. On this day the enemies of the Jews had hoped to overpower them, but now the tables were turned and the Jews got the upper hand over those who hated them. (9:1)*

The day had finally arrived for the decrees to be carried out — and God's people were ready. Although the enemies of the Jews had hoped to overwhelm them, the enemies were themselves overwhelmed.

**Who were these enemies? How were they described at the very end of the verse?**

_____

Notice that they were not innocent government officials or soldiers dutifully carrying out a royal decree. They were instead *those who hated them.* These enemies were virulent antisemites, men who had determined to seize the opportunity afforded by the first decree to destroy the Jewish people and plunder their property. Yet that's not the way it turned out.

*The Jews assembled in their cities in all the provinces of King Xerxes to attack those seeking their destruction. No one could stand against them, because the people of all the other nationalities were afraid of them.* (9:2)

The text now provides some detail. Throughout the empire, the Jews *assembled in their cities;* in other words, they formed militias.[3] The Jews were organized, and they were effective. The English word *attack* suggests that the Jews went on the offense, which of course they were not authorized to do. The Hebrew literally says that they assembled *to send the hand against* or *strike* those seeking their destruction. The Jews were fully prepared to strike back against anyone who would strike at them.

**Why did *all the other nationalities* fear the Jews?**

_____

_____

There was a power behind the Jewish people that no one could oppose — a power that was not a matter of swords and shields. Even those who hadn't actually converted to Judaism feared their God.

> *And all the nobles of the provinces, the satraps, the governors and the king's administrators helped the Jews, because fear of Mordecai had seized them.* (9:3)

Recall what we learned several weeks ago about the government of the Persian Empire.

**Who were the *nobles of the provinces*? What was their ethnic background?**

_____

As we learned in week one, Persia was ruled by a small group of Persian families. In all likelihood, the phrase *the nobles of the provinces* was referring to members of these ruling families.

**Why would these people — relatives of the king — fear the new prime minister?**

_____

_____

Rather than supporting the first decree, nobles and government officials at all levels supported the second — which was not surprising given recent developments at the palace. How did they help the Jews? The text does not say. But whatever form their help might have taken, their motivation was clear. They were not driven by a fear of the king; they were driven by the fear of Mordecai, and ultimately Mordecai's God.

*Mordecai was prominent in the palace; his reputation spread throughout the provinces,*
*and he became more and more powerful. (9:4)*

As Mordecai's influence within the palace grew so did his reputation throughout the provinces. It is doubtful that Mordecai's legal powers exceeded those of Haman, or that those powers were expanded while he was in office. How, then, did his power grow?

**What do you think?**

_____

_____


Legal authority was one thing; practical authority was another. As government officials throughout the empire saw the power of God at work, they no doubt realized that this was a man to be taken seriously — and they obeyed him fully. But then, having seen Mordecai's faithful and courageous demonstration at the palace gate, we shouldn't be the least bit surprised.

*The Jews struck down all their enemies with the sword, killing and destroying them,*
*and they did what they pleased to those who hated them. (9:5)*

Although this verse may make the actions of the Jews sound gratuitous, almost ghoulish, that was not at all the intent. The Hebrew picks up on the tone of the two decrees, describing the victory as *a slaughter, a killing, a destruction.* By using these words, the writer was demonstrating how thoroughly God had turned the tables on those who would *slaughter, kill, and destroy* His people. The passage also notes that the Jews *did what they pleased* to those who hated them. Recall the king's words to Haman in Esther 3:11, when he told him, as the Hebrew puts it, "*The silver and the people are given to you to do with as is pleasing in your eyes.*"[4] This brief verse is filled with irony.

*In the citadel of Susa, the Jews killed and destroyed five hundred men. (9:6)*

Now the narrative focused in on the action in the capital city of Susa, where the Jews killed five hundred of their enemies. And once again we can hear in the words the echo of the decrees. Does it surprise you that the king would allow fighting to go on in the citadel itself?

**Why might the king have ordinarily considered that an unacceptable risk?**

_____

_____

_____

For one thing, armed conflict could easily have gotten out of hand. More significantly, armed men loyal to the prime minister waging battle in the capital city — that's a risk that most kings would have been unwilling to take. That Xerxes allowed it demonstrated the king's confidence in the loyalty of Mordecai.

> *They also killed Parshandatha, Dalphon, Aspatha, Poratha, Adalia, Aridatha, Parmashta, Arisai, Aridai and Vaizatha, the ten sons of Haman son of Hammedatha, the enemy of the Jews. But they did not lay their hands on the plunder.* (9:7-10)

Included among those who had attacked the Jews were the sons of Haman, mentioned earlier but named for the first time here. Regrettably these young men seem to have shared the antisemitic views of their father. Although their mother had recognized the futility of opposing the Jews, they did not. Recall that having many sons was a source of great pride in Persian culture. Even months after his execution, Haman's pride was still being dealt a deadly blow.

The passage concludes by mentioning that the Jews did not take the property of Haman's sons even though the second decree had given them the right to do so. The concern of the Jews was not plunder, after all, but survival and justice. Note also that these sons had personal property even after Esther was given control of Haman's estate — a testimony, perhaps, to her kindness and generosity.

God calls us to take great risks, but in return He gives even greater victories. Today, begin to apply these truths by reflecting on a great victory, especially a "table-turning" type of victory, that God has given you. What did God do? How did that victory turn your situation around? How did it impact you and the people around you?

**Tell about a time when the "tables were turned" in your life — a time when a situation that appeared to be going against you suddenly turned around and began going dramatically your way.**

_____

_____

_____

_____

**How did this "turning of the tables" impact the attitudes and perceptions of the other people involved?**

_____

_____

_____

**Describe how you were impacted by this event. Did you become more trusting of God, more bold? Why or why not?**

_____

_____

_____

_____

## PRAYER SUGGESTION

Tell God the story you shared in today's first question. Tell Him how you were feeling as the crisis grew and especially before the tables turned in your favor. Tell Him what happened in your life and heart as the tables began to turn. Describe to Him the impact all of this had on you as well as on the other people involved. Finally, ask Him to help you trust Him for more moments like that. Confess to Him that sometimes, before those moments come, you start to give in to doubt and discouragement. Ask Him to use the "table-turning" times of your past to strengthen your faith in the future.

# Victory!

**PASSAGE: Esther 9:11-17**

The victory was now almost complete. Those who would have destroyed God's people were themselves being destroyed. Once again God had demonstrated His faithfulness, but only after His people demonstrated their faith. Trust in God always comes before victory, because God gives His greatest victories to those with the greatest faith.

**READING ASSIGNMENT: Esther 8:1-9:17**

**FOCUS FOR TODAY: Esther 9:11-17**

> *The number of those slain in the citadel of Susa was reported to the king that same day.* (9:11)

Not surprisingly, the king was staying informed about the progress of the fighting, particularly right there in his capital city. He was informed that five hundred enemies of the Jews had been killed, including, as we shall see, the sons of Haman. Why were no Jewish casualties mentioned?

**What do you think?**

_____

_____

_____

_____

Would it be too much to hope that not a single Jew had been killed in the fighting? Perhaps it is. God's protection of His people has never included their absolute invulnerability. Many Jews as well as many Christians have lost their lives in the furtherance of God's plan for His people. It was, after all, the survival of the race that was at issue, rather than the survival of each and every individual. The emphasis here, then, was quite appropriately on God's protection of the race rather than on what were, one can hope, only isolated losses.

*The king said to Queen Esther, "The Jews have killed and destroyed five hundred men and the ten sons of Haman in the citadel of Susa. What have they done in the rest of the king's provinces? Now what is your petition? It will be given you. What is your request? It will also be granted."* (9:12)

The king reported the figures to Esther. But more than that, he expressed wonder at what must have been going on in the rest of the provinces. Was he feeling regret? Perhaps he was. Any leader would. By having allowed himself to be taken in by Haman, the king had unleashed terrible violence among his subjects. Even if Xerxes cared little for his subjects as human beings, a king so recently defeated by the Greeks might well have regretted the loss of so many potential soldiers.[5]

Having given Esther the latest count of casualties in the citadel, the king did something remarkable.

**What did he do and why was it so remarkable?**

_____

_____


Surprisingly, the king asked Esther if she had any other requests — if there was anything more that she would like to see done. Unless we are to assume that Esther had come before him to make a request, and there is no indication that she had, it would appear that the king did this entirely on his own initiative. Why might the king have made such an offer?

**What do you think?**

_____

_____


I can only suppose that the king wanted to resolve the conflict fully and finally. He did not want any loose ends.

> *"If it pleases the king," Esther answered, "give the Jews in Susa permission to carry out this day's edict tomorrow also, and let Haman's ten sons be hanged on gallows."* (9:13)

Esther was ready with her answer. Perhaps she had already discussed the situation with Mordecai. Her request was for the Jews to be permitted to defend themselves for one more day.

**Why might this have been necessary?**

_____

_____

Perhaps Mordecai had made Esther aware of pockets of antisemitic opposition that seemed determined to fight on, despite the fact that the first decree was about to expire. It would have been dangerous, then, for the Jews to disarm before these groups had been dealt with fully.

Esther also asked that Haman's ten sons be hanged on the gallows. But weren't these men dead already? Yes, they were. Why was Esther now suggesting that their bodies be mounted in public view? Presumably as a warning to anyone else who might consider threatening the people of God. As ghoulish as this may seem in light of modern sensibilities, there was some precedent for this in Mosaic law. (See Deuteronomy 21:22-23.)

> *The king commanded that this be done. An edict was issued in Susa, and they hanged the ten sons of Haman. (9:14)*

Esther's request that the bodies of the sons of Haman be hanged was granted and carried out.

> *The Jews in Susa came together on the fourteenth day of the month of Adar, and they put to death in Susa three hundred men, but they did not lay their hands on the plunder. (9:15)*

As Esther had requested, the fighting was allowed to continue for one more day, and although they were able to kill three hundred more of their enemies, the Jews still refused to take any plunder. Why was it important that this lack of plundering be emphasized?

**What do you think?**

_____

_____

> *Meanwhile, the remainder of the Jews who were in the king's provinces also assembled to protect themselves and get relief from their enemies. They killed seventy-five thousand of them but did not lay their hands on the plunder. (9:16)*

The edict that allowed the fighting to continue might have embraced the rest of the empire as well. When the fighting was finally over, seventy-five thousand enemies of the people of God had been killed. Certain evidence suggests that the cities of Samaria and Shechem, long-standing enemies of the Jews, were destroyed right about this time.[6] It may well be that these cities were wiped out in the Jewish counteroffensive.

> *This happened on the thirteenth day of the month of Adar, and on the fourteenth they*
> *rested and made it a day of feasting and joy.* (9:17)

The opposition had been defeated, fully and finally. And then the Jews celebrated.

In today's application, begin to reflect on the principle that God's greatest victories are usually reserved for those with the greatest faith. Think back on a time in your life when God demanded the greatest level of trust in Him. Perhaps it was the illness or even death of a loved one. Perhaps it was a job loss and the resulting financial struggles. Perhaps it was a severe conflict that threatened to divide you from family or friends. Whatever it was, take a moment to recall an incident that demanded of you the greatest level of trust in God. Then reflect on the victories that followed.

**What time in your life required the greatest trust in God? Briefly tell the story.**

_____

_____

_____

_____

**Why was your trusting God in this situation such a challenge?**

_____

_____

_____

_____

**How did God resolve the crisis in the end?**

_____

_____

_____

_____

_____

**Looking back now, what kind of victory did He give you? (Even if it was not the victory you requested!)**

_____

_____

_____

**What did God accomplish in your life that He could not have accomplished through a lesser challenge?**

_____

_____

_____

### PRAYER SUGGESTION

Thank God for loving you enough to draw you close and grow you up — no matter what it takes. Thank Him that He cares about you more than He does your finances, your comfort, your health, or any other earthly thing. Thank Him that He has been working throughout eternity on your behalf, and that you can trust Him with everything that happens, no matter how painful it may initially seem.

Thank Him, too, for the victories He brings. Thank Him that even though the pain was often great, the victory was greater.

✝
## WEEK EIGHT
## NEW CHALLENGES, NEW VICTORIES
# Small Group Discussion Guide

Haman, the enemy of the Jews, had been hanged. Yet Esther and Mordecai were then faced with the even greater challenge of saving the Jews from the decree ordering their destruction. Does it ever seem like new challenges are all lined up just waiting to take their shot at you? Well, sometimes they are! In today's study, we are going to learn how to turn new challenges into new victories.

**TODAY: Esther 8:1-9:17**

**I. Expect new and greater CHALLENGES.**
**KEY PASSAGE:** Esther 8:3, 5-6 (read it aloud)

**DISCUSSION QUESTION:** What new and greater challenge did Esther bring to the king's attention following the execution of Haman?

_____

_____

**PRINCIPLE:** In real life, real people have real problems. So expect it!

**SUPPORT PASSAGE:** John 16:33 (read it aloud)

**APPLICATION:** As you enjoy deliverance and victory over a recent crisis, what new and perhaps greater challenges do you see ahead?

_____

_____

**II. Look for new and greater PROVISION.**
**KEY PASSAGE:** Esther 8:1-2, 7-10 (read it aloud)

**DISCUSSION QUESTION:** What provision to meet this new challenge has God already made?

_____

_____

**PRINCIPLE:** Problems are certain, but so is God's provision. So look for it!

**SUPPORT PASSAGE:** Deuteronomy 31:8 (read it aloud)

**APPLICATION:** As you consider your new challenge, what new provision can you see that God has already made?

_____

_____

## III. Prepare for new and greater INVOLVEMENT.
**KEY PASSAGE:** Esther 8:11-17 (read it aloud)

**DISCUSSION QUESTION:** How was God demanding greater and more widespread involvement in Esther's new crisis than He had in the crisis over confronting Haman?

_____

_____

**PRINCIPLE:** God's solutions usually involve our participation, and participation requires preparation. So prepare for it!

**SUPPORT PASSAGE:** 1 Chronicles 28:20 (read it aloud)

**APPLICATION:** How might your new crisis demand even more of you than did your previous crisis? How are you going to have to grow and develop to meet those demands?

_____

_____

## IV. Trust God for new and greater VICTORIES.
**KEY PASSAGE:** Esther 9:1-3, 5, 16-17 (read it aloud)

**DISCUSSION QUESTION:** What new and greater victory did God give His people?

_____

_____

**PRINCIPLE:** God assures us that in Him we have _overcome the world_ (John 16:33; 1 John 4:4; 5:4-5) and that He always leads us in _triumphal procession_ (2 Corinthians 2:14). So trust God for it!

**SUPPORT PASSAGES:** John 16:33; 2 Corinthians 2:14; 1 John 4:4; 5:4-5 (read them aloud)

**APPLICATION:** What new and greater victory is God offering you?

_____

_____

# A Miracle Remembered

Day 1 — Celebration

Day 2 — Remembrance

Day 3 — What's in a Name?

Day 4 — Family Traditions

Day 5 — Lasting Impact

What had begun as a great crisis had ended as a great victory. Haman had been hanged, his sons were dead, and his fellow antisemites had been overcome. The Jews had been victorious over their enemies and could now enjoy peace. So why doesn't the book of Esther end there? What unfinished business could there possibly still be? The answer is the unfinished business of celebration.

We are usually much better at asking God for deliverance than we are at thanking Him and celebrating when it finally comes. Even if we do, we quickly set the celebration aside and move on with our lives, never revisiting that wonderful moment when God was so tangibly there for us.

This week's study will show you how to be a good "celebrator." You will learn how to say thank you to God. And you will learn how to do it this year, next year, and the year after that — so that the full impact of God's deliverance never fades.

# Celebration

**PASSAGE: Esther 9:17-19**

The Jews had been delivered from a terrible crisis, and rather than just take God's deliverance for granted, they celebrated. God has delivered us countless times. How often do we respond with celebration? Today's lesson has much to teach us about how to show God our gratitude.

**READING ASSIGNMENT: Esther 9:17-19**

**FOCUS FOR TODAY: Esther 9:17-19**

> *This happened on the thirteenth day of the month of Adar, and on the fourteenth they rested and made it a day of feasting and joy.* (9:17)

We looked at this verse last week, but let's look at it again. We will discover in a moment that this verse is referring to the Jews in the provinces. It begins with the words *this happened*; to what event is it referring?

**Looking back in chapter nine, to what are the words *this happened* referring?**

_____

When did these events take place? As we learned in week three, the month of Adar extended from the middle of February to the middle of March. The first decree, the one issued by Haman, specified that the genocide was to occur on the thirteenth day of the month of Adar, or roughly around the end of February. The second decree, that of Mordecai, specified that the Jews were to defend themselves that same day. This was exactly the way things turned out in the provinces. Both the attack on and the defense by the Jews took place on the day specified.

So in the provinces, both the attack and the defense came on the thirteenth of Adar.

**What did the Jews do on the fourteenth day of Adar?**

_____

**In case you didn't make this point in your previous answer, how specifically is this celebration described? Three or four things are specifically mentioned.**

_____

_____

There is a lot to learn here, but hold those thoughts until we look at the next verse.

> *The Jews in Susa, however, had assembled on the thirteenth and fourteenth, and then*
> *on the fifteenth they rested and made it a day of feasting and joy.* (9:18)

Verse seventeen describes what happened in the provinces. In Susa the situation was a bit different. As we saw last week, Mordecai and Esther asked the king to allow the Jews in Susa to defend themselves against their enemies for one additional day, thus extending the fighting in the capital city to the fourteenth. Although the reason for this extension was not given, it was doubtless intended to give the Jews the opportunity to deal with their enemies in a way that would virtually eliminate any future threat. Consequently the Jews in Susa celebrated their victory not on the fourteenth, but on the fifteenth.

**What did the Jews in the capital city do on the day following their victory?**

_____

**How did they celebrate? Again, three or four things are specifically mentioned.**

_____

_____

Don't miss the details of this wonderful scene. Let's work through the last part of the verse to get the full impact. The phrase begins with the words, *they rested.*

**What can we learn from this phrase?**

_____

_____

Next we are told that they *made it a day of....*

**What can we learn from this phrase?**

_____

_____

Then we see the word *feasting.*

**What does this tell us?**

_____

_____

Finally, we come to the word *joy*.

**What can we learn from this word?**

_____

_____

What do I see here? Let me begin with what I don't see. I don't see people just congratulating each other, shaking hands, or patting each other on the back as they headed for home. I see a lot more than that!

I see grateful people. I see people who threw a party! I see people who celebrated on purpose. First of all, they rested. They were *focused*. They stopped doing whatever else they were doing to focus on thanking God. Second, they made it a day of celebration. They were *deliberate*. They didn't stand around hoping a party would break out — they threw one! Third, they feasted. They were *extravagant*. They didn't scrimp on this party; they put resources and effort into the event. Finally, they celebrated with joy. They were *expressive*. They didn't stand around a buffet, holding a plate in one hand and a cup of punch in the other, engaging in idle chitchat. They cut loose! Although the passage doesn't expressly say so, I'm sure there was music and dancing.

They had the right idea! Too often we allow our relief at the passing of a crisis to substitute for a celebration. Don't do that! When God delivers you from a crisis, do what the Jews did — celebrate it!

> *That is why rural Jews — those living in villages — observe the fourteenth of the month of Adar as a day of joy and feasting, a day for giving presents to each other.* (9:19)

The Jews in the provinces celebrated their victory a day earlier than the Jews in Susa, but they too celebrated it with feasting and joy and, we now learn, with the exchange of gifts.

**What does the exchange of gifts tell you? What can we learn from this?**

_____

_____

Let's add one more item to the list we began above: They were *generous*. They didn't just celebrate what God had done for each of them as individuals; they celebrated what God had done for all of them as a people, as a family. It's as though each person were saying, "*I* wasn't delivered; *we* were!"

**What does this verse suggest to you about how often this celebration was held? Do you get the feeling that it was a one-time event, or that it was celebrated each and every year at that same time?**

_____

The verse implies that the celebration became customary, an annual event. This will turn out to be the most significant point of all, for reasons we will discover later in the chapter.

✛

When we encounter a crisis, we are quick to pray. Yet when God resolves the crisis, we often seem slow to celebrate. Let's resolve to change that! In today's application, take the time to stop and prepare to celebrate on purpose.

**Think back to the most recent time that God delivered you from a crisis. What did you do to celebrate? If you forgot to celebrate, what could you plan now?**

_____
_____
_____

**One way or another, God will deliver you from your current crisis. Express your commitment to Him that when He does deliver you, you will celebrate.**

_____
_____
_____

**Start planning your celebration right now. Specifically, tell how you will be _focused, deliberate, extravagant, expressive,_ and _generous._**

_____
_____
_____

### PRAYER SUGGESTION

Confess the times that you have failed to celebrate God's deliverance. Ask Him to remind you of the celebrations that you missed and commit to Him that you will not miss the next one. Ask Him to help you be _focused_ as you set aside distractions. Ask Him to help you be _deliberate_ as you make it the kind of celebration it should truly be. Ask Him to help you be _extravagant_ in proportion to His provision for you. Ask Him to help you be _expressive_ of your joy, both with Him and with others. Ask Him to help you be _generous_ as you celebrate not only what God did for you, but what He did for everyone else who was involved as well. Then, finally, invite Him to the party!

# WEEK NINE † DAY TWO
# Remembrance

**PASSAGE: Esther 9:20-23**

When victory was finally theirs, Jews throughout the empire broke into a spontaneous celebration. Seeing this, Mordecai had an idea: Wouldn't it be appropriate to celebrate this amazing deliverance next year as well? And why not the year after that? Even when we remember to celebrate the deliverance of God, after a few months or years go by, we may forget what it was we were celebrating. Determine not to allow that to happen by taking a lesson from Mordecai.

**READING ASSIGNMENT: Esther 9:17-23**

**FOCUS FOR TODAY: Esther 9:20-23**

> *Mordecai recorded these events, and he sent letters to all the Jews throughout the provinces of King Xerxes, near and far…* (9:20)

**Why was it so significant that Mordecai recorded these events? What would surely have happened if he hadn't?**

_____

_____

_____

Often we tend to obsess on our crises. When we are in the middle of a tough time, it is all we think about. And when God finally delivers us, we cannot imagine ever forgetting the details of our crisis and of what God did to deliver us. But we do. Important details of events that dominate our lives for months can, mere months later, be lost forever. Mordecai didn't let that happen. He wrote everything down.

Does the phrase *Mordecai recorded these events* suggest that Mordecai wrote the book of Esther? Probably not. He may well have written the book — the author is never identified — but this verse was referring not to the book of Esther — it referred to Mordecai's second letter to be distributed throughout the empire. (His first was addressed to all peoples and contained the decree authorizing the Jews both to defend themselves and to plunder the property of those whom they would defeat.) This second letter was addressed to the Jews, and it did two things. The first is mentioned here in verse twenty.

**What was it?**

_____

First, it recounted the events of the thirteenth and fourteenth of Adar, doubtless providing details of the victory as it had been reported from around the empire. But it did something else as well. It issued yet another decree, as the next verse indicates.

> ...*to have them celebrate annually the fourteenth and fifteenth days of the month of Adar*... (9:21)

Now we discover Mordecai's second reason for writing the letter.

**What was it?**

_____

_____

Inspired by the spontaneous celebrations that had broken out in Susa, Mordecai decreed that this great victory should be celebrated annually on the fourteenth and fifteenth of Adar. Was Mordecai even aware at this point that celebrations had already broken out not only in Susa, but throughout the empire? It's possible that he was, given the extensive network of signal towers that linked the empire. Yet it's also possible that he saw the celebration in Susa and simply decided that this was something that should be repeated each year by Jews everywhere in the empire.

**Why was it so important that the decree to observe the celebration annually be accompanied by a complete description of the events being celebrated?**

_____

_____

_____

_____

Unless we remind ourselves each year of the reason for our celebration, the tradition will either fade or become empty.

*…as the time when the Jews got relief from their enemies, and as the month when their sorrow was turned into joy and their mourning into a day of celebration. He wrote them to observe the days as days of feasting and joy and giving presents of food to one another and gifts to the poor.* (9:22)

Mordecai's letter included the reason for the celebration, something we will look at in more detail in tomorrow's study. He also indicated the nature of the celebration. It was to be a time of feasting, joy, and the giving of gifts, especially food. The gifts were to be given not only to friends and family, but to the poor as well. In other words, the Jews were to have a party!

**Why would it have been inappropriate for the occasion to be a time of mourning and fasting?**

_____

_____

_____

The important point, however, was that Mordecai made the celebration an annual event. He had a sense that this incredible deliverance was something that the Jews should not allow themselves to forget. And the best way to remember to celebrate something is to put it on your calendar.

*The Jews agreed to continue the celebration they had begun, doing what Mordecai had written to them.* (9:23)

Having received Mordecai's instructions, Jews throughout the empire agreed to observe the celebration annually.

There's one thing we all learned in school: If we don't plan to remember something, we are almost certain to forget it. Even when the "something" is an amazing deliverance from God, our memory of the event will inevitably fade unless we do something to keep it fresh.

During the days following my wife's diagnosis and throughout the days of her surgery and recovery, we kept a detailed journal with dates of everything that happened, including information on all the wonderful people who helped us in so many different ways. What a treasure that journal will be in years to come!

Don't let your precious memories of God's faithfulness fade. Do something to capture those memories right now.

Is the anniversary of a deliverance from years past approaching? Can you remember the date? Reconstruct the dates as accurately as you can, and then transfer the results to your calendar.

_____

_____

_____

What will you do to celebrate the next anniversary?

_____

_____

_____

What more recent deliverance do you need to record right now so that you will remember it next year?

_____

_____

_____

## PRAYER SUGGESTION

Ask God to remind you of events that you have forgotten. Mention some specific events, then ask Him to help you and others who were involved remember the details so that nothing will be lost in the retelling. Commit to Him that you will take the time to record these events as fully as possible and ask Him help you find the time to follow through. Then promise Him that you will take action to recall and reflect on those events in years to come.

# What's in a Name?

**PASSAGE: Esther 9:24-26**

Mordecai had decreed that the celebration of God's deliverance of His people would be an annual event. But what would the annual event be called? In this passage we learn not only the name of this event and its significance, but also a helpful suggestion on how to remember the special deliverances of God in our own lives.

**READING ASSIGNMENT: Esther 9:17-26**

**FOCUS FOR TODAY: Esther 9:24-26a**

> *Haman son of Hammedatha, the Agagite, the enemy of all the Jews, had plotted against the Jews to destroy them and had cast the pur (that is, the lot) for their ruin and destruction. (9:24)*

Why should the people observe this annual celebration? What was it they were celebrating? The writer retells the story. But surely the reader hasn't forgotten already! Why in the world would the writer of the book of Esther retell the story here?

**What do you think?**

_____

_____

I think there were two reasons. First, the details explained the name of the celebration. Recall from chapter three that Haman had originally determined the day of his failed genocide by casting lots, the Hebrew word for which is *pur*. As we will see in a moment, the name of the celebration was derived from this word. There is a second reason for retelling the story.

> *When the plot came to the king's attention, he issued written orders that the evil scheme Haman had devised against the Jews should come back onto his own head, and that he and his sons should be hanged on the gallows. (9:25)*

As the story is retold, we not only learn the reason for the name of the celebration; we are reminded of the events themselves. After a little time has gone by, most of us struggle to remember the details of events. We might remember what God did in general terms, but we can easily forget the sequence of events, the details, and even the names of the people involved. Before long the story gets shortened, fuzzy, and distorted. And sometimes the story gets lost entirely.

**What can you do to make sure this never happens? How can you guarantee that the real significance of your celebration, complete with all the wonderful details, is never lost?**

_____

_____


It is a good idea to celebrate each deliverance from God. It is a better idea to celebrate each deliverance annually. It is an even better idea to retell the story each and every time we celebrate it. We can even do what Mordecai did: Write it down. That is the only way the story will stay vital and alive with detail.

Yet the Jews went beyond even recording and retelling the story at the annual celebration. They gave the celebration itself a vividly significant name, as the next verse explains.

*(Therefore these days were called Purim, from the word pur.)* (9:26a)

Now we learn the name of the celebration: It was to be called *Purim*, a word derived from *pur*, the Hebrew word for *lot*. The lots, as you may recall, were the ancient equivalent of dice. So the event was given a name, and the "Celebration of the Dice" would be observed annually on the fourteenth and fifteenth days of Adar, corresponding to the end of February or beginning of March on our calendar.

Wasn't this an odd choice? "The Celebration of the Dice" — just try to put that one on the church calendar!

**Why did they name the celebration after dice? (Hint: Reread Esther 3:7.)**

_____

_____

_____


But doesn't this seem like an obscure, even insignificant detail?

**Why would the Jews pick the lot as the symbol of God's deliverance? (Hint: Read Proverbs 16:33.)**

_____

_____

_____

Proverbs 16:33 suggests the answer: *The lot is cast into the lap, but its every decision is from the Lord.* In other words, God is sovereign. He is in control. Even when a pagan official has the priests of a false religion cast the lot, God is still God. Haman could not get around the power and plan of the God of Israel by throwing the dice. So the name of the celebration was to remind the people both of the events and of God's role in bringing them under the control of His will. By naming the celebration after the lot that was cast against them, the Jews were reminding themselves of the sovereign power of God.

✛

It is wonderful to celebrate the times that God has delivered us from crises. It is even better to make those celebrations annual events. But if we don't write down and retell the stories behind those celebrations, we will soon forget what they are all about. Or even if we remember the reasons, those reasons will cease to be central to the celebrations — something that has already happened for many people with Christmas and Easter.

**What stories of God's deliverance in your life do you enjoy retelling?**

_____

_____

_____

_____

**What stories have you almost forgotten that need to be remembered and retold?**

_____

_____

_____

_____

**What new stories of recent works of God in your life do you need to begin telling?**

_____

_____

_____

Here is a fun exercise: Look back at some of the more significant and exciting crises from which God has delivered you, then think of a name for a corresponding celebration of each. You might want to make each name a little unexpected. Not only will that make it more memorable; it will be a great conversation-starter! Here is a chart to help you get going.

EVENT                         NAME

_____ : "Celebration of the _____"

_____ : "Celebration of the _____"

_____ : "Celebration of the _____"

_____ : "Celebration of the _____"

## PRAYER SUGGESTION

Ask God to refresh your memory about the stories you remember and to remind you of the stories you have forgotten. Ask Him to give you the boldness to share those stories with others. Also ask Him to remind you to retell those stories at your celebration each year. Finally, ask Him to help you come up with a memorable name for your celebration, something that will help you remember the event and even start conversations about it.

# Family Traditions

**PASSAGE: Esther 9:26b-28**

Purim was to become an annual celebration of God's faithfulness to His people. But unless the people embraced that celebration, unless they told the story and handed it down from generation to generation, the incredible deliverance that they had experienced would have been forgotten. Wouldn't it be wonderful if our children and grandchildren could benefit from the demonstrations of God's faithfulness in our lives? They can, but only if we make it happen.

**READING ASSIGNMENT: Esther 9:17-28**

**FOCUS FOR TODAY: Esther 9:26b-28**

> *Because of everything written in this letter and because of what they had seen and what had happened to them…* (9:26b)

Since Mordecai was the prime minister, his letter had considerable force. But there was much more at work here than just a letter or the authority of a prime minister.

**What made the events recorded in Mordecai's letter so compelling for the average Jew?**

_____

What made Mordecai's account and decree so forceful was that they reflected the experiences and sentiments of the Jewish people themselves. So, because they had personally witnessed and experienced the events, and because the prime minister had so decreed, the Jews took action.

> *…the Jews took it upon themselves to establish the custom that they and their descendants and all who join them should without fail observe these two days every year, in the way prescribed and at the time appointed.* (9:27)

The Jews were only too happy to make the celebration of Purim an annual event. Notice that the text says, *they took it upon themselves to establish the custom.*

**Why was that important?**

_____

_____


Decrees don't establish customs; people do. Apart from action on the part of the people, Purim would have been nothing more than a good idea and a missed opportunity. But Purim was established as a custom precisely because the people *took it upon themselves* to establish it. What exactly did they do? We aren't told. But we can be sure that they did whatever was necessary to ensure that each fourteenth and fifteenth of Adar, the celebration would actually be held and that it would be done right.

Who would participate in the annual celebration of Purim?

**What does the verse say?**

_____

_____

_____


I see three groups: the Jews, their descendants, and *all who join them* — in other words, future converts to Judaism. In case this wasn't clear enough, the writer made the expectation emphatic.

> *These days should be remembered and observed in every generation by every family,*
> *and in every province and in every city. And these days of Purim should never cease*
> *to be celebrated by the Jews, nor should the memory of them die out among their*
> *descendants.* (9:28)

The expectation is clear: Every Jew of every generation of every family of every city of every province was to observe Purim from that day forth.

**Why was the wording so emphatic?**

_____

_____

_____


If the Jews didn't take these steps, the memory of the event would have died. The memory of the event might have lived on for as long as that generation lived, and perhaps their children might even have kept the memory alive for a time. But before long the memory would die —

unless someone took the necessary steps to keep it alive. This is precisely what Mordecai had instructed the people to do.

✠

What were the most significant spiritual events in the lives of your parents? How about your grandparents? How about your great-grandparents? Do you see the problem? The same thing will happen with the great spiritual events in our lives as well — unless we do something about it.

**What steps do you need to take right now to assure that your list of celebrations will be more than a list tucked away in a long-forgotten Bible study guide? What do you need to do to *establish the custom*?**

_____

_____

_____

**What memories of God's deliverance need to be retrieved from your parents or grandparents and celebrated as part of the traditions of your family?**

_____

_____

_____

**Who should be included in your next celebration? What family members or friends would benefit from hearing your story? Write your guest list below.**

_____

_____

_____

### PRAYER SUGGESTION

Ask God to give you such gratitude for what He has done in your life and such a heart for your friends and family, that you will see to it that the stories of His faithfulness in your life are told and retold, perhaps even for generations to come. Thank Him for how He worked in the lives of your parents and grandparents and ask Him to help you retrieve their stories so that those stories can be told and retold. Finally, ask Him to give you a sense of the enormous faith-building benefit that you and your family will experience as you recount the stories of God's faithfulness for years to come.

# Lasting Impact

**PASSAGE: Esther 9:29-10:3**

Mordecai wrote to explain the events and issue the decree concerning Purim. Esther wrote to add her voice to Mordecai's. Her account of the events would lend support to the incredible story related by Mordecai as well as provide encouragement for the people to take up the annual celebration of Purim. The courageous faith of Esther and Mordecai had an impact on the Jewish people that was both immediate and lasting. They were "difference-makers." They lived their lives outside of their usual comfort zones — and history was changed. We would all like to think that our lives will have a lasting impact, that the world will never be the same because we passed through. If that is going to happen in and through your life and mine, we are going to have to follow the example of Esther and Mordecai and live with courageous faith.

**READING ASSIGNMENT: Esther 9:17-10:3**

**FOCUS FOR TODAY: Esther 9:29-10:3**

> *Queen Esther, daughter of Abihail, along with Mordecai the Jew, wrote with full authority to confirm this second letter concerning Purim.* (9:29)

Queen Esther wrote a separate letter, this one with the *authority to confirm* Mordecai's letter concerning Purim. How are we to understand this authority and confirmation? It was doubtless not a matter of legal authority, since Esther, as the queen, would have had little real authority, particularly when compared with Mordecai, the prime minister.

**As she recounted the story, what kind of *authority* would Esther have possessed?**

_____

It seems likely that Esther was writing with the authority of an eyewitness, to testify to the incredible series of events that had led to the deliverance of the Jewish people. She might even have filled in a few details of her own. But there might have been something more here. Note the phrase *daughter of Abihail*.

**How would that reminder have been likely to encourage the readers of Esther's letter?**

_____

_____

By using her father's name, Esther was emphasizing her Jewish heritage. Remember that the name _Esther_ was Persian, not Hebrew. Her Hebrew name was _Hadassah,_ yet it was by her Persian name that she was known as queen. (See Esther 2:7.) Esther's readers would have been enormously encouraged by her reminder that she, the queen, was one of their own people. Although Esther had no legal authority, her personal authority as an eyewitness and her credibility among the Jewish people, especially at this point, would have been enormous.

> _Mordecai sent letters to all the Jews in the 127 provinces of the kingdom of Xerxes —_
> _words of goodwill and assurance... (9:30)_

Apparently the letters from Mordecai and Esther were sent out together. The letters were said to have contained _words of goodwill and assurance._ But _goodwill and reassurance_ for whom?

**What do you think?**

_____

_____

We might at first suppose that the assurance was intended for the regional officials who, as we learned last week, had come to fear Mordecai. (See Esther 9:3-4.) But that couldn't be the point, since we learned in verse twenty that these letters were sent to the Jews.

**Why would words of goodwill and assurance have been necessary for the Jews?**

_____

_____

It seems likely that the letters were intended to provide Jews throughout the empire with an assurance of the goodwill of the imperial government. Given all that they had experienced during the previous twelve months, such assurances would be welcome indeed.

> _...to establish these days of Purim at their designated times, as Mordecai the Jew and_
> _Queen Esther had decreed for them, and as they had established for themselves and_
> _their descendants in regard to their times of fasting and lamentation. (9:31)_

The ultimate purpose of these letters was, of course, to establish the celebration of Purim. The words *fasting and lamentation* refer not to Purim, which was to be a time of feasting and joy, but to the other days of special observance already occupying the Jewish calendar. In other words, Mordecai and Esther wanted to make sure that Purim was given its proper place among all other Jewish religious observances. But were they allowed to do that? The events on the Jewish calendar had been established by God Himself. By what right did Esther and Mordecai add another observance to the sacred list?

**How would you respond to this question?**

_____

_____

I would simply say this: God has never punished anybody for praising Him. We can get so caught up in our religious scruples that we forget what really matters to God. Sure, Esther and Mordecai were taking it upon themselves to add a new celebration of God's faithfulness to the Jewish religious calendar. But they were not upsetting God; they were delighting Him.

> *Esther's decree confirmed these regulations about Purim, and it was written down in the records.* (9:32)

Esther's decree confirmed the account and decree of Mordecai. The most important phrase for us is the final one: *and it was written down in the records.* We take for granted our knowledge of God's mighty acts on behalf of His people. But would we know about the parting of the Red Sea if Moses had not written it down?

Who will know what God has done in your life if you don't write it down? Every work of God in your life is absolutely unique. Have you ever thought about that? There has never been and there will never be another you. You are a unique creation of God. That means that everything God does in your life is a "once-in-eternity" act of God — never done before and never to be repeated. That makes them immensely significant. Yet the truth is, even we will begin to forget the details if we don't write them down immediately. Don't let the memory fade! Write it down! The book of Esther concludes by revealing that God's blessing on and through Mordecai didn't end with the events we've just studied.

> *King Xerxes imposed tribute throughout the empire, to its distant shores. And all his acts of power and might, together with a full account of the greatness of Mordecai to which the king had raised him, are they not written in the book of the annals of the kings of Media and Persia?* (10:1-2)

Apparently the incident in which Mordecai exposed the assassination plot was not the only time Mordecai's name would be recorded with distinction in the annals of the court. Note, however, that the emphasis in these verses was not on Mordecai, but on Xerxes. Why would the book have been concluded with an emphasis on the accomplishments of the king? The next and final verse explains.

> *Mordecai the Jew was second in rank to King Xerxes, preeminent among the Jews, and held in high esteem by his many fellow Jews, because he worked for the good of his people and spoke up for the welfare of all the Jews.* (10:3)

These verses were included in closing to demonstrate how King Xerxes continued to prosper with Mordecai as his prime minister. We, of course, are to understand that this blessing came ultimately from God. His concern for His people didn't end with the events of Purim.

Over the years God has delivered you from crises of all kinds. In virtually all of those instances, He called on you to trust Him and take action. As you stepped forward — ignoring your fears and keeping your eyes fixed on God and His promises — you saw doors open, barriers fall, and crises fade from view.

These types of moments have likely had an obvious and lasting impact on you. But what impact have they had on the people close to you, the people you care about? How have the people in your life been blessed by your faith during the tough times? In what ways has your deliverance blessed and even delivered them?

**Think back on a recent crisis. As God delivered you from that crisis, how were the lives of the people around you touched? What positive influence have they reported?**

_____

_____

_____

**Think farther back to a crisis that happened long ago. How has God's deliverance from that crisis permanently impacted your life and the lives of those who are close to you?**

_____

_____

_____

**What can you do to safeguard and even enhance your long-term impact as God delivers you from your current crisis?**

_____

_____

_____

## PRAYER SUGGESTION

Thank God for the ways He has used the crises of your past to impact yourself and others. Thank Him for the fact that you would not be the person you are today if He hadn't allowed some struggles and provided abundant deliverance in your life. Mention a specific instance or two of how His faithful deliverance changed your life and the lives of those around you for the better. Then ask Him to remind you of a time or two when He used the faith and His ultimate deliverance of someone else to touch your life. Then go thank them for it, too.

# Preparing for Your Small Group Discussion

As you complete your personal study of the book of Esther, take some time to prepare for your next Bible study or small group meeting. Notice that I did not use the word *final*. I am trusting and praying that you have fallen in love with small group life, and that as your group completes this study of the book of Esther you will already have decided what you are going to study next.

To that end, allow me to offer you some advice and encouragement from years of experience: Don't lose your momentum! "Taking a break" in your small group meetings can be fatal. If your life is anything like mine, your schedule abhors a vacuum. As soon as you clear out that evening or that hour or two in the morning, something else will surely rush in to take its place. So take a short break if you must, but schedule your next meeting first. Then stick with it!

If you are completing this study of the book of Esther on your own, I encourage you to continue your pursuit and study of God's Word.

✝
## WEEK NINE
## A MIRACLE REMEMBERED
# Small Group Discussion Guide

As the book of Esther ends, God's people were celebrating. They were not at all content to accept God's deliverance and then return to business as usual. Instead they took steps to remember the miracle. They did what it took to guarantee that they and their descendants would never forget the faithfulness of God.

**TODAY: Esther 9:17-10:3**

**I. When God delivers you, CELEBRATE.**
**KEY PASSAGE:** Esther 9:17b-18 (read it aloud)

**DISCUSSION QUESTION:** What did the Jews do to celebrate their deliverance?

_____

_____

**PRINCIPLE:** When was the last time you had a party to celebrate God's faithfulness? Plan one!

**APPLICATION:** Think back to the most recent time that God delivered you from a crisis. What did you do to celebrate? If you forgot to celebrate, what are you planning now?

_____

_____

**II. Don't just do it once. Do it ANNUALLY.**
**KEY PASSAGE:** Esther 9:20-23 (read it aloud)

**DISCUSSION QUESTION:** What did Esther and Mordecai do to guarantee that this deliverance of God's people would never be forgotten?

_____

_____

**PRINCIPLE:** What good thing did God do in your life about this time last year? Celebrate it again!

**APPLICATION:** Are you coming up on the anniversary of a deliverance from years past? Can you remember the date? What will you do to celebrate that anniversary?

_____

_____


### III. When you celebrate it, TELL THE STORY.
**KEY PASSAGE:** Esther 9:24-26a (read it aloud)

**DISCUSSION QUESTION:** What did Mordecai do to make certain that the annual celebration would remain meaningful?

_____

_____


**PRINCIPLE:** What good things has God done in your past that need to be retold? Retell them!

**APPLICATION:** What stories of God's deliverance in your life do you enjoy telling? What stories have you almost forgotten that need to be remembered and retold?

_____

_____


### IV. Be sure to include YOUR FAMILY and FRIENDS.
**KEY PASSAGE:** Esther 9:26b-28 (read it aloud)

**DISCUSSION QUESTION:** Who was to be included in the annual celebration of Purim?

_____

**PRINCIPLE:** Who would benefit from hearing about how God has blessed you? Include them!

**APPLICATION:** Who should be included in your next celebration? What family or friends would benefit from hearing your story?

_____

_____

**V. Above all, write everything down IMMEDIATELY.**

**KEY PASSAGE:** Esther 9:29-32 (read it aloud)

**DISCUSSION QUESTION:** What did Esther do to lend her support to the establishment and annual observance of Purim?

_____

_____

**PRINCIPLE:** Which is better: your intentions or your memory? Don't wait! Record everything now!

**APPLICATION:** When will you start? Make a commitment right now and share it with the others in your group.

_____

_____

✢

# Conclusion

Exactly six weeks had passed since Julie's surgery. It was Fellowship Group night and we were enjoying the company of some very special people. God had used many, many people to love and care for us during the previous weeks. The people sitting in that circle were some of the most faithful, the most loving ones of all.

We enjoyed dessert. We laughed. We talked. And we reflected on the weeks that had just passed. Although the memories were still fresh, I took a moment to reminisce about the things God had done, especially the things He had done through these friends. And I thanked them all.

It was a sweet moment, the kind of moment that makes you grateful that you don't face the tough times alone. Julie still had a long way to go in her recovery, but we felt so secure that night. We have a good God and good friends, and we are absolutely confident that there will always be plenty of arms to hold us close and enough love to keep us warm.

As we began to share our prayer requests, a newer couple in the group opened up for the first time. They told us about a crisis in their life, a crisis which in its own way was every bit as serious as ours. As they shared, I saw the love and concern that we had experienced from the group reach out to embrace them. I saw the relief on their faces as they realized that other people really did care. I saw their burdens shift to us, and our strength shift to them.

By the time the evening ended, this couple had new hope — you could see it in their eyes. They were ready to face their crisis with a fresh strength and a new courage to trust God.

As I write this, I have no idea how their crisis will end. But I do know this: As they meet their "moment of trust" with courageous faith, God will give them the victory.

# ✣

# Notes

## Week One

[1]Herodotus, *The History, Books 6 and 7.* In *The Great Books of the Western World,* Ed. Robert Maynard Hutchins, (Chicago: Encyclopedia Britannica, Inc., 1952).

[2]Ibid., 214-259.

[3]Ibid., 260-314.

[4]Howard F. Vos, *Ezra, Nehemiah, Esther: Bible Study Commentary* (Grand Rapids: Zondervan, 1987), 149.

[5]D. J. Clines, *Ezra, Nehemiah, Esther: The New Century Bible Commentary* (Grand Rapids: Eerdmans, 1984), 277.

[6]Herodotus, *Book 9.*

[7]Francis Brown, S. R. Driver, and Charles A. Briggs, *A Hebrew and English Lexicon of the Old Testament* (Oxford: Oxford University Press, n.d.), 255, 278; and Joyce G. Baldwin, *Esther: An Introduction and Commentary. Tyndale Old Testament Commentaries.* Ed. D. J. Wiseman (Downer's Grove, IL: InterVarsity Press, 1984), 59-60, 150.

[8]Ibid., 150.

[9]R. Laird Harris, Gleason Archer, Jr., and Bruce Waltke, *Theological Wordbook of the Old Testament* (Chicago: Moody Press, 1980), 346; and Brown, Driver, and Briggs, 525.

[10]Harris, Archer, and Waltke, 284; and Clines, 280.

[11]Vos, 152.

[12]For more on Xerxes' reputation as a womanizer, see Will Durant, *Our Original Heritage,* Volume 1 of *The Story of Civilization* (New York: Simon and Schuster, 1954), 381.

[13]Herodotus, *Book 8,* 98.

## Week Two

[1]Brown, Driver, and Briggs, 269.

[2]See also Esther 8:8 and Daniel 6:8,12,15.

[3]Harris, Archer, and Waltke, 137.

[4]Baldwin, 64.

[5]Clines, 285.

[6]Brown, Driver, and Briggs, 598.

[7]Ibid., 213.

[8]Ibid., 64.

[9]Josephus, the Jewish historian, places the number at roughly 400, while one contemporary scholar puts the estimate as high as 1,460.

[10]Durant, 351, 356.

[11]Clines, 289.

[12]Herodotus, *The History, Book 8.*

[13]We might mention Daniel and his friends as examples of those who resisted a king and put their trust in God. (See Daniel 1, 3, 6.)

[14]See 2 Samuel 3:7; 5:13; 15:16. For more on concubinage in ancient Israel, see "Concubinage," *Baker Encyclopedia of the Bible*, Ed. Walter A. Elwell (Grand Rapids: Baker Book House, 1988), Vol. 1, 504-505.

[15]Clines, 285.

[16]Clines, 286.

## Week Three

[1]Although we do not know the precise year the assassination plot was exposed, there are some clues. The banquet in chapter one occurred in the third year of Xerxes' reign (Esther 1:3), or 483 B.C. Esther became queen in Xerxes' seventh year (Esther 2:16), or 479 B.C. The events of chapter three occurred in Xerxes' twelfth year (Esther 3:7), or 474 B.C. So roughly nine years have passed since Vashti was deposed in chapter one.

[2]A. K. Helmbold, "Agagite," in *The Zondervan Pictorial Encyclopedia of the Bible*, Ed. Merrill C. Tenney (Grand Rapids: Zondervan, Regency Reference Library, 1976), Vol. 1, 68; and Vos, 158-159.

[3]Baldwin, 71-72.

[4]That "Agagite" could carry this derogatory sense is widely attested, as in "Agagite," *Baker Encyclopedia of the Bible*, 35.

[5]This discussion of Persian greetings is based on Herodotus, *Book 1*, 134.

[6]Clines, 294.

[7]Ibid.

[8]Ibid., 295; Carey A. Moore, *The Anchor Bible: Esther* (New York: Doubleday, 1971), 38; and Vos, 160-161.

[9]Vos, 161.

[10]The sense is, *scattered* [among] *and* [yet] *divided* [from], the other peoples of the empire. Cf. Brown, Driver, and Briggs, 808, 825.

[11]Herodotus, *The History, Book 3*; cited in Clines, 296.

[12]Baldwin, 74.

[13]Herodotus, *The History, Book 1*; cited in Durant, 376.

[14]Herodotus, *The History, Book 1*; cited in Clines, 298.

## Week Four

[1]Brown, Driver, and Briggs, 277.

[2]*The Septuagint: Greek and English*, Trans. Lancelot Brenton (Grand Rapids: Zondervan, 1970), 655.

[3]This translation from the Hebrew is my own.

[4]Flavius Josephus, *Antiquities*, Book 11, Chapter 6, in *The Works of Josephus: Complete and Unabridged*, Trans. William Whiston (Peabody, MD: Hendrickson Publishers, 1987), 299.

[5]*Webster's New World Dictionary of Quotable Definitions*, 2nd edition. Ed. Eugene E. Brussell (New York: Prentice Hall, 1988), 114

[6]Cf., for example, Clines, 302.

[7]See Clarence Bass, "Fast, Fasting," in *Baker Encyclopedia of the Bible*, Ed. Walter A. Elwell (Grand Rapids: Baker Book House, 1988), Vol. 1, 780-781.

## Week Five

[1]For a description of the rooms in that part of the palace and their adjacencies, see Clines, 303-304.

[2]Esther 4:11.

[3]Josephus, 299.

[4]Herodotus, *The History, Book 9*, 110-111.

[5]Durant, 375-376.

[6]For more on the Hebrew word for *glory*, see Harris, Archer, and Waltke, 426-428.

[7]After the Babylonian exile, the Jews were hesitant to utter the personal name of God. So when they read the Scriptures aloud and encountered the name *Yahweh* they would say the word *Lord* instead. In fact the Hebrew texts we have today reflect this practice, since the consonants are those of the word *Yahweh* (*YHWH*), while the vowels, in effect, are those of the Hebrew word for *Lord* (*Adonai*). The combination of the consonants of the one word with the vowels of the other accounts for the origin of the word *Jehovah*.

## Week Six

[1]Herodotus, *The History, Book 8*, cited in Vos, 169.

[2]Clines, 308.

[3]Ibid.

[4]Brown, Driver, and Briggs, 314.

[5]Walter Bauer, William F. Arndt, and F. Wilbur Gingrich, *A Greek-English Lexicon of the New Testament and Other Early Christian Literature*, 2nd ed. (Chicago: University of Chicago Press, 1957), 427.

[6]Bauer, Arndt, and Gingrich, 528.

[7]I am sorry to say that I don't recall where I first heard it put this way. I can only say that it is not original with me.

[8]The best explanation of the "kenosis" of Christ I have ever come across is found in Karl Barth, *Church Dogmatics*, Volume 4, "The Doctrine of Reconciliation, Part 1." Trans. G. W. Bromiley. Eds. G. W. Bromiley and T. F. Torrance (Edinburgh: T&T Clark, 1956), 180-183.

[9]Bauer, Arndt, and Gingrich, 428.

[10]If you are looking these up, you will need to know that the word is a form of *lambano*. Ibid., 464.

## Week Seven

[1]Although I don't know whether it is original with him, I first heard this from Pastor Rick Warren of Saddleback Church in his "Purpose-Driven Church Conference" in May 2000.

[2]The Hebrew word emphasizes not just the terror, but also its startling suddenness. See Brown, Driver, and Briggs, 129-130, and Harris, Archer, and Waltke, 122.

[3]Dr. and Mrs. Howard Taylor, *Hudson Taylor's Spiritual Secret* (Chicago: Moody Press, 1989), 112.

[4]The Hebrew word basically means *hot*, and in this context emphasizes a burning rage. See Brown, Driver, and Briggs, 404.

[5]Clines, 312.

[6]Brown, Driver, and Briggs, 404.

[7]To recline at tables was customary at Persian banquets, and indeed throughout the ancient Near East. See "banquets," *Baker Encyclopedia of the Bible*, Ed. Walter A. Elwell (Grand Rapids: Baker Book House, 1988), Vol. 1, 256-257.

[8]Clines, 312.

[9]Baldwin, 93.

[10]This translation from the Hebrew is my own.

[11]This translation from the Hebrew is my own.

[12]Allen P. Ross, *Creation and Blessing: A Guide to the Study and Exposition of Genesis* (Grand Rapids: Baker Book House, 1988), 598. Ross's excellent insights are more widely available in his commentary on Genesis in Vol. 1 of *The Bible Knowledge Commentary*, Eds. John F. Walvoord and Roy B. Zuck (Wheaton, IL: Victor Books, 1985), 15-101.

[13]Ibid., 609-610.

[14]I am quoting Pastor Rick Warren from his "Purpose-Driven Church Conference," Saddleback Church, May 2001.

[15]Ibid.

## Week Eight

[1]Clines, 314.

[2]Ibid., 318.

[3]Vos, 180.

[4]This translation from the Hebrew is my own.

[5]Baldwin, 106.

[6]Vos, 118.

# ✠ About the Author

Keith Bower (B.A., Th.M., M.A., Ph.D.) is the senior pastor of Grace Community Bible Church in Fort Bend County, Texas, southwest of Houston. He also serves as an adjunct professor in theological studies at Dallas Theological Seminary, Houston extension, and as founding chairman of the Grace International Children's Foundation, an organization dedicated to the construction and operation of homes for the children of AIDS victims in east Africa. Keith, his wife, Julie, and their children, Emily and Stephen, reside in Katy, Texas.

# Real Problems... Real People... Real Life... Real Answers...
# THE INDISPUTABLE POWER OF BIBLE STUDIES

**Through the Bible in One Year**
Alan B. Stringfellow • ISBN 1-56322-014-8

**God's Great & Precious Promises**
Connie Witter • ISBN 1-56322-063-6

**Preparing for Marriage God's Way**
Wayne Mack • ISBN 1-56322-019-9

**Becoming the Noble Woman**
Anita Young • ISBN 1-56322-020-2

**Women in the Bible — Examples To Live By**
Sylvia Charles • ISBN 1-56322-021-0

**Pathways to Spiritual Understanding**
Richard Powers • ISBN 1-56322-023-7

**Christian Discipleship**
Steven Collins • ISBN 1-56322-022-9

**Couples in the Bible — Examples To Live By**
Sylvia Charles • ISBN 1-56322-062-8

**Men in the Bible — Examples To Live By**
Don Charles • ISBN 1-56322-067-9

**7 Steps to Bible Skills**
Dorothy Hellstern • ISBN 1-56322-029-6

**Great Characters of the Bible**
Alan B. Stringfellow • ISBN 1-56322-046-6

**Great Truths of the Bible**
Alan B. Stringfellow • ISBN 1-56322-047-4

**The Trust**
Steve Roll • ISBN 1-56322-075-X

**Because of Jesus**
Connie Witter • ISBN 1-56322-077-6

**The Quest**
Dorothy Hellstern • ISBN 1-56322-078-4

**God's Solutions to Life's Problems**
Wayne Mack & Joshua Mack • ISBN 1-56322-079-2

**A Hard Choice**
Dr. Jesús Cruz Correa • Dr. Doris Colón Santiago
ISBN 1-56322-080-6

**11 Reasons Families Succeed**
Richard & Rita Tate • ISBN 1-56322-081-4

**The Fear Factor**
Wayne Mack & Joshua Mack • ISBN 1-56322-082-2

**Embracing Grace**
Judy Baker • ISBN 1-56322-083-0

**Courageous Faith**
Keith Bower • ISBN 1-56322-085-7

**5 Steps to Financial Freedom**
James D. Wise • ISBN 1-56322-084-9

# Problemas Reales... Gente Real... Vida Real... Respuestas Reales...
# EL INDISCUTIBLE IMPACTO DE LOS ESTUDIOS BÍBLICOS

**A través de la biblia en un año**
Alan B. Stringfellow • ISBN 1-56322-061-X

**Preparando el matrimonio en el camino de Dios**
Wayne Mack • ISBN 1-56322-066-0

**Mujeres en la Biblia**
Sylvia Charles • ISBN 1-56322-072-5

**Parejas en la Biblia**
Sylvia Charles • ISBN 1-56322-073-3

**Decisión Difícil**
Dr. Jesús Cruz Correa & Dra. Doris Colón Santiago •
ISBN 1-56322-074-1